Now We Are Thirty

Now We Are Thirty

Women of the Breakthrough Generation

MARY INGHAM

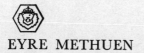
EYRE METHUEN

for Frank

First published 1981
by Eyre Methuen Ltd
11 New Fetter Lane, London EC4P 4EE
Copyright © Mary Ingham 1981
Printed in Great Britain by
Richard Clay (The Chaucer Press) Ltd,
Bungay, Suffolk

British Library Cataloguing in Publication Data

Ingham, Mary
    Now we are thirty.
    1.   Women – Great Britain – Social conditions
    I.   Title
    305.4'216'0941   HQ1593

    ISBN 0–413–47750–9
    ISBN 0–413–49300–8 Pbk

When Anne and I go for a walk
We hold each other's hand and talk
Of all the things we mean to do
When Anne and I are forty-two

(**A. A. Milne,** *Now We Are Six*)

Contents

Acknowledgements

Towards the end of 1976 I set out to trace and interview the women who had been in my year at school, three forms of 11-year-old grammar school pupils in 1958, who would be 30 in 1977. I succeeded in tracking down, interviewing and corresponding with forty-five of them, whose thoughts and experiences – under fictitious names where quoted – I have drawn on to write this book. On one level this book is a very personal account. It would have remained only that, a very narrow exploration of what it was like to grow up through the 1950s and 1960s and become an adult in the 1970s, without the overwhelmingly generous and open response of all my interviewees to my pesterings. I should like to thank them all for making my research work so rewarding, absorbing and enjoyable, and also thank our retired headmistress and French mistresses for their valuable assistance in jogging my memory and digging out addresses.

I owe especial gratitude and thanks to Annie and Ian, without whose hospitality and interest I would never have started the research, let alone finished it; to Bob Woodings, for having faith in the rough outline of the idea and for his guiding efforts to help me shape it; to my mother, father and aunt for bringing the past to life for me; and last but not least to Christie, Christina, Elsbeth and Sue for their loyal support and unflagging encouragement.

I am also grateful to the Department of Employment, Department of Education and Science, and the Office of Population Censuses and Surveys for the use of their library facilities.

In the course of background research, I found the following books most useful and likely to be of interest for further reading:

A Woman's Place by Ruth Adam (Chatto & Windus, 1975), a social history of women, 1910–75; *Bombers and Mash* by Raynes Minns (Virago, 1980) on women during World War II on the domestic front; and *Ecstasy and Holiness* by Frank Musgrove (Methuen, 1974) on the counter culture.

Acknowledgement is gratefully made to the following for permission to quote from songs: ATV Music Ltd and Northern Songs for an extract from 'Ticket to Ride' by John Lennon and Paul McCartney, on p. 94; EMI Music Publishing Ltd for an extract from 'The Young Ones' (copyright © 1961 Harms-Witmark Ltd; sub-published by EMI Film and Theatre Music Ltd) on p. 71; Warner Bros. Inc. for extracts from 'If You Gotta Go, Go Now' by Bob Dylan (© 1965) on p. 109 and p. 110; and Edward Kassner Music Co. Ltd for extracts from 'You Really Got Me' and 'All Day and All of the Night' by Ray Davies on p. 90.

Introduction

thirty, the female dilemma, for a special generation — a decade of developments in women's rights

> *To be twenty-nine and unmarried, to be a failure,*
> *child-less, insane too, and no writer*
> Virginia Stephen (Woolf)

Thirty, for a woman, is a sensitive age. If she is expecting her first child she will be clinically dubbed an 'elderly primigravida' and probably coerced into having the baby in hospital, because of the risks attendant upon her advanced age. A childless 30-year-old faces the fact that if she wants to start a family, she hasn't got much time left, and perhaps, just as all these thoughts occur, her career is beginning to take off. A 30-year-old mother finds her family beginning to grow out of their dependence upon her and as they emphasize their individuality so she is forced to ponder her own. Who is she? What has she done with her life? Her children might scoff at the suggestion that she goes back to work, and she might privately agree. It's hard to make a fresh start at 30. Opportunities tend only to exist for younger people. And, at 30, one is more prone to ask 'what if I fail?'.

It's not just timidity born of experience, or realization of advancing age. At 30 it's difficult to change direction because at 30 somehow one's identity is formed. Thirty is a turning point, a milestone, not simply the dividing line between youth and the slippery slope towards 40. Thirty is a threshold, a ledge in life where you pause to look at yourself as an adult. You gain a sense of who you are, as much through the things you've not done as through what you've achieved. A housewife feels more of a housewife because she never finished her training to be a dentist; a single woman with an enviable career feels the lack of a family. Where are the wife and mother she once saw in herself? This is what the crisis is all about. Well, here you are, an adult over 30. This is your life. You've had certain chances, and choices, what have you made of them?

Those of us now in our early thirties belong to a special generation. Labelled as the postwar 'bulge', we were born to celebrate the return of family life (Johnny sleeping in his own little room again, as the wartime song promised) and the golden future glimpsed beyond the grim reality of postwar Britain. We grew up alongside nationalized industries and the Welfare State. We were forced to swallow lukewarm milk through straws, chew on gristly school dinners and stare at lumpy semolina. Along with the milk, we all received free secondary education, according to our age, aptitude and ability, courtesy of the 1944 Education Act. And we started going out on Saturday night in the sixties, that daring decade of affluence and excitement.

What did it mean to be part of the 'bulge'? The word conjures up a soft, fat polystyrene-filled cushion, a slow expansion, quantity rather than quality, and a sort of muffled, muted sagging swell of numbers, anonymity in overflowing classrooms. Yet some of us made a very sharp-pointed impact with student demonstrations, aggressive music, outrageous clothes, long hair and disregard for sexual morality and most of the values our parents had carefully built up in our interests. Now we've grown up we're no longer the younger generation. We are the responsible ones now, who characterize the conventions of the society we live in.

I was one of a privileged small percentage of that generation, creamed off for grammar school education at 11. Now, in our thirties, I see my contemporaries becoming established and successful in professions and businesses. Or is it only my brother's contemporaries? What about *my* schoolfriends, now intelligent, educated grown women? What have they done with their lives?

The conflict between a woman's childrearing capacity and

her capability of earning her own living stems from the way in which industrialized society separates work and home. It must be no accident that the first stirrings of the women's movement began within fifty years of the onset of the industrial revolution. The movement for the emancipation of women did not gather momentum, however, until the turn of this century, along with advances in and acceptance of contraceptive methods, giving a woman a measure of control over that side of her nature which made her dependent. The diary of women's history shows an impressive list of achievements in the early part of this century, including militant demonstrations for the vote, strikes for higher pay. Women won the vote and changes in the law, giving married women a measure of independence. But then, in the thirties, the diary goes blank. Nothing significant happened, either in the advancement of women's rights or any agitation by women in the name of their own equality with men.

More and more, the women's movement appeared to have been the frenetic obsession of a minority of women, over-privileged, over-educated, upper-class ladies, bored by their role as decorative dolls. Most women, it seemed, accepted their lot, bound by their biological role. Then, suddenly, forty years after women won the vote, something stirred.

Since our generation left school, over the past ten to fifteen years, so many opportunities have been opening up for women. In 1967 abortion, in certain circumstances, became legal; 1970 saw the first national conference of the Women's Liberation Movement in Britain and the passing of the Equal Pay Act, to become law in 1975; in the early 1970s, women began to demonstrate for better job opportunities, nursery places, free contraceptives. In 1974 British women married to foreigners were given the same right as British men for their spouses to live in this country. Contraceptives became available free in 1974 to single as well as married women, who were now taking advantage of newly developed, more reliable methods, like the pill and the coil. In 1975 the Sex Discrimination Act became law. In theory, at least, women cannot now be discriminated against on the grounds of their sex in employment, advertising and the provision of goods, facilities and services.

Have any of these changes affected our lives, or the way in which we are handling the dilemma of women who have reached 30? And was it merely coincidence that the women's movement spoke up once more when our generation found its voice, that all these developments have coincided with our adult lives, as a generation of women?

*images of adult life – mid-1970s mixed flat reality – was it only me? –
tracing my year at school – meeting our mothers*

Like most girls, I imagine, I grew up picturing cameo images
of my future adult self, a set of expected milestones in relation to
the opposite sex. I imagined being married at 22, quite old
really, and settling down to raise a family at 25. But at university, 22 suddenly didn't seem so old, so all the images shuffled
forward a few paces. Marriage was now 25, children at 27, 28;
I would be bound to have them before I was 30.

Where would I be at 30? I'd be married to an attractive man
in a creative but stable career – an architect, say, or a graphic
designer. We'd have a couple of kids, of course, and we'd live,
for a few years at least, in London, in a street of elegant, terraced houses with black railings and sash windows, not too
far away from my friends. I'd have a large kitchen full of herbs
and earthenware pottery. My girlfriends would have gone
their separate ways, of course, but we'd meet over a cup of
coffee, or invite one another round for dinner or to babysit.
Our kids would grow up playing together. What I would be
doing was never quite clear – something vaguely arty and
interesting – it was never worth trying to define it too sharply;
after all, so much depended on the man.

I knew I was getting older because I had to keep writing my
age down on forms, but in some way I had set in my second
year as a student – I felt eternally 19. I hardly noticed, therefore, that 25 came and went without the wedding and 27 without the children. Not looking where I was going, I had tripped
over my milestones, but nothing had happened.

I was 27 in 1974, sharing a flat with five others, mostly also
ex-students, in an inner London suburb. The house was

imposing, if somewhat dilapidated, part of a Regency crescent overlooking a park. A table cluttered with fifty letters for previous tenants long 'gone away' and a shabby settee ejected by the occupants of the ground floor flat sat in the hallway. A very worn staircase led to the upper floor where six of us lived in what would have been described as a mixed flat. To me, I simply lived with friends of both sexes. We were all in our mid-twenties. Martin was a student again, studying art this time; Sharon and Ros worked for publishing companies; Terry was on the dole, having dropped out of teaching; Doug worked for a charity for the homeless; Sarah was training to become a polytechnic lecturer; and I had shelved a career in social work to work on a little newspaper.

We each had our own rooms and shared a living room, kitchen and bathroom. A large table dominated Ros's room, with boxes pushed away underneath, the spoils from her broken engagement – electric mixer, sewing machine . . . Sarah and Terry shared a big, dark room at the top of the house, sprouting waxen green foliage and loud high-fidelity David Bowie. Sharon lived among books and pieces of flowered pottery; Doug with fluff from his candlewick bedspread and Beethoven; Martin in pale pink order and the smell of oil pigment. Our rooms were little jewels in a dull setting. The common areas of the house and their neglect struck me as a statement about the way we lived. When we did get around to decorating them, it was the lowest common denominator of taste which was expressed, nobody's choice, by the time everyone had been consulted.

In theory we were very organized. We took turns in shopping, cooking and cleaning. But men seemed to have lower standards of cleanliness and culinary skill. Resentments arose. Once you had taken on a domestic task, we discovered, you got stuck with it because other people then never noticed it needed doing – like defrosting the fridge.

Meeting and talking to try to iron these problems out never seemed to bear much relation to what went on the rest of the time. But even though they never solved anything, communal meetings, summoned out of some kind of separate tension, soon dissolved into a warm familiarity. We became a kind of family for one another, only one where the tie consisted of a month's notice and helping to find a replacement flatmate. We exchanged presents before Christmas and ate a meal together, but each slunk away to parents for the event itself, and the house became an eerie, empty shell.

Most of the time it throbbed with life, mid-seventies city life. Crowding into the smokey local to listen to the latest pub band, sauntering down to the late-night cinema, or the Sunday morning market, arguing about entry to the Common Market, marxist politics, astrology; meeting fringe theatre actors and media people at noisy parties overflowing with wine, garlic bread and vegetarian delights; fervent social workers clomping in and out in their platform-sole boots, long peasant dresses and baggy trousers, setting up women's groups and neighbourhood law centres. I felt I had really arrived. There were always transitory guests, someone sleeping on the dirty, salmon-pink settee in the living room that we never did get around to recovering. With so many distractions the tendency was to sit around the kitchen table half the evening, leaning on elbows, with plans, possibilities, fantasy paraphernalia that never come to pass.

One evening, staring across the supper plates, over my stoneware coffee mug, I watched Sarah unfold a beautiful unicorn-patterned tea towel, muttering 'Don't know what I was saving this for', and over the weeks it gradually got raggy round the edges, where people let it trail in the flame when they used it to pick the kettle off the gas.

Ros must have been aware of this too. She brought out her gadgets to prepare a meal, but quickly washed them up and stowed them back under her table afterwards. I began to realize I too was holding something back, not investing in the present, but waiting for a time when I could bring out my fancy tea towel and it would be appreciated; hoarding my hopes, meantime, under the table, like Ros.

It struck me that something didn't fit, between my image of the future and the path I was actually on. And yet what nudged me was that there *was* something familiar about the way we lived . . . Regency house, with big sash windows, pot plants, earthenware pottery in the kitchen . . . I was there, in the house in London. One of the milestones had materialized, but not quite in the way I'd always imagined. Where was my husband? My friends were certainly around, but our kids couldn't play together because we hadn't any. The house wasn't ours, and the kitchen didn't quite have that Habitat/country cuisine charm. It was stuck all over with the reality of all those greasy places down the side of the cooker that nobody bothered to reach, because nobody else bothered to reach them.

That summer my brother got married. I am the youngest of four children, a girl and a boy born before the war and my brother and I born just after it. This brother was now 30. I dressed up that morning in a long flowing smock, simulating femininity and fertility, as was fashionable then, and stepped out of a taxi into the morning freshness of West Hampstead for the wedding. I imagine my relations all said what was expected – 'You next.' My parents stayed on in a hotel and paid me one of their rare visits. I hustled them through the dingy hallway and awkwardly introduced them to Sharon. They were polite and bewildered, like tourists in a foreign country, which they were. I thought of my mother at my age, with two children and a home of her own, bought by my father, proudly cared for as the main preoccupation of her day.

However much I'd decorated the image, with architect and town house in London, I'd always seen myself the same. What had gone wrong? Where had I stepped out of line, out of my mother's plans for me, out of my elder sister's footsteps?

But perhaps it was not so strange after all, that my lifestyle was utterly at odds with everything I had been nurtured towards, encouraged to expect. So much of what I was groomed and rehearsed for just didn't apply by the time I grew up, because so many new opportunities had opened up for women: free, reliable contraception, abortion, easier divorce, job opportunities. My close female friends and I were all single, liberated women, sympathetic towards the women's movement because it underlined our independent spirit. But were we simply eccentrics, part of some amazonian vanguard of displaced, well-intentioned yet misguided representatives of our sex, neatly rearranging life for the others who frankly rejected the stalwart singleness we stood for? Life was so much simpler if you didn't have to map it out yourself, if it came cut out in the simplicity of the happily-ever-after.

I knew that more married women were going out to work, but a Feiffer cartoon stuck in my head. Mornings I hate, she says, slumped over a typewriter. I hate travelling to the office. I hate work. Sometimes I just sit and dream about getting away from it all, getting married. And then I remember, I am married. It was tempting to assume that women had merely joined the rat race by doubling up on their domestic role, settling for second-rate jobs. I could see so many women like that, dashing out at lunchtime, armed with shopping bags.

But surely, out of the rest of our year at school, it wasn't just my friends and I who were different? After all, we were all part of a special generation, who burst out of the mould our parents had lovingly cast for us, in the sixties. But then every age has its nonconformists, and my mother had been part of a special generation herself: women given a new freedom, the freedom to vote on equal terms with their male peers, and it didn't seem to have affected their lives very much.

I began to wonder what other women of my generation had made of the predicament of being a woman as well as a person (the over-defensive mid-seventies label, not so frequently used now). Perhaps they'd not even felt it as a predicament. I decided I wanted to talk to a cross-section of ordinary, intelligent women my age, who'd had the educational opportunities I'd had, although not necessarily stayed on in the sixth form and gone to university as I did. The idea stayed just an idea, as ideas often do, for a couple of years. And then, in the summer of 1976, at that critical age of 29, I bumped into someone I had not seen for ten years. Annie and I had been at school together. She introduced me to her husband and her young daughter. She was back in our home town, teaching, and invited me to visit them some time. There were quite a lot of familiar faces still around the town, she mentioned in passing, others from our year at school.

I knew I had found the women I wanted to interview, women with whom I'd shared seven years of grammar school, through first periods and boyfriends, before branching out our separate ways into the world, as adults. I wouldn't just be a stranger with a tape recorder, and I'd enjoy meeting them again.

I did, although it took some time to track about half of them down. Finding the three forms of the 1958 intake of 11-year-olds who'd passed the 11-plus, my year at school, turned out to entail a certain amount of detective work. Married women are women living under an assumed name, and in most cases I had no idea what that name would be. The most effective way of tracing them turned out to be through their parents, often still living at the same address recorded on the school register. These parents, at first sight, seemed very much like my own. Retired couples, the man pottering round the garden, the wife exuding the same comfortable image as my own mother. My image of my mother is that cosy mum image; mum who had no idea what was going on in the outside world, never had to fend for herself, had no opinions, unless they were on how you got stains out of things, or cooked new potatoes, mended a tear. Mum whose domain was the house, who ruled the roost and all those in it, who comforted and rescued from nightmares and darkness, who stroked away temperatures and coaxed back appetites, who knew best, but knew nothing, beyond the family circle.

I'd always assumed that my mother's generation had happily copped out, been given the vote and simply asked their husbands, in the way you get someone to use their brain to work out something you're too lazy to work out for yourself; trotted back into the house because the modern world happened to be a threatening place. In spite of the rousing efforts of the suffragettes, the great morass of women had voted with their high heels, declined the challenge, slipped back into the groove as society nudged them, comfortable, off the main line. It was only meeting some mothers, and hearing my contemporaries talk about their mothers, that I began to wonder whether I'd got the image wrong. What were our mothers really like, and what effect did they have on our lives?

This book is an exploration of the lives of a number of women, now in their thirties. But if the next two chapters appear to stray into the past, it is because that is where our development as a generation of wives, mothers, lovers and people is rooted. Also, in some ways I want to redress the balance. The mute, martyred generation of our mums, blanked out in the diary of women's history, holds the key to the continuity between the two seemingly separate waves of the women's movement this century.

2 My Mother/Someone Else?

1907–47   Edwardian childhood – First World War – spinster war-workers and hardworking housewives – elementary education – 'oh no, Winifred, you'll get married' – 'Pop said he trusted us' – wives don't work – Second World War – conscription of homemakers – working mothers – 'don't you know there's a war on?' – Royal Commission on Equal Pay – a nation's workers and the New Look – what do women want?

My mother was born in 1907; she was nearly forty when she had me. I accepted her and her cuddling indulgence without question when I was little. When I started school, from the distance of our new separateness, I became aware that she was older than most of my friends' mothers, old-fashioned and overweight. As the gulf between us widened, my criticisms increased. She stood for most things I disdained: uninformed opinion, repressed sexuality, narrowminded morality; the implacable belief that a woman's destiny lay solely in getting married and having babies, saving yourself for the simple self-sacrifice of wiping up after others; the stereotype housewife and mother who denies she exists in her own right. I never thought to ask why, let alone ask *her* why.

In recent years we have come closer, understand one another better, partly because I have come to realize, through talking to her, that my mother was partly simply defending the limited status that social circumstances had dictated for her.

My mother was born in Birmingham, in an Edwardian lower middle-class household where a woman's place was in the home under the protection of her father, until a stranger, whom she would commit herself to honour and obey, offered to cherish her while she reared his children. But my mother was also born into a society where a woman's place had begun to be questioned. In Manchester the Pankhursts had formed the Women's Social and Political Union and catapulted the sedate (and largely ineffectual) women's suffrage movement into vivid and open conflict with the social system it had been politely questioning since the late-eighteenth century, when Mary Wollstonecraft published her *Vindication of the Rights of Woman*. Married women had gained certain basic human rights in the 1880s (they could retain their own property after marriage and also sue deserting husbands) and now women wanted to assert themselves in the men's world by demanding the vote.

But it was only a certain class of women, who had the time, the education and the means to question their role in society. Change, for the majority of people, is slowly absorbed through the skin from the altered atmosphere around them. Like a car on a motorway sliproad, it has somehow to be smoothly incorporated into the running motion of ordinary life.

My mother remembers the suffragettes vaguely, pictures of 'wild women' and newspaper stories of hunger strikes and their shop-window smashing, but says most women were too busy to take it seriously: 'Mother thought it was a lot of nonsense. There was enough to do at home, and no easy way of doing it. Vacuum cleaners had been invented, but they were an inaccessible luxury in most homes, which didn't even have electricity. Elbow grease was the main active ingredient of household equipment. You beat the carpets in the yard, knelt on a mat with a scrubbing brush and a bar of Monkey soap to clean the floors.'

When war broke out in 1914 the suffragettes gave up smashing things and patriotically joined the war effort although, like other women, their offers of help went unheeded at first. But in 1915 Lloyd George woke up to the fact that here was a vast, untapped source of labour, freeing the men to go and do their duty. On her way to school, my mother began to see women working as bus conductors, tram drivers, men's jobs previously. But it was only the single women, who did not have homes to run. Life for wives and mothers went on much as before, except for the empty place at the head of the table and the new habits of economy they acquired – learning to be better managers, waiting in long queues when the butter came in at the Co-op.

My mother and her two sisters spent school holidays with Gran (my great-grandmother) in the country, away from the menacing feeling of the Zeppelin raids. Gran had worked as a housekeeper until she married her employer, stopped getting paid, and bore him nine children. Now a widow with two spinster daughters left at home, Gran was a lady, albeit one who dropped her aitches. But her life still symbolized the oppression of women: deadend job, borrowed social status, responsibilities she could not morally neglect. Every morning Gran rose at five, when the first trolleybus went past, and fastened her bodice, whalebone corsets, woollen stockings with garters, two taffeta petticoats and finally her working dress.

Female servants were increasingly hard to get, because the expansion of shops and offices offered more congenial work for women, so with the help of her daughters, Gran cleaned the whole house herself (bar the front step, which she paid a woman to come and scrub). Down on her hands and knees, she rubbed up the redtiled kitchen floor with diluted milk. She even made her own pork pies. It was go, go, go, all physical energy and Gran was as hard a taskmaster as she was a worker, inspecting all the slats of the venetian blinds after Aunt May had wiped them. Respectable young women didn't go out to work in those days. When they weren't learning house crafts, they sat sewing single thread embroidered pictures or went walking. My mother's Aunt May grabbed at the opportunity for a bit of life. She volunteered for work at the munitions factory at Dudley, striding down to the station in an old suit and bouncing back in the evening, grime clinging to her skirts. She loved it, going out into the world. 'Better than slaving over lemon curd tarts for you lot to gobble up,' she said. She loved the camaraderie at work, the jokes and the goings-on, and the freedom the money gave her to waltz out to the pictures. But it was only for the duration of the war. Too independent to take the first man who offered her marriage, May found she had joined the 'old maids', the surplus women of a generation, whose marriage partners had not survived. She took a job as a companion to an older woman. The days of fun were over.

Meanwhile, the mould in which my mother's life was to set had begun to take shape. My grandmother's health was poor. Had Rose, my grandmother, been part of Gran's generation, she would probably have died in childbirth, but the dirty secret of contraception was slowly spreading. The birth rate had fallen from 36 per thousand in 1876 to 28 per thousand in 1901. Now that she had some say in the matter, a woman's liberation from confinement, breastfeeding, weaning, training and supervision of a succession of demanding little dependants had begun. By the time Rose was 30, she had sent her three children off to school.

My mother's elementary education was unlikely to propel her towards any career. And staying off school to cope with housework her mother was not well enough to handle, she fell behind. The school attendance officer turned a blind eye; after all, the girls were being trained for housework. In their final year, when they were 14, they had two full days of domestic training per week, one in the kitchen and one in the laundry.

They learnt to soak the clothes in hard soap, shredded up, scrub on the scrubbing board, then boil on the gas. After boiling, everything went into the 'dolly tub'. You'd 'post' the dolly (a wooden stick perforated at the bottom) like the agitator of a washing machine, up and down, except that you had to stand over it, doing it yourself. Then came rinsing, starching, wringing everything out, and finally ironing. This was a mammoth job, because women wore clothes right down to their ankles, and layers of petticoats. My mother, dunce of the class, came top. But still, although she was over the moon, housewifery wasn't seen as being clever. It was just part of the training you had to be a good wife.

It was all very well to look after your own home, but cleaning someone else's was too much like being a skivvy. When my mother left school in 1921, she went into an office. Routine office work had opened up working opportunities for respectable girls without qualifications. My mother started as a messenger, but when she was promoted to the invoice department, she was terrified of being given some reckoning up that she couldn't do. If she had been a boy there would have been no alternative but to stick it out, and in the process gain self-confidence, but for my mother, there was a timely escape route: 'Mother dying got me out of that office, but I was ecstatic when the invoice manager said they were sorry to lose such a good worker.' The encouragement, unfortunately, came too late. My mother had left work, at 16, in 1923, to take on the role of housekeeper for her father and sisters. She never went out to work again.

Kathleen worked as a shorthand typist, Phyllis commuted to a bank in Birmingham operating a ledger-posting machine, and my mother began to discover some of the drawbacks to staying at home. Both sisters were buying their own clothes, but my mother only had the money she could keep back out of the housekeeping, which made her feel like a thief, although in other ways she was becoming freer. To Gran's horror (she wore the same long skirts until she died) hems slid up to the knee, showing gleaming silk stockings, when the swinging, fringed short skirts came to stay in 1925. My mother and her sisters sat rolling up strips of wallpaper, threading them on to cotton to make long strings of beads. And they started wearing make up. All Gran had ever done was rub a bit of glycerine and rosewater into her hands. 'Mother did put powder on, rubbed off those little leaves you bought in a booklet,' my aunt remembers, 'but she hid behind the wardrobe door, so that no one would see her do it. Lipstick and eyeshadow were really common and nail varnish, well, only whores wore that!'

The freedom of the fashions echoed the freedom of young people who met at Sunday school and cycled off for picnics together. They posed coyly in cloche hats, their shimmery knees clung modestly together and pointed strappy shoes flung carelessly apart, for the young man in cricket flannels to take a snap. The pose reflected the confusions of the time. They were provocatively revealing themselves in a way women had never done before, casting aside cumbersome clothing, roaming around on bicycles. It scandalized Gran, but gone was the era of the authoritarian parent. For if marriage was now a freer arrangement between protector and protected, the parent-child relationship had changed too.

'Pop used to say he trusted us,' my mother explains. 'We respected that and didn't abuse it.' The new morality was no longer mute obedience. It was choosing for yourself, being responsible for making your own decisions – based on ignorance and fear. 'One of us had been out late to a party,' she remembers. 'Pop lined us all up in the sitting room next day. He cleared his throat and muttered "Damn fine cheek your mother had, leaving me with you three girls." Then all he said was, "There are only two things that are real in this life – birth and death." We knew what he meant.'

But did they? Some of my schoolfriends' mothers, who grew up ten years after my mother, remember the innocence of thinking that you could get pregnant by sitting on a man's knee. Penalties against a woman exploring her own sexuality were still too great. 'Getting into trouble' was still the most probable consequence, and therefore shameful proof, of 'having relations'. So there was safety in numbers. Young people went on holidays together, sailing and hiking. 'We were too scared of what people would think to risk doing anything we shouldn't.'

My parents met at 18, but didn't marry until they were 25 when my father could afford to keep a wife. My mother was unaware of belonging to a special generation of women who, when they turned 21 (in 1928), became the first women free to exercise the same voting rights as their male peers; the only freedom she was interested in was the freedom of her own home.

It was what every woman yearned for, but when they married in 1933 it wasn't quite the contented independence my mother had envisaged. 'We'd spent our honeymoon on the Norfolk Broads and when I put the sheets out to dry, the flapping in the wind reminded me of the sails of our boat . . . but it wasn't like our honeymoon. I was miles away from my family and friends; the flat was much easier to run. Washing was quicker and easier with soap powders, and with the vacuum cleaner I got all the cleaning done by eleven o'clock. I got very bored and lonely.'

My father had left home and friends in search of promotion. The splintering of communities had begun during the 1914–18 war, and the depression accelerated it, when people moved in search of jobs. My father began to make new contacts through his job, but it was not so easy for my mother. She wanted to get a job in the local hospital, but my father wouldn't hear of it.

It would look as if he couldn't afford to keep his wife. For the sake of social convention my mother sat at home.

Isolated and undermined, she got so depressed she went to see the doctor, a lady who sympathized, and took her on her rounds to get her out meeting people. But it was only a short-term solution, a palliative. The problem remained – until my mother got pregnant. 'I could see her lip tighten when I started to talk about the baby. I don't know why, but she gradually stopped taking me out. It didn't matter, though. I had the baby to occupy my time.' My mother's 30-year path of childrearing had begun, orbiting round my father's career search, the modern nuclear family unit, the satellite I would be joining in 1947.

Most of the women who were to become the mothers of my contemporaries were at school during the depression of the 1930s. Shirley's mother grew up in the north-east where many men were out of work. Shirley's grandmother became the family breadwinner, but although her grandfather felt the stigma of sitting at home while his wife supported the family, she wasn't considered to be taking work away from the men – frying and serving in a fish shop was woman's work. Equally, although Shirley's grandfather was at home all day and helped out a little, he would never be seen doing it – housework was woman's work. Role identification ran deep.

Although girls' secondary education had been pioneered in the 1870s, it was considered an unnecessary luxury for most girls who would, after all, only become housewives. But along, perhaps, with the increasing individual freedoms, girls were developing a sense of resentment at this sort of restriction on their ambitions. Sandra's mother resented the fact that wanting to go to grammar school and become an infant teacher was summarily dismissed: 'I can remember my father saying, "Oh no, Winifred, you'll get married, so it doesn't affect you, but as long as Ted's all right . . ." ' Ted was her brother.

Helen's mother was luckier. She got to grammar school, following in her mother's and grandmother's footsteps. She wanted to be a doctor, but her father saw no point in investing £1,000 for her training, so the next best thing was nursing, which she started in 1938. Even so, this career could only continue as long as she was single. The middle-class stigma against married women working had, during the depression, become an actual ban – the marriage bar – rationalized by the immorality of two incomes going into the same home, and the contaminating effect of a worldly-wise married woman upon innocent young girls: 'One girl had done three years children's nursing training and three years general, but she married when the war broke out, because her fiancé was called up. She made the mistake of telling the matron, who said, "You'll have to leave at once. I might be talking to a pregnant woman." "I wish she had been," the girl said bitterly. With a career spoilt, what was there left? Getting married ruined anyone's career, because you were expected to go back to domestic life. But I married when I was 25, during the war, so I carried on working.'

The Second World War broke the barrier, the either/or choice for a woman between the sexual and emotional fulfilment of self through marriage and the personal, individual fulfilment of going out to work.

When war broke out again in 1939, the women's offers of help outside the home once more went unheeded. It had become the accepted thing for single women to work before marriage, so most single women were already out at work. Some of them were even made redundant in the transfer to wartime heavy machinery production, rather than the female-dominated light textile industries. All this rapidly changed, with the threat of invasion from Germany, with a population of over 75,000,000 compared with our 47,500,000. When more hands were needed during the First World War, the single, unattached women without responsibilities had answered the call. Now the only untapped labour supply were the wives, the homemakers.

Improved living standards resulted in the streamlining of many household tasks, with electric irons and vacuum cleaners; better products, like soap powders which were quicker and easier to use; and public amenities like laundries and automatic washing machines had taken over from the labour-intensive methods of handwashing at home or in public washhouses. Although changing fashions had dispensed with drawn thread work, what did remain to keep women occupied in the home were the skilled housecrafts, the caring rituals of creating a comfortable home life for husbands and families, another of the luxuries to go now that there was a war on.

Propaganda now encouraged women to view their household responsibilities as necessary chores, to be squeezed around their commitment to working for their country, a commitment which became, for some married women, a compulsory one. Conscription of able-bodied young women (between 19 and 30) was brought into force at the end of 1941. Bright girls like Susan's mother (who'd gone without grammar school education and had to take a monotonous job as a shop assistant) sprang to the stimulation and challenge of joining the Land Army, learning to milk cows and handle machinery, and substituted for men in many industrial and light engineering jobs which were entirely new to them, much as the girls had done during the First World War. Women not only widened their experience of the outside world, but had to learn to be more independent, abandon home altogether as they could be sent anywhere in the country where labour was needed. But the vital difference in this war was that women who had assumed that once they married the working phase of their lives was over and they would now devote themselves for life to their homes, now found themselves called upon to go out into the working world again; to regard domestic responsibilities as passing chores to be accomplished as quickly as possible, rather than a fulltime vocational labour of love. Manufacturers emphasized the time-saving advantages of their household equipment; cheap tinned foods were no longer a betrayal of a woman's self-esteem. Out of political and economic necessity women were being persuaded by the policymakers that their place was no longer at the cooker and the kitchen sink. Old attitudes and habits had to be overcome almost overnight. The response that met any clinging to traditional customs was 'Don't you know there's a war on?'

But if the Second World War demonstrated the part-time concertina'ing of domestic duties, it also exposed the real nature of women's home responsibilities. The early panic evacuations of city children (instigated by a male-dominated government which took the mother's role in the home largely for granted) overlooked the traumatic effect of this disruption of the close family bond, and the extent to which secure home life was a necessary component of normal adjustment. And the first conscription schemes for women overlooked what many young married women in their twenties were preoccupied in doing.

Conscription compelled young women to work or join the forces, with the exception of mothers of children under 14 – which instantly took care of many of the age-range chosen for the call-up. So the call-up was extended to include almost all women, from teenagers of 18 to 50-year-old grandmothers, women whose families had grown up. Mothers of young children were now among the minority left at home, which the endless making-do and mending, the wartime shortages and economies, had made a very cheerless place, despite the way in which women used their ingenuity, faking appetizing meals out of spun-out meagre rations, or creating dance dresses out of net curtains. The only consolation, increasingly, the only brightness in a world of blackout and drabber and drabber clothing, was the company of others, the camaraderie of life itself. The home fires were kept burning in cheerful hearts outside the home, rather than at the hearth.

After the failure of evacuation, mothers demonstrated for more nursery provision to free them to volunteer for part-time work. The government's positive response, because these women's efforts were needed, was nevertheless clumsily slow. The end of the war was almost in sight (in people's minds if not in actuality) by the time makeshift day nurseries, playcentres, school meals services, canteens and a national string of restaurants and (more rarely) special shopping facilities had been organized to relieve the burden on working mothers. Schools opened in the holidays as playcentres, and by October 1944 68,000 children under 5 were attending 1,500 day nurseries, and over a million children stayed at school for their midday meal, enabling two-and-a-half million married women (750,000 of whom had children under 14) to work in British industry. (1943 had seen the maximum participation of women in the workforce – 9 out of 10 single women and 8 out of 10 married women with children over 14.)

Women were learning to be more independent and self-supporting than they had ever been before. Going out to work was achieved through their own energy and efficiency rather than any help from the men, who were either absent or still inhibited about helping out in the home. One man, in the northeast, where traditional role assumptions were more fixed than elsewhere, was assumed to be signalling to the Germans when he was seen hanging nappies on the line. The Second World War saw the birth, not of equality of responsibility and opportunity between the sexes, but of supermum who juggled a job and household chores.

What reward were the women going to get for their sterling efforts this time? And what was it that women themselves looked for when the war ended? Hanging around, waiting to be posted or sheltering from air raids, the best morale booster was discussing peacetime prospects, the kind of society everyone was fighting for. And with food rationing, people had acquired a taste for fair shares.

Although women substituted into men's jobs enjoyed earning more than they had done previously employed on 'woman's work', it did not pass unnoticed among some that there was a discrepancy between what they were paid and what a man earned, doing the same job. In September 1942 the TUC unanimously backed a resolution for equal pay for equal work after the war and the same training facilities and rights of reinstatement as men. The TUC Women's Advisory Committee was considering the prospects for women when the war was over, and half of the Women's Trade Unionist annual conference in April 1943 was devoted to a discussion of this topic. The feelings of those who concerned themselves with women's rights were summed up at the time in a book published by Vera Douie:

> The demands of women fall under three heads. As workers, they want a fair field and no favour; as homemakers, they want their work in the home valued; as citizens, they want to be able to make unhampered their full contribution to the community, and, above all, to have their share in planning the peace.
>
> As workers, what women have long asked for is the right, whether married or unmarried, to work on equal terms with men

in the field of common employment. For some jobs, men may prove more suitable; for some, women, but they ask that no artificial barrier to their employment should be erected, and that they should not be discriminated against merely on the grounds of sex or marriage. They ask also that, where their work is equal in value to that of men, they should receive an equal recompense.

(*The Lesser Half*, 1943)

But not all spokeswomen for their sex were in agreement. Mary Ferguson asked (*Westminster Newsletter*, 'Women and Postwar Industry', 1945):

Who is preparing safeguards for the millions of women who will be searching for security in postwar jobs at the same time as millions of men will be demanding re-establishment in industry? Who?

But she went on to assert:

. . . it is essential for the nation's good that the nation's mothers get back home and stay there . . . Industry must not re-organise on the assumption that married women will be in the market for jobs. If married women are allowed to compete in the labour market with single women and married men, nothing but sorrow will result.

As a single woman Mary Ferguson felt that independent breadwinners' livelihoods should not be threatened by the material assumptions of those whose responsibilities lay in the home and whose immediate needs for food and shelter were already provided. If a woman chose the fulfilment of marriage and children, then that was what she should be content with.

The government, uneasily aware that everyone had done their bit, but that the returning heroes would not tolerate the shambles of demobilization after the first war (when survivors came home to reclaim their jobs only to find that they had been replaced), tried to discover what the women themselves wanted when the war was over. The war had dislodged a lot of the generalized assumptions about women's roles. Rattling around, they rang pretty hollow. Would they neatly drop back down into the same old slots? In 1943 the Office of the Minister of Reconstruction authorized Geoffrey Thomas to conduct an enquiry into the 'attitudes of working women towards postwar employment, and some related problems'. His conclusions tended to echo the words of a pamphlet issued by the Conservative Women's Reform Group that 'though still regarding the home as the centre of their wellbeing . . . [women] no longer regard it as their boundary'.

His findings showed that although more than half the number of single women interviewed disapproved of married women going out to work, less than half of those who were married concurred with this prewar attitude. Married women found work a problem when it conflicted with their home responsibilities ('too much to do all round') which came first, but were much more positively disposed towards the advantages of going out to work. Thomas concluded that those with less home responsibility (older married women whose families were more independent) wanted to stay at work after the war. But he recognized that women's attitudes were affected by the lack of opportunities for them:

> Few women, *even now*, appear to look upon work as a career so long as all the disadvantages attaching to their sex, and to work after marriage, remain . . . A discussion on choice of work can only be made conclusive, therefore, if it is known whether, *given a greater choice*, women would prefer to marry and/or stay at home, rather than work. The reasons for choice of job given by women who were working would then bear a direct relationship to their attitude to work as a whole.
> (*Women at Work*, 1944)

Geoffrey Thomas recognized that lack of opportunities greatly affected women's choices about going out to work, compared with staying at home. Poor prospects in women's work before the war had connived to perpetuate the middle-class housewife as a status symbol stay-at-home. Otherwise, what job could she take up commensurate with her husband's social position? Equal pay for women would mean the beginnings of better opportunities through more equal status. Women like Shirley's mother, a lowly ward-maid before the war, gained self-respect and independence through the responsibilities of warwork as government munitions factory inspectors. Would women like these choose to stay at work if they had the chance, and employ domestic help to take care of their homes?

The representatives of women's rights were demanding equal pay as the just reward for women's proven equal efforts during the war. The government, under pressure, appointed a Royal Commission in 1944 to look into the question of equal pay. It was regarded by many as a typical delaying tactic; the issue was after all rather more thorny than the demand for the vote, but the fact remained that it had a lot of support. The deciding factor, in the end, would be which way the women themselves chose to jump at the end of the war: whether they were going to trot back into the home, or keep their foot in the door of the working world and demand their just rights within it. The women had proved themselves as equals while the men were away. A lot depended upon how they viewed themselves when the breadwinner returned.

The Royal Commission on Equal Pay reported in 1946, grudgingly in favour of the idea in principle, although its application in practice would be too inflationary to be carried out immediately . . . The technical victory had been won. Women only needed to put their weight against the barrier that remained. But as we all know, it took another twenty-five years, the space of a whole generation to grow up, before the Equal Pay Act was passed. The assumption, particularly among those who were instrumental in the real, more recent victory, has been that women ratted out after the war, meekly withdrew into the home to make way for the men again. But it wasn't quite like that. It wasn't so simple for those who were there at the time.

A lot of the old traditional assumptions about a woman's place had been affected by the war. Emergency measures implemented purely for the duration had become a way of life after the six long years that the war had lasted. The argument seemed to come to a head in 1947 when, after the report of the Royal Commission, many people assumed that equal pay would be bound to come before long. Letters written to the newspapers at the time reflect the fact that the argument that a man should earn more as a 'breadwinner' had been eroded, partly by the prewar decline in the birth rate and partly by the increasing intervention of the state (consolidated by the Welfare State provisions after the war) taking over family responsibilities.

What remained was the argument that a woman only had half her mind on her job and would eventually desert her employer:

> . . . no woman works as well in a trade or a profession as a man. A job to a woman is an incidental continuity until she gets married. A woman experiences neither the needs nor the incentive to climb to the top. Most women enter business with their ambitions fixed on achieving independence in a kitchen as some lucky man's wife while most men start a job with the desire to do well enough to provide the kitchen. An employer cannot command the same attention from two such differing minds. Nor does he expect to. Faces of female workers change from year to year but in the main sheer necessity causes the males to take root from the feet up. Are fleeting faces worth the same money earned by men who by steady application to their jobs know the firm's business inside out?

> J. J. Dryden, Surrey.
> (Letter to *Picture Post*, 5.7.47)

Women had been issued with a challenge at the end of the war. Where did their priorities lie? The issue came to a head when, shortly after the Royal Commission's report, the government began flooding newspapers and magazines with appeals to women to stay at work, or return to work. It seemed that the demands of postwar production had not been satisfied by the phased demobilization of the men; a perfect moment to hammer in the claim for equal pay again and make it stick. In 1947 the Women's TUC voted unanimously in favour of equal pay for women. It represented about 1·75 million female workers. Mrs T. Keep of the AEU pointedly said: 'Women are not prepared to go back into industry under the present conditions.' Meanwhile each individual woman, now that the war was over, now that no one was saying 'don't you know there's a war on?' any more, was solving her own private problems in her own personal way.

The divorce rate soared at the end of the war, as couples faced the reality of infidelities and differences accumulated during their separation. But many couples were also getting married, wanting to re-create the family life the war had disrupted, consummating wartime romances or hastily contracted weddings before he left for the front. Romantic magazines like *Woman's*

Weekly ran stories that showed that women could combine work and marriage, like that of the dedicated young nurse in Ann Lorraine's 'Twelve Hours a Day' (5.7.47) who says when her doctor boyfriend proposes: ' "Resign – me?" she demanded indignantly. "Why I adore the hospital Bill! The only thing that worries me is that there are only twelve hours in every day!" '

Now that the men had come home, and everyone wanted a better life, women were facing the practicalities involved in setting up home. What did they do if they wanted to carry on working, and yet were still expected to do all the housework? And what did you do if you wanted to carry on working, but your husband whisked you off to the other end of the country? The war had made the population so much more mobile. The chances were that you had met while he was temporarily based nearby. Sandra's mother suddenly found herself living in the midlands, leaving behind her job in the west country, her family and her friends. Other women had even harder choices to make. The lifting of the ban on fraternizing with POWs enabled hundreds of couples to marry, but in doing so the girls lost their nationality and the ex-POWs had to return to Germany and Italy, taking their war brides with them. All my grandmother had done when she married was move round the corner, but thousands of GI brides were flocking across the Atlantic, deserting jobs, family, roots, sacrificing, in effect, their identities. For a few the romance and the better standard of living lost out in favour of their own familiar lives, but the majority gave it all up and went. They went because they were pursuing something they had been deprived of, while they were toiling away in turbans and square-shouldered suits. There had been the makeshift glamour of now-or-never flirtations, but what women had been starved of was a feeling of their own femininity. Some people thought this was incompatible with their stand for equal rights, that it symbolized the fly-by-night frivolity of which women had always been accused.

To those who had been waiting for the happily-ever-after of the postwar world, the continuing austerity and the bitter winter of 1946–7 came as a dispiriting blow. The men had at last come home, but what had they come home to? And what had women got to look forward to? *Picture Post*'s Mrs Average wanted 'more leisure, more colour, more food and clothing, less weary work. But most of all she wants hope. That is why she is sadder than during the war . . .' Women were looking for something wonderful and exciting around the corner; which was when Dior introduced the New Look.

'. . . it all began when the word *femininity* crept back . . .'

Now that the men were back, women were looking in the mirror again, and the scrubbed face, box suit and sensible shoes didn't flatter. Pearson Philips, writing in *Age of Austerity*, described the New Look, emphasizing small waists with long flowing skirts, '. . . like a new love affair, the first sight of Venice, a new chance, in fact a new look at life . . .' Dior gave women back an image which reflected 'no longer Amazons, but nymphs; no longer Cinders, but Cinderella'. He also waved a red rag in the faces of those fighting to keep women toeing the line in a man's world. They saw the New Look as an irresponsible waste of material, symbolizing a regression to non-emancipated woman. The trouble was that the New Look sold.

> You can't move in the Home Counties without hearing arguments about the New Look. You'd think that after all these austere years no one would grudge us this small token of pleasanter things to come. It's possible to wear skirts down to your ankles and still be one of the world's workers.
>
> (Miss Norah Alexander, 13.3.48, *Daily Mail*)

> Can anyone imagine the average housewife and businesswoman dressed in bustles and long skirts carrying on their varied jobs, running for buses and crowding into tubes and trains? The idea is ludicrous. Women today are taking a larger part in the happenings of the world and the New Look is too reminiscent of a caged bird's attitude. I hope our fashion dictators will realise the new *outlook* of women and will give the death blow to any attempt at curtailing women's freedom.
>
> (Mrs Mabel Ridealgh, MP)

Philips, from the vantage point of the early sixties, summed up the New Look as typical of the late forties – aspiring towards the future while gazing nostalgically at the prewar period:

> photographs of those first bold bearers of the New Look make them seem strangely lost and bewildered, as though they had

mistaken their cue and come on stage fifty years late. There was a revolution going on all around them which they didn't seem to be part of. This, of course, was what it was. In musical terms it was the ghostly restatement at the end of the first movement of the 20th Century of the theme which had been heard at the beginning of it. It was Orpheus turning round to have a last look at unemancipated Eurydice. And, having looked, we knew that we should never see her again.

(Age of Austerity 1945–51)

(Excusably – or perhaps not – this paragraph was written in 1963, seven years before maxi skirts. Whatever its theme was, the ghostly restatement would be heard more than once; unemancipated Eurydice wasn't going to lie down that easily, either.) In 1947, whatever the New Look itself signified, the furore it created crystallized the dilemma of our mothers' generation – torn between the desire to establish equality with men and the longing to indulge *la différence*. How was it, then, I wondered, since the New Look meant so much at the time, that my mother couldn't remember wearing it, nor any of the other mothers to whom I spoke.

And then it struck me. When Dior launched his nipped-in waists on 12 February 1947, it's hardly surprising my mother didn't rush out to buy one. She was, after all, about to give birth to me. The New Look had become a symbol, particularly in the minds of feminist MPs, of women's regression to their dependent roles, as decorative dolls in society's toybox. They argued that not only were long skirts a shocking waste of precious resources (never mind the men spending their coupons on beer and cigarettes) but that they would hamper women going out to work. Our mothers had already put themselves out of the job market anyway. They were all bulging and busily pregnant – with us.

1947–57   a new look, as mothers – 'we need the women at work' –
government campaign and canvassing women – Royal Commission on
Population – bringing up the bulge – equal pay for our teachers – 11–
plus – hopes deferred to daughters

I like to think of myself as unique, but 241,421 of us blinked on
to a blurry white world to be tucked into prams and pushed
out into the snowcovered rubble of postwar Britain in the
first three months of 1947. The birth rate for the first quarter
of that year was higher than any quarter since June 1921:
22·8 births per thousand of the population, compared with an
average of 16·1 for the first quarters of 1941–5.

The *Economist* enquired placidly on 3 May 1947:

> Does this mean that before the Royal Commission on Population,
> appointed in 1944 [to investigate the falling birth rate] issues its
> report in a few months time, the population problem will have
> solved itself?

The birth rate had been steadily nosediving since the twenties, so
much so that the Royal Commission sent out a questionnaire to
a million wives asking them why they weren't having children.
Not enough females were being born to maintain the population
as future mothers. Couples were apparently taking advantage of
better contraceptive methods and opting for a better standard of
living – a car rather than a third child. The social and economic
causes of the declining birth rate were widely discussed. Then
suddenly the birth rate began to creep up again in 1943.
The *Economist* pondered whether this meant that children were
being 'borrowed' from the future because couples were marrying earlier, or if the size of the family was actually rising.

Paradoxically, the rising birth rate during the later war years had been a symptom of the disruption of normal family life. After four years of war the most loving relationships were strained by the enforced separations, however romantic couples could be by post and on leave. Wives felt the need to plug the gap, for something to hold on to, in case he didn't come back, and sweethearts felt the same. The illegitimacy rate shot up, partly because a shotgun wedding wasn't so easy to arrange in time for the arrival of the little stranger. The extenuating circumstances of the war broke down a lot of moral barriers. People developed a greater tolerance for others' weaknesses, now-or-never outbursts of passion. Daughters who had been protected primarily through innocence found this a rather inadequate defence against the romantic allure of a uniform, the excitement of sudden physical proximity, huddled in air raid shelters, the need for a reassuring touch.

Peace didn't bring the rosy glow of contentment as automatically as people desperately needed it to. The continuing shortages and the difficulties of adjusting to being together again only increased most people's desire for some tangible confirmation of their security. They were tempted to sentimentalize prewar habits and attitudes, to think in terms of a return to what had been before. Women started slotting back into the old ways of thinking, that life came in two phases and you married for your home life. The war had been an emergency measure and, anyway, they felt like a change. The men had had a change, coming back and putting on their demob suits, but what had the women got to show for the peace?

Rationing was worse than during the war. But there was one freely available way of relieving the drabness, the most tangible way of reinforcing family feeling and starting a new life, by doing just that – having a baby. Women like Sandra's mother, who'd been uprooted from their jobs, had no reason to wait. Shirley's mother had waited long enough: 'We planned to start a family right away, because I was getting older. That was when the big "bulge" was, when the men were being released out of the forces.'

The forecasters had already guessed (having consulted statistics for the period after the Great War) that the uphill curve would just be a 'bulge' on the graph, and the line would track gently downward again. By late 1947 they were beginning to be right. The baby boom was subsiding although its reverberations were only just beginning to be felt. If any single force was going to pull women back into the home, we were it. Not the wasp waists of the New Look, but the tug of tiny fingers on skirts. Thousands and thousands of women were taking a new look at themselves, as mothers.

Meanwhile, between June and September 1947, the government launched an appeal to recruit married women back to work. Hospital workers and shorthand typists for the new welfare services, labour for the textile and light industries were needed, for the postwar production boost to get the country back on its feet again. The Minister of Labour broadcast a special appeal; advertisements appeared in newspapers and magazines ('We Can't Get on Without the Women and That Means You . . . We *Need* the Women Back At Work Again', *Picture Post*, July 1947), film trailers at the cinema, posters in town centres; conferences and public meetings were held.

Geoffrey Thomas once more canvassed the women. On behalf of the Ministry of Labour and National Service he interviewed nearly 3,000 women, two-thirds of whom were going out to work, on the 'problems of recruiting women to industry'. In 1943 the number of women going out to work had reached nearly eight million. In June 1947 it had dropped to just over six million, although 65,000 women were officially registered as unemployed. As many single women as married women had dropped out, presumably to get married, conforming to the old ways of thinking, like Sandra's mother: 'I never thought about being an infant teacher after I married. You married for your home life, and after the war we were ready to give up work and settle down. Your husband went out to work and you looked after him and had his meal ready when he got home and you never thought of working unless you were very hard up and went cleaning or did home dressmaking. I'd carried on working after we married because we were apart, but directly my husband came home, our married life started. Working had been one part of your life, and then you married, and gave it up, and made the home for your husband and family.'

Geoffrey Thomas' investigations confirmed this attitude. Marriage was several times more important than children as a disincentive to going out to work, because women felt their responsibilities as wives came first, and were not prepared to wear themselves out as they had during the war. Most women felt that a woman should only go out to work if she could also carry out her duties to her husband and family, and nearly 90 per cent of the married women interviewed had a home to run as their sole responsibility. However, half the women interviewed felt that a woman *should* go out to work if the home could be looked after, and only a very small proportion (less than 10 per cent) were against the idea of two incomes going into the same home, or unfair competition with men. Attitudes had changed, and if women were against combining work and marriage, it was simply because they felt the weight of their responsibilities as homemakers came first.

Two thirds of the 'unoccupied' women said they had recently thought of getting a job, but nearly all of them decided against it because of their domestic responsibilities as wives and mothers. Less than half the sample felt that a woman definitely *shouldn't* work if she had young children. Many women said they would work if there was more part-time work, nurseries and special shopping facilities available.

Most of the makeshift back-up nursery, playcentre and shopping facilities had been closed down when the war ended. By 1948, most of the playcentres which had catered for 20,000 schoolchildren had closed, although 250,500 state-run nursery places and classes still existed.

Geoffrey Thomas concluded that readiness to take up work was not associated with having children as such. A third of the mothers of under school age children said they would use nursery facilities if these were available. He estimated from his survey that about 100,000 women were ready to take up full-time work, and 350,000 part-time. If nurseries were provided, a further 450,000 would find it easier to work part-time. He discovered that the majority of those ready to work were wholly responsible for their households, had children, with a high proportion under 5. A third of the women under 35 said that their responsibility to their children had prevented them from going out to work.

Approximately 9,500,000 women of working age were 'unoccupied' in 1947, nearly a quarter of whom had recently considered taking part-time employment and decided against, mainly because of their duties to homes and children. About 330,000 were not working because there were no jobs available – only 75,000 of these wanted full-time work. He therefore recommended that 900,000 women might be persuaded to take up work in part-time as well as full-time jobs if enough nurseries could be provided, and suggested the provision of laundries and special shopping facilities. The result of the government's campaign was that 14,187 women volunteered for work, and just over 17,000 were known to have gone out and got a job direct. This obvious discrepancy with Geoffrey Thomas' estimates hinted at a large pool of would-be workers, wanting some kind of part-time work and sharing of the burden of their domestic responsibilities.

But the Minister of Labour pointed out firmly that his appeal was not directed at women with young children, nor those with domestic responsibilities; the labour shortage, although urgent, was only temporary. Women were being once more treated as a pool of surplus labour. The government was not prepared to invest in special facilities for women to enable them to go out to work, but of course private industries were free to do so. Some did, but there was indeed little incentive to invest in a temporary part-time work facility which women were not really pressing for, now that they had their young babies to occupy their time, and the jobs melted away.

Ironically, when the Royal Commission on Population (which had been set up when the birth rate was declining to the level where the population was in danger of not reproducing itself), finally published its recommendations, they included family grants, home helps, babysitters, free day and residential nurseries, facilities for holiday playcentres, special travel facilities for mothers and children, and free contraceptives. But because women had volunteered their services as mothers, no support was now forthcoming. In one fell swoop, by returning to the home-centred lives of the prewar days, and being absorbed by the responsibility of our newly arrived presence in their lives, women had lost their foothold in the working world, the lever which would have forced the equal pay issue into actuality.

There was, however, one group of women for whom the baby boom gave their working position ballast rather than detracting from it by its conflicting pull. That was the women teachers. Following the 1870 Education Act, educated women had flooded into teaching in the same way that secretaries had flooded into office work. Teaching, particularly of infant and junior school children, was an acceptable extension of a woman's natural role, just as cleaning, cooking and working-dressmaking were acceptable commercial extensions of her housecraft role. Men did not automatically resist the influx of female teachers; after all they still dominated the higher levels and the top jobs. Women teachers were paid less and accepted this inferiority because the rise of the trade union movement was based on the idea of a 'decent living wage' for a man who had to support a family.

However, with the formation of the National Union of Teachers, the position of the female teacher in a male-dominated profession altered radically, because force of numbers carried motions rather than superior status, and six out of ten teachers were women. In 1904 one headmistress, who handled the union's benevolent fund, pointed out a discrepancy in benefits between men and women, although both sexes contributed the same: the battle for equal pay had really begun. Despite the scorn and hostility of the men, the Equal Pay League was founded, along with the formation of an all-male, anti-equal pay splinter group from the NUT – the National Association of Schoolmasters.

The important outcome of all this was the confrontation which effectively became a platform to debate the previously unquestioned assumptions about the difference between men's work and women's work and how much they should be paid. This debate allowed the argument of remuneration for individual effort rather than family responsibility to emerge from the thicket of opposing interests. The contribution of women workers during the war added fuel to a fire which had been lit by the women teachers back in 1904 before the suffragettes. In 1942 an opinion poll showed public approval of equal pay for the teachers.

With the wartime efforts of women fresh in mind, an equal pay clause to the 1944 Education Act very nearly passed in to law, having survived the committee stage, and was only withdrawn after it had been made the subject of a government confidence motion. Churchill had prepared a speech likening the equal pay clause to putting an elephant in a perambulator; Churchill himself apparently regarded the clause as an 'impertinence' but he could not ignore its support: hence the Royal Commission which, although a delaying tactic, paved the way for the acceptance of the principle of equal pay. All that now remained was for there to come a time when public pressure insisted on its application. The grim postwar period, when people looked only to put the country back on its feet again, and for the comfort of familiar home surroundings, was not the time for the majority of women to rise up and demand equal pay. But the time was soon to come when the teachers would be in a perfect bargaining position to do so.

By a majority of over two million, the 1950 TUC conference voted that the time was right to implement equal pay and a large demonstration was held in Trafalgar Square in July 1951. But the government could afford to continue making excuses about its inflationary effect because it was immune from any real pressure from women themselves. However, the raising of the school-leaving age and the arrival of our generation at school in the early 1950s created an urgent need for women teachers, which verged upon panic. A campaign, offering part-time work, was rapidly launched to attempt to lure women back into teaching, but the response was not sufficient to meet the demand. In 1952 married women comprised one third of the teaching profession. In a debate about the difficulty of securing women teachers the issue of equal pay was raised. In 1955 (when we were swamping junior schools and threatening to converge on the secondary schools) the Burnham Committee agreed to phase-in equal pay for female teachers, to be fully implemented by 1961.

The National Union of Women Teachers (organized to fight
for equal pay) wound itself up with a victory dinner. Women in
teaching had gained a lot: a proper evaluation of themselves
as workers in their own right, the possibility of part-time work to
fit in with their domestic commitments, and a working day that
enabled them to meet their own children out of school, as well
as the rationale that they were needed and necessary for the
welfare of other people's children to combat any criticism against
them for possibly neglecting their own.

Nurses were another category of workers urgently needed.
'My husband was a clergyman,' says Helen's mother, 'and we
didn't have much money, so I started work when my daughter
was old enough to go to school. I got a job at the maternity
home – I had to take what I could to be home when the children
got in. My mother had been very houseproud, polished everything every day, whereas I dashed round dusting before anyone came. People were very fussy in those days, and they really
frowned on mothers working, because they had seen what the
crèches and day nurseries had done during the war. But if you
were a teacher, or a nurse, they forgave you, because teachers
and nurses were needed.'

A few of our mothers were teachers or nurses; some of them
worked because they simply had to, they were widows, but for
most of our mothers, however much they enjoyed the stimulation of working during the war, that phase of life was over
now, home responsibilities took precedence, and we arrived.
Our presence consolidated their sense of devotion to home and
family, smoothed over any difficulties of adjustment they might
have had: 'I went straight from working full-time to being a
housewife,' says Shirley's mother, 'and fell pregnant almost
right away. I felt a bit bored, because there wasn't enough to
occupy me, but you keep yourself going thinking you'll have
more than enough to do when the baby arrives. You plan
ahead, for a different way of life, because that's what life's
made up of, phases. I'd earned six times my prewar salary
when I was a bomb inspector, nearly bought my own house,
so it did feel a bit strange, at first, not having money of my own.
I had to get used to sharing, trusting my husband.

'Besides, the memory of how much I missed my mother when

she was out working stayed with me, during the war. I'd seen little toddlers going to the nursery, in the blackout on winter mornings. It didn't seem like the way to bring up children to my mind, pushing them out into the cold with hats and coats and gloves on and handing them over to complete strangers. I wanted to bring my children up myself.'

For most of us, the strongest early image of our mothers was their all-embracing presence, 'always there'. My earliest memory is of separation from my mother, when she went out to feed the chickens and, because it was raining, left me behind indoors, gazing at her through the french windows. Our mothers devoted themselves wholeheartedly to their children, not so much because they had been pushed back into the home, but because they were eager to rebuild what had been demolished during the war. People were reacting to the unsatisfactory emergency arrangements imposed on their lives during the war. They associated parking children in nurseries with all the other privations of the war. Institutional care had underlined the inherent insecurities of a situation in which children suffered as uncomprehending spectators of the instability and distress. And the war had shown the value of a secure, loving home life, of a mother's role. These sentiments were reinforced (rather than imposed from outside, as subsequent feminist literature seems to like to assert) by the focus upon child psychology which the disruptions of the war had triggered off. The importance of the mothering role, having been temporarily withdrawn, was now fully acknowledged, if perhaps too much so, by the writings of Dr Spock and John Bowlby, which emerged during the early fifties.

The trouble was that in their over-enthusiastic emphasis upon the needs of the child these commentators ignored the needs of the mother, largely because of the ingrained acceptance of the lack of necessity for married women to go out to work. In the fifties it didn't matter so much. There was still the neighbourliness of feeling you were all in the same boat, although the common enemy had disappeared. Televisions were few and far between – you all crowded in next door for the coronation, nipped over the fence and borrowed sugar when you ran out of coupons.

But over the Atlantic, in a more affluent (and therefore enclosed) home world, one contemporary of our mothers was beginning to question what she felt was the myth of a glorious, contented home life. Betty Friedan had lost a stimulating job to a war veteran and turned to marriage and having babies, just like the mothers of our generation. But the contrast made her think:

> At home you were necessary, you were important, you were the boss, in fact – the mother – and the new mystique gave it the rationale of career . . . more comfortable, more safe, secure and satisfying – that year and for a lot of years thereafter than that supposedly glamorous 'career' where you somehow didn't feel wanted, and no matter what you did you knew you weren't going to get anywhere.
>
> . . . we could be virtuous and pure of compromise, and even feel a smug contempt for the poor man who could not so easily escape the ulcerous necessity of really conforming and competing. For a long while it looked as if women had gotten the best part of that bargain. It was only later that some of us discovered that maybe we had walked as willing victims into a comfortable concentration camp.
>
> I still feel the pains of guilt caused by leaving my first baby with a nurse when I went back to work. Would all that guilt have been necessary if Dr Spock hadn't said . . . 'If a mother realises clearly how vital [safety and security] is to a small child, it may make it easier for her to decide that the extra money she might earn, or the satisfaction she might receive from an outside job is not so important after all.'
>
> (*It Changed My Life*, 1977)

The war had broken the either/or barrier between marriage and a career, but it hadn't solved how women juggled their dual responsibilities, to themselves and to their husbands and children. If any of our mothers felt the conflict, they didn't act upon it like their American contemporary by starting to write a book over the dining-room table (a book which would be published just as we were leaving school), although some of them were able to juggle the two, as she did. Did they express any of the missed opportunities they felt they'd had, in the way they began to bring us up, their daughters?

Recent research into sex-role stereotyping has shown how

mothers subtly reinforce sex differences by their expectations of and responses to their children's behaviour, even as tiny babies. Our mothers, in the days of the smocked and frilly fifties, were certainly no exception: 'I didn't bring Shirley and Michael up differently, but well, there is a difference between a boy and a girl. A newborn boy is all punch, you can feel the strength in him and little girls are always wanting to do something round the house – so feminine, aren't they?'

The role models were there for us to pick up on, when we were little. When Daddy was out at the office, the man with the case full of tins and brushes used to call, and give the little girl a tiny sample tin of polish for her dolls' house. The differences were also emphasized at junior school, not only by segregation for games and in the playground with its separate lavatories, but inside in the classroom as well. I came top at primary school, the year before we left. When Mrs Peers read out the results, she added 'We do find the girls do well at this age, but later on the boys take over.' This remark hung in the air with all the weight of the assumption that we were only playing at competition and success, whereas for the boys one day it would be deadly earnest, sink or swim. They had to be encouraged to succeed, at our expense.

I left the junior school before everyone else did. My parents moved many times in the course of their married life as my father's career progressed, trailing removal breakages, lost friendships, disrupted schooling with every fresh uprooting. But my father waited, this time, before shunting us all from the green belt to a grimy midland town, until I had sat the 11-plus. The 1944 Education Act, which had so narrowly missed giving women teachers equal pay, gave us an opportunity our mothers had missed: free secondary education, according to our age, aptitude and ability, for which we competed equally with the boys.

I stared once again, feeling lonely, through a rain-splashed window, this time from my bedroom in the new house, after we had moved. I spent one term at the new junior school on a hilltop overlooking the town, its gesture of faith in the new generation growing up, in a world fast acquiring all the material things its parents had had to go without. It was here that I first met some of the girls who were to become the interviewees in my sample of women from the 'bulge' generation. I began to make friends, but it was a difficult time.

Now that parents did not have to weigh up a costly personal investment, they could freely look to sons and daughters alike to fulfil their own missed opportunities. Daughters suddenly found themselves under the kind of pressure that previously only sons had felt. Angela: 'My father thought he had missed out, he wanted me to have the opportunities he'd never had. If I hadn't had the push from him, the dread that I wouldn't please him, I probably wouldn't have worked so hard to pass. He would have been very humiliated if I hadn't.'

And some of our mothers still felt the injustice of their own limited education. They weren't writing a book to put things right, they were encouraging their daughters to succeed where they hadn't had the chance. Deirdre: 'My mother felt she'd missed out. She was bright, but her parents couldn't afford to let her go on to grammar school, so she lived her ambitions through me in a way; she didn't push me, she just encouraged me an awful lot.'

Sandra: 'My mother always said there was absolutely no difference between the girls and the boys in our family. She always felt the ridiculous unfairness of her own lack of formal education, and she determined it wasn't going to be like that for me. Mum got annoyed when people assumed all the brains came from Dad, because she won all the prizes at elementary school.'

Christine: 'My mother wanted me to get on, because my father had had a grammar school education and she hadn't. They coached me like mad to get through the 11-plus.'

Friendships wilted or blossomed on the strength of what was going to happen to us the following autumn.

4   Educate a Woman . . .

*1958–63   high school girls – homework, not home work – TV, the
catalyst for change – friends and fashions – culture and the cult of
sensation – pop music, grapevine for a growing generation – the
permissive society – sex education*

Over ninety of us started our secondary schooling at the Girls'
High School, in a middle-sized midland town, in September
1958. We had been creamed off, set apart, lined up for the
best education the state could offer. The propaganda assured
everyone that the 11-plus was simply an aptitude test, but
everyone still saw it as an exam, one which I knew I'd passed
and a lot of the boys, in spite of the primary school teacher's
predictions, had failed. Although we were to be educated
separately, the boys who passed had not been given preferential treatment for the sake of their future careers.

The High School's history only went back as far as the end
of the last century (whereas the boys' grammar school, on the
hill, dated back to the sixteenth century), but the High
School had developed quite a reputation over the years. I
gazed at the names inscribed in gold in the entrance hall, when
we all went separately with our mothers for the introductory
interview with the headmistress before the term began.

Behind the curtained doorway to the headmistress's office
hung a sepia-tinted framed photograph of a group of dedicated blue-stockings clustered intimately with several stal-
wart-looking ladies. Outside in the corridor hung the evidence
that secondary education was now free – the unfurled spread
of five hundred fresh faces from all parts of the town, lined
up in front of the school building.

The High School's reputation ironed on the moment you

donned that distinctive dark uniform which made you the
butt of taunts from former friends who'd been banished to
the secondary modern. We were here because we were clever.
But we were never allowed to lean back on our laurels. They
constantly spurred us on to do better, dug out any pockets of
complacency with their pickaxe criticisms.

The charioteers in this grim race were the clique of single
women teachers, long hair firmly controlled under a hairnet and
twisted into plaits or a bun, long box-pleated tweedy skirts
and sturdy lace-up shoes. These were the women whose own
education had been hardwon, in the teeth of opposition.
Out of a stifling tangle of aimless, creeping dabblers, the ambitious ones hacked a way to university and the one profession
within a woman's reach. No wonder they were obsessed with
qualifying and matriculating examinations. How were we to
know, on Speech Day, when they flitted about in their fur-
tipped gowns, that although we were taking the Cambridge
GCE examinations *en masse*, women were first admitted as
full members of that university only in 1947, and then the
proportions were strictly limited, one woman for every ten
men.

I don't remember noticing I had moved from a mixed school,
although the only man at the High School – bar the care-
taker – was the art master. But I'm glad I went to a single sex
school. We had our own world, and you could go right to the
top of it. With the boys I feel sure we should have shrunk into
the old stereotypes, where they forged ahead while we froze
into giggling self-consciousness or frittered ourselves away on
dog-like devoted attentiveness in class. They would have claimed
physics and chemistry, leaving us to potter on with soft-
bellied biology, and of course the arts. But the only candidates
for the newly furbished science laboratories were us, and we
were actually encouraged to take physics and chemistry
because they carried more weight at 'O' level than biology.

Our education did differ from the boys': while they learnt
woodwork and played athletics, cricket and football, we did
needlework, dancing, rounders, hockey and netball. But woe
betide the games mistress who allowed the bell to go while we
were still on the field in games kit, thereby eating into a *real*

lesson. We were pursuing learning for its own sake, or rather, for the number of GCEs it gave you. Non-exam subjects languished in cracks in the timetable like weeds tolerated in crazy paving.

Compared with my mother's two-day domestic training, my preparation for my future role was two forty-minute periods, which I took as a chance to relax. It took me a whole year to finish a rather grubby smocked apron. I was too busy talking. I met my oldest friend in the first form needlework class. Jane was a guide. The Norwood Report on Education (published in 1943, when traditional roles had been over-turned) had recommended that 'girls should have an opportunity of learning handicraft and boys domestic subjects'. Such facilities were already available in 'co-ed' schools, but the report felt that 'Scouting' or 'Guiding' could answer such a need not met in single sex schools.

However, by the time we joined the Guiding movement, in the 1950s, responding to the tomboy impulse, we began to be instilled with ideas about who does what. Jane: 'At that age, I went out and built dens. Christine and me had boys' names, we played games of spies and French resistance workers. That was what appealed to me about Guides, learning to fend for yourself, rough it, going off camping. But helping around the house was how you won the badges – "cook", "baby-sitter", "housewife", "knitter" – while they got them for being adventurous and enterprising.'

The little girl who helped me finger the sewing in the least industrious manner became a firm friend, partly because my mother propelled me towards her. It was whispered around that her mother had just died, and my mother knew what that meant. But my friend's experience was somewhat different from my mother's. There was no question that Jane would miss school to look after the house – even if she had wanted to. Her elder sister, away at university, was also immune from what had been the traditional blackmail for a single daughter.

The school attendance officer had turned a blind eye to my mother's absence from school in 1919, but the problem itself was not ignored. In 1926 the Board of Education published a report which dwelt on the burden of domestic responsibilities which weighed more heavily on girls than boys. In 1947 a

widower was forced to send his daughter to school, after keeping
her at home cooking three-course dinners. When Jane's mother
died, in 1959, her father took over the responsibilities of the
shopping, got a 'woman' in to clean, and took turns with Jane in
getting the tea.

Home life differed for all of us, but only within certain limits.
Hardly anyone lived in a flat, and I didn't know anyone
whose parents were separated or divorced. Family life was
sacrosanct, you stuck with it. And the alternative for a woman
was not very bright. When I was quite small, it had dawned on
me that although we, the children, were all related, my parents
had once been total strangers. We were the family, not them.
But it never occurred to me that anything could separate them
or alter their relationship, just as it never struck me that my
mother could do anything but look after the house, cook,
write shopping lists (1lb toms, a nice lettuce, 1 t-roll) and thumb-
lick through pattern books at the drapers.

The traditional role distinctions were there, in black and
white. The only difference was that I was not being com-
mandeered to act them out. At school they sandwiched an
attempt to teach us to cook into two lessons a week for two
terms. The closest we came to concocting a meal was Cornish
pasty, cauliflower cheese and apple pie. While the novelty
lasted I made these snacks at home, on request, but otherwise
the most I had ever done was stir the gravy. My mother found
it hard to delegate in the kitchen, relinquish her total control.
I would retreat in frustration when she tried to show me how
to do something and ended up doing it herself. I couldn't
have deputized for her in her absence, even if I'd wanted to.

When I was 15, she had to go into hospital. I stayed to
school dinner then, and the daily help arrived with apple
pies and tarts on Pyrex plates. I have a dim recollection of us
all wandering into the cold kitchen and foraging in the larder,
like forgotten pets. I was then almost the same age my mother
had been when she left work to run a house. I attempted to
cook lunch for my brother and father – egg and chips. The
chips were pale and raw and the eggs stiff and leathery – I
had no idea how to time a meal.

Mothers were never normally inconsiderate enough to be

ill, and then they soldiered on until it was convenient to withdraw. Sandra's mother remembers being ill once in eleven years: 'Luckily it was Easter, so I came home quickly, hoovered round, changed the beds, went up to the shops and stocked up with food, by which time I'd missed the doctor's surgery, so when Daddy came in at five o'clock, I said "Cheerio, I'm off to bed".' When mothers dropped in their tracks, it was fathers, not daughters, who took over. Janet's mother was ill a lot when they were young, so her father cooked, bathed them, ran the house. Janet: 'He started off doing it when she was ill, then gradually took it over as his role. My mother was happier working in an office (I've no idea what she did, I never asked her). She was good at her job, whereas at home she never had been. I admired my father for doing so much around the house, when other people's came in, put their slippers on and watched the television. But I didn't admire him workwise, because he never made a great success of his career, and I can remember feeling sorry for him having to be so domesticated, whereas nowadays, I would feel it was the accepted thing.'

Jane's father, although he came from the north-east, believed that women should be able to drive cars and men cook dinners, although he preferred to have a wife around to do it for him. These men were exceptional. Most dads deputized, in dire emergencies, but with varying degrees of distaste and ineptitude. They were, after all, strangers to domesticity and home affairs. Mine was a figure in dark, formal suits, sometimes seen brushing his own shoes in the morning scramble when my mother juggled breakfasts, clean uniforms, dragging us out of bed. Or a hand, reaching out from behind the newspaper for the next sandwich to appear on his plate. Away at meetings in the evenings, he missed most of the family dramas over which my mother presided. She held him up as the ultimate deterrent, but it was she who dominated our lives.

Only after Sunday lunch did my father ceremoniously put on a special plastic apron which clutched at his waist rather than tying with strings. The saucepans he thought he'd washed up often had to be ditched back into the bowl. His tea was milky and insipid, and once contained desiccated coconut instead of sugar. If any of us was sick or ill, he would light a cigarette and walk away. I could never understand how such an influential person could be so incompetent.

Not that housework was anything I was interested in becoming proficient at. Some of us had jobs around the house, delegated to sons as well as daughters, but many of us, like myself, were waited on hand and foot by our mothers, boys and girls alike. Sometimes in the holidays I helped clean the brasses. Usually I made sure I didn't have to lift a finger. When the washing up needed doing I was already halfway up the stairs with my homework. I never made my bed. If you leave something long enough, I discovered, it will miraculously do itself for you, so why bother?

When my mother called from the steamy realms of the kitchen to where we sat in front of the television: 'What do you want for your tea?' the safest reply would be: 'Anything you like', so the onus was on her to prevent me from starving while I carried on watching the programme. She had the annoying habit of joining us halfway through and expecting to be told what was happening.

In 1959 my father had succumbed to family pressure and begun renting a television. The Englishman's castle was surrendering *en masse* at this time to invasion by the new mass-communication medium. From one in ten in 1960, the number of households centred around the box rather than the hearth had increased to two out of three by the end of the decade, a symptom of increasing affluence and standards of living during the production boom of the 1950s and 60s. But the 'telly', 'TV', 'goggle box' and all the other affectionate nicknames it acquired, was more than a harmless toy. This hypnotizing, glaring intruder was a revolutionary catalyst in a process of rapid social change which would affect all our lives, including our mothers'.

During the postwar recovery period, when raw materials became available again, manufacturers started looking for marketable uses for some of the technological innovations made during the war, to persuade people into parting with the extra pounds, shillings and pence they now found in their pockets. The monitoring of people's attitudes and experiences during the war (by Mass Observation) gave rise to a new approach to selling and advertising goods – the market research survey. Although only about 25 per cent of all married women were going out to work in the mid-fifties, statistics showed that it was women who went out shopping. They accounted for 60 per cent of consumer spending power and were the obvious targets for expanding markets.

The wooing of the housewife with new labour-saving gadgets began in the early fifties, with the appearance of paper tissues in 1952, and the long-handled sponge mop in 1954. Their advantages over boiling up dirty handkerchiefs and bending, mopping, scrubbing are to us instantly apparent, but people carried on blowing their noses into white cotton and women stayed on their knees on rubber mats. The trouble was that people still felt the effects of long years of making a virtue of thrift (disposability spelled waste) and housewives trained as our mothers had been distrusted anything not tried and tested. People were, in those days, creatures of habit. It had taken the war to dispense with time-consuming rituals like spooning jam into fluted dishes, making preserves and bottling fruit, and that had been in the interests of economy.

What commercial television did, when it appeared in the mid-fifties, was persuade people of the advantages of new ways of doing things by showing them a live demonstration. When extra-powerful detergents were advertised in 1958 for their wipe-away effect on dirty floors, the obvious applicator was not a sensitive hand clutching a wet cloth, but the elegant, efficient absorbent sponge on the end of a long handle, operated without bending now that elbow grease was unnecessary and demonstrated by the patronizingly smug lady who then went and irritated her next-door neighbour, still slaving away with the old method. Sales of the mop rocketed immediately.

Housewives needed similiar persuasion to invest in spray polish (developed from wartime insecticide aerosols used by the Americans in the Far East): the extra expense was worth it, because the polish was more economically distributed. Dry cake mixes and dehydrated foods had been developed (and detested) during the war, but when Viota drew attention to their Tea Cakes Mix 'for busy mothers', during a fifteen-week intensive TV campaign in 1959, the easy transformation from packet to mouthwatering end-product had the desired effect – they went like hot cakes. And when families starting to take holidays in Spain returned home, mum could try out the exotic dishes they'd tasted without the palaver of searching for unusual ingredients. Even I enjoyed the novelty of watching the hard little knobs in the packet swell into succulent morsels of paella in the saucepan.

Between 1949 and 1959 the number of families owning a vacuum cleaner doubled, home-owned washing machines increased tenfold and fridges trebled. People began to turn to electric fires and central heating and away from the dust and mess of coal fires. You bought sewing machines that did button-holing and embroidery, what little you had to embroider any more. In an increasingly affluent society many of the house-crafts that had been cultivated during the war were dispensed with to keep up appearances. You didn't darn elbows or mend socks, you consigned the garment to the duster drawer and bought new. Spin dryers whirled the effort out of Monday, as did steam irons and the new non-iron fabrics – bri-nylon and crimplene.

Now that housework was much less laborious and time-consuming, what were 'busy mothers' busy doing? Some women were beginning to go out to work again. They couldn't exactly leap into the careers they'd once dreamed of, because of their continuing domestic responsibilities, but more and more married women began going out to work part-time. They had to take what opportunities there were, capitalizing on what experience their years in the home had given them, but even then they were impeded by lack of self-confidence outside the family circle. Brenda: 'When we were about twelve, my mother started helping in the shop up the road, part-time. Then she taught herself shorthand and typing and became a school secretary, so she could be home in the holidays. She got very nervous before she started, not knowing whether she would be able to cope. But she's the bursar now, in charge of three other school secretaries.'

Christine: 'My mother tried to get a teaching certificate to teach cookery, but it was too much, in her forties, going to college and trying to keep the home running, so she took a

job as a reception class assistant, having not worked since the
war (when she drove a GPO van and shinned up telegraph
poles). She's doing the same job now.'

Sandra's mother also took a part-time job, helping at a
training centre for handicapped children. She'd got very un-
happy at home all day with the children staying to school
dinner, but was very nervous at first, because she hadn't
worked for about fifteen years: 'But I really enjoyed it. It
led on to what I'm doing now, supervising a playgroup. In a
small way, I'm doing what I originally wanted, which was to be
an infant teacher. It made up for a lot of the disappointments
I'd had. But it was definitely unusual for a married woman to
go out to work then, I think people automatically assumed
we were hard up. I mean, we all like money, but I did it
because I wanted to get out of the house, have an outside
interest.'

The middle-class taboo against working wives persisted,
partly because job opportunities in part-time employment
were limited, so it wasn't easy for a wife to find a job commensurate with her husband's status. 'At the age when men are
making their way up the ladder, most women are bringing
up their families' (*Financial Times*, 1959, 'It's Still a Man's
World').

As my father became more absorbed and successful in his
career, his affluence and our growing independence were
making my mother increasingly redundant in hers. But she had
no qualifications or skills, other than that of an office junior, or,
in her own words, skivvy. She had been out of circulation for
too long. It was hard enough for her to handcream her work-
roughened hands, adjust her normal bustling stance to a long,
brocade evening dress and tiny clutch bag and her earthy
conversation ('where are your dirty knickers?') to the loftier
issues of the outside world, when she had to accompany my
father to social functions which were too rare for her to acquire a
facility for them. She posed for the group photograph clutching a bouquet of roses, a dazed party to my father's professional
success. She was still just washing socks.

It was easier, less threatening for middle-class wives like
my mother to donate their services to voluntary community

help organizations, like the WI, the Mothers Union and the WRVS. One or two mothers got professional, reasonably paid work, with hours to suit their family commitments. These were, of course, the mothers who were trained teachers.

Their children's experience was light years from my own. Catherine's mother was a teacher, and Catherine remembers sometimes wishing that her mother had time to make her clothes, but at the same time relishing the independence it gave her, of doing things for herself, being able to put a meal together from the age of 10. Whereas my mother's response, lacking the vestiges of self-confidence, work experience and initiative other mothers had hung on to over the years, was to retreat into making more and more of her role as a mother, to occupy her time and justify her presence as an indispensable slave to her family.

The trouble was that housewifery, my mother's proud skill, had become reduced to boring mechanical tasks, relieved by the novelty of buying things rather than the satisfaction of making them. In the evenings my father stalked the house, switching out lights. My mother was marvellously extravagant, in comparison. Dr Edith Summerskill called these housewives 'the Cinderella(s) of the Affluent Society'. They were also to become the alienated, kleptomaniac compulsive consumers, or the phobic neurotic ones, reaching for the bottle of anti-depressants.

As people became more affluent, they also became more self-sufficient. The television, which brought so many marvels into the home, kept people there instead of going out or dropping round on neighbours. There was no excuse now that you didn't need to borrow next week's sugar ration. The housewife became increasingly isolated as her children grew older and she no longer saw them to school, chatting with other mothers; as the family clustered around the set in the living room, she was left alone in the kitchen. The gate to the outside world seemed further down the garden path. Even shopping was becoming much more anonymous, with supermarkets springing up in new shopping centres. It hardly seems surprising that many of our mothers reacted by making more of the important and vital responsibility that remained.

It never struck me, when I got home from school always

greeted by a fresh cup of tea, that my mother might be lonely
and bored, waiting under the dripdry shirts on the airer
for me to appear. I brushed aside her cross-examination about
my day because the questions betrayed her ignorance of my
world. Other mothers may have been better educated than
mine, but they too were often cloistered inside the daily demands
of domesticity. When we needed help with our homework,
they had either forgotten, or the subject was one which, at
elementary school, no one ever learned. Our parents indulged
us in schooltrips to visit penfriends when they themselves had
never set foot on foreign soil. Perhaps it was at this point that
they began to lose their hold as all-knowing, worldly wise,
figures of authority . . .

Only in the holidays did I enter into my mother's hollow
world, surfacing about eleven o'clock to a polished mausoleum
with a cold, empty grate. I was driftwood, washed up on the
desolate shore of domesticity, but I had the consolation of being
able to closet myself with my records and daydream, or, offering to do some shopping, snatch the excuse and the busfare to
meet my friends in Boots café or the wilder Wimpy bar in town.

The end of the holidays would invariably be a sunny,
leaf-dancing September morning, as my father offered my
brother and me a lift, since we were lumbered down with
games bags and holiday homework. I tried to pretend we
were setting off on holiday, instead of taking the same old
route to a plate of indigestible facts we had to regurgitate on
demand. The constriction of the uniform, the seriousness, the
grind sweeping over us again – horrible. But it was also talk,
talk, talk, excitement muffled among the coatpegs and sweaty
shoes. I was growing with influences outside the home, not
just school, but the friends that I found there.

After all, we were growing up. At first, when I was 12, 13,
my friends simply came round for tea. We played games and
dressed up in my mother's old dance dresses, stuffed with old
stockings at the top. But my own personality was stirring
and it would carry me away from her influence. My schoolfriends sharpened my own tastes. I looked at myself in the
mirror of their gaze and decided I didn't like the tartan trews
and brown laceups my mother had chosen.

On the uniformed face of it school was more or less the same for everyone, just as everyone looked more or less alike. But friendships based on the accident of sitting next to one another began to dovetail towards common interests, along with streaming and subject choice of concentration upon arts or sciences. Some of us were loners, but most of us moved within a circle of friends, or had one close confidante, with whom we started going out . . .

It was at weekends that the different strains of social butterflies began to emerge. We all responded differently, as we grew up and began to go out on Saturday night in the early sixties. We could be identified by how fashionably we dressed, how much make-up we wore, the music we liked, whether we went to Sunday school, youth club, or the local church hall dance or the coffee bar, and last but not least, by our attitude towards the opposite sex.

The council estate girls were all going steady at 13, setting their hair in rollers, wearing natty suits and lipstick and stockings, and generally flaunting their femininity long before my friends and I did. Other groups were more sporty than mine, quieter, or more serious, less obsessed with crushes on elder brothers at the grammar school.

Our own identities began to form within the supportive influence of our group of friends, each one of us becoming someone neither the teachers nor our mothers quite knew. I was the lazy slut my mother put up with. I was the shy, conscientious worker the teachers wrote reports on, somewhat 'diffident' in class. The 'real me' I only shared with my friends.

We were developing beyond our mothers' realms of knowledge through our education, but we couldn't really identify with the teachers because of a whole area of experience which they chose to ignore. They forbade us to wear our hair loose, or run along corridors, but always called us 'girls'. Our development into young women and the self-consciousness that accompanied it were brushed to one side. Only the needlework mistress, a motherly married woman, actually listened to our agonies over spots, curly hair, freckles, small eyes, big noses, fat arms and thighs and assured us all that we would grow into swans.

Otherwise, budding femininity and the frivolity that went with it were crushed and confiscated. No jewellery (the girl who got engaged in the fifth form wore her ring around her neck in scandalous secret) or nail varnish (straight down to the chem lab for a bottle of acetone), let alone the slightest hint of make-up. We did our best with modifications of the summer shirt-waisters to accommodate hooped and net petticoats underneath, but the following summer term, when the headmistress made an announcement that stiff petticoats would not be allowed because we couldn't all fit into the hall for assembly, we were all busy running up shifts, straight as a die.

The 1959 Crowther Report, commissioned to reconsider secondary and higher education in the light of changing social and individual needs, had recommended that education should acknowledge adolescent girls' interest in dress and courtship, but the little our teachers knew of fashion betrayed how out of touch they were with our world. Those who went into town on Saturday morning, bare ankles brushing against Marks & Spencer American Tan stockings, either dreaded bumping into a teacher or defiantly relished the prospect. Fashion was something on which we, not they, were the experts. We knew that dresses had to be hipster with box pleats and, equally firmly later, that the only style you could possibly wear was wide and waisted, then the empire line, and squeezing your feet into a succession of slingbacks, winklepicker stilettos, spade or chisel-toed shoes.

The fashion dictates we grew up under brand us, more than anything else, as children of that fascinating phenomenon, the sixties. Attempts to recapture its atmosphere often dissolve into a mush of goggle-eyed superlatives about 'swinging London' and its celebrities, with a sprinkling of chopped-up newspaper stories centred around cult heroes like John F. Kennedy and seamy scandals like the Profumo affair. But for the generation growing up under its glare, the most vital ingredient of the sixties was the cross-fertilizing effect of the mass media in the way that it focused upon us and our peers. The excitement of going out on Saturday night may have been tied down by the limited offerings of provincial night-life – the youth club or the bowling alley – but it soared on the air current of what was happening simultaneously in London and Liverpool. Previous generations, in the mild ambiance of the church youth club or the tennis pitch, were never exposed to such startling sophistication.

Amidst the clamour about affluent teenagers exploited by unscrupulous and cynical advertising men, Peter Laurie (in a wonderful evocation of the sixties, called *Teenage Revolution*, written in the thick of it all – 1965 – but with a foreigner's detached insight) pointed out that sixties' teenagers were much freer than previous generations to spend their pocket-money on luxuries like clothes and records, because of the paradoxical influences of growing up under the comforting umbrella of the Welfare State and an aggressively capitalist consumer economy. Whether the marketing men actually did plot against us with Clearasil, Panstick and pop records is in one sense irrelevant. The fact was that they fed our fantasies, eclipsing the influence of our parents and teachers in the process.

My mother indulgently capitulated to my insistence on fake snakeskin fashion boots that weren't sensible enough to keep the wet out, and let me straighten the curls she coveted so much. She risked her reputation in the town by the sight of me in a black shiny mac, face masked deathly white and eyes blackened like a prostitute, because of the force of our numbers, the insistent logic of acceptability – 'everyone else did'. Our teachers may have found it easier to forbid these appurtenances, but their own efforts to point us in the right direction in a strange way only served to accelerate the opposite effect.

As we, the Bulge, progressed up the school like a mouse swallowed by a snake, the building was forced to expand, literally, to accommodate us. A new block was tacked on the back, with more science labs, a bigger sixth form room and dining-room, and brand new showers began to be built inside the old quad, next to the gym. Through its windows the young workmen stared in at us. We couldn't imagine how such shiny-nosed, blotchy-skinned schoolgirls in navy knickers and ankle socks could possibly interest them, and we dreaded the day when the building work was finished because we would have to display our bodies to one another.

One well-developed girl didn't wear a bra and wobbled

unconcerned into everyone's view in the changing room, but most of us were our mothers' daughters still, sharing the humiliation of naked exposure. You could be excused from showering if it was the 'wrong time of the month'. Many of us suffered from over-regular periods thereafter, but were forced out of some of our shyness, the result of so much modesty at home.

Romantic comics, *Roxy, Mirabelle* and *Romeo,* which I devoured between home and school and then hid under my mattress (imitating my brother with his *Spick and Span*), were banned at home as 'common trash' and at school as an insult to our intelligence. Yet I have a sneaking feeling it was simply because they were concerned, underneath all the simpering froth of dreamy looks and innocent romantic clinches, with the base bodily undertow we were beginning to feel. But our parents couldn't so easily cut off the food supply on which forbidden thoughts flourish.

Culture could combine with the cult of sensation. In 1960, when the M1 had just opened, we went on an educational trip to London and visited the National Gallery. Sandra saw 'all these people sitting on the gallery steps with no shoes on, and I thought how wonderful'. Back at home she bought black stockings and persuaded 2/6 out of an indulgent neighbour to buy some black eyeliner.

School texts may have been abridged, but not the performances we witnessed on group outings to Stratford, or the late night BBC Shakespeare history plays we insisted on staying up to watch, because they were part of the GCE syllabus. A friend banished to relatives in the holidays earned her parents' approval and relieved her own boredom by dedicating herself to a history book. She wrote in a letter: 'In case you think I'm cracked, *Kings of Merrie England* although history is so bloodthirsty, sex-mad and like an epic film that it's great reading. Edward II was a queer and I won't tell you how he died cos it's the most brutal murder in history. I read in a recent crit of the Marlowe play that grammar schools like to do it to see how far they can get with the last scene before the headmaster intervenes. I must get a copy.'

Such apparent obsession with sex was simply part of our normally encouraged natural curiosity. We were outside the

door to the inner sanctum, the temple of the adult world.
When I was little, banished to bed, I used to hang over the
banisters for a glimpse of what went on down there. Later,
when I found out where the action really was, the focus shifted
back upstairs, although only metaphorically. Parents were too
successfully discreet. We had to turn to books, films, and the
television to find out.

The English mistress encouraged us to watch current
affairs programmes like *Panorama* and the much more enticing
Tonight, which offered mirages of masculinity, Robin Hall and
Jimmie MacGregor strumming in open-necked shirts. Similarly,
she encouraged us to use part of the wall of our formroom as a
current affairs corner. I had the task of chopping all the news
items out of the previous day's paper before I went to school,
and pinning them up when I got there. I never bothered to
read the close, small type of the *Daily Telegraph*, except for one
court hearing in 1960, which I pinned up religiously every day
and which everyone clustered round to read.

The liberal permissiveness of the new Obscene Publications
Act which excluded works of art from the penalties of suppres-
sion as 'mere pornography' was to be tested by the trial of
Penguin Books for publishing *Lady Chatterley's Lover*. It was an
open forum to discuss eroticism, sensuality, and, in the words of
the Bishop of Woolwich, 'quite astonishing sensitivity in the
beauty and value of all organic relationships' – a fitting way of
ushering in the secular, sensational, swinging sixties. It was not
just 'honesty' and 'realism', the growing openness about sex,
defended by respectable intellectuals, which allowed us to pin it
up on the wall in school, to openly declare our interest in sex.
While the trial continued our excitement was about the idea of
the book, that sex was not a taboo, 'dirty' subject. When the
prosecution was defeated by a jury of ordinary people, someone scawled 'Congratulations, Lady C' across the blackboard.
The young, married English mistress smiled, but the elderly
spinster who took us for scripture flushed and clucked, in spite
of the Bishop of Woolwich, and ordered it to be smothered off
with a duster. However, she couldn't smother the fact of its
availability.

I brazenly ordered a copy from the newsagents on the way

home. I imagine I hid it in my desk at school. The phoenix on the cover and the title were now so notorious I couldn't have risked taking it home. I only read the salacious bits. But it wasn't the titillation of reading rude words that fascinated me, as my father drily dismissed it. It was the revelation that sex for a woman could be an incredible physical experience, not just an artificial, romantic, airbrushed ecstacy, guilt-ridden surrender in sordid circumstances. We wouldn't be lying back, thinking of England.

Two years later we were also the children of the Cuban crisis, the sudden threat of nuclear war. The question was what to do with your last four minutes on earth, and the consensus of opinion was to rush out into the street and grab a man. One self-possessed sophisticate said that she didn't reckon it would be all it was cracked up to be, but still, you didn't want to die without knowing. Please God, don't let me die a virgin. You huddled among the coats in the cloakroom and wondered what 'it' would really feel like.

The reality was that we were all at different stages in the game of going out with boys, just as our taste in pop music split us into very different factions – liking Roy Orbison's heightened romantic stuff, Brenda Lee's gutsy, gritty battle for emotional survival, Cliff and the Shadows' rather tame (to me) efforts, or the more blatantly erotic messages of Billy Fury and Elvis, and of course the complete rejection of all this in favour of *Fingal's Cave*, marked us out as blatantly as any label could have done.

Music, like perfume, is so magically evocative. Old singles act like a fixing solution for the events of almost twenty years ago. Music reaches long dead sensations, emotions, moods, binding a generation of separate upbringings simply because the same record played everywhere – Boots record booths, the Wimpy's juke box, Alan Freeman's 'Pick of the Pops' and Radio Luxembourg Top Twenty late on Sunday night under the pillow. Our transistors tuned us in to all the others of our age. The adolescent was no longer the solitary misfit of the family group.

Music was an escape from cerebral pressures, sinking into the senses and channelling the energy our mothers had to stifle, the amazing energy of youth. It was, as Peter Laurie expressed it, 'the pulse and flow of teenage life'. And dancing was its expression. It was still unthinkable for a girl to go out on her own, like the boys could, but unlike our French and German penfriends we had the freedom to go out in the evening to church hall dances, just a group of girls. At first it meant trying to learn how to jive with your girlfriend, and having to play wallflower when a boy butted in. Then Chubby Checker saved us with the Twist. A group of you did it in a circle, getting off with a boy was no longer such a putdown to your best friend. And the opposite sex was the interest most of us shared. I never confided in my mother about boys – she might have injured my shaky confidence by patronizing or mocking me. A friend wrote to me in 1962 and bracketed the bits I shouldn't read out to my mum. By 1964 the P.S. at the head of her letter read: 'I haven't marked the bits you can't read to your mum, cos you can't read any . . .'

The 1962–3 academic year had been a turning point in our lives, not simply because it was the year we all took 'O' levels and some of us stepped off into the adult world, but because it was the year our school made two concessions towards our need for social skills in that world, both of which outlined the gulf between us and the older generation.

The first was ballroom dancing classes, held on Monday evening during the autumn term, culminating in a dance at Christmas. The girls clung to one side of the hall and the grammar school boys to the other, until the physics mistress winkled them out and propelled them towards us. I only ever learnt the man's part, partnering my girlfriend in preference to a clammy hand behind your waist that didn't support you when you spun round. Then one Monday evening, it was rumoured that a new group called the Beatles were going to be on television, on a local programme called 'People and Places'. My friend and I knew what came first. We faked the excuse of the fog – it was chilly November 1962 – that our mothers wanted us home before dark and dashed back to the television.

The Parlophone red label 'Love Me Do' that we bought between us, sounds thin and raw today beside the sophisticated popular singers at the time – Elvis, Gene Pitney, Billy Fury – with their well-orchestrated amplification. But these four angular figures in their collarless suits were so appealing because they seemed so much closer to us than the superstars. They made up their own songs, they'd lived here, taken GCEs too. Because there were four of them, we could share them out equally, each dream of marrying a Beatle without competing with our best friend.

1963 was the year the pop music scene burst into raw life, with the emergence of the Rolling Stones and the tidal wave of Liverpool groups in the Beatles' wake. Many of these groups did the circuit of church hall dances – my friends and I did the Shake to the live music of the Kinks, the Four Pennies, the Mojos and Faron's Flamingos. The rest of the time we had to console ourselves with enormous double-page photos out of *Fabulous* and *Big New Beat*, a huge face contorted by the middle fold and pockmarked with staple holes. This obsession with men-gazing was innocent enough, except that we were releasing a voyeuristic appetite for them as sex objects, and later responding more passionately because they never got near enough in reality to threaten to seduce us – all within the context of an increasingly 'permissive' society in which a controversy raged between the repressive moralists and the liberal free-thinkers.

Our generation was old enough to go and see the daring X films of the early sixties: *Only Two Can Play*, *Saturday Night and Sunday Morning*, *A Taste of Honey*, *The L-Shaped Room*. Though relatively tame in terms of films today, all sympathetically explored taboo subjects, including shameless adolescent female sexuality, which was the subject of *Term of Trial* (1963).

But we didn't need to go out to absorb the new open-ended attitudes. Parental control over 'scandal papers' which had been stopped before they reached the letter box was seriously undermined by the invasion of the television, which even lent an air of authority to those sections of society of whom they most disapproved. The irreverent attacks of 'TW3' ('That Was The Week That Was'), the adventurous satirical review programme put out by that revered institution, the BBC, overrode all their feeble tuts and clucks. The BBC even interviewed Dr Alex Comfort, now famous for his sex technique manuals, whose *Sex in Society* was republished in 1963. The book dealt with sex from a frank and humanistic point of view, advocating the foolishness of denying its pleasure.

Our teachers could no longer hold their heads in the sand and ignore the fact that we were growing up in such a world. They had to concede that we were no longer protected by innocence, and they decided to give us the full facts, assuming that knowledge of the dangers of pregnancy would deter us, and reduce the taboo element that was so fascinating. At the end of the fifth form we each carried home a note to our parents, informing them that we were about to have sex education lessons.

Very few mentioned the note, although they knew we knew what it contained. Some managed to say, not without some embarrassment, that they didn't have to say anything, did they, because we knew what was right and wrong. Their embarrassment betrayed the simplicity of their own early tuition. One mother, having been crudely enlightened by a wartime propaganda film warning of the dangers of promiscuity and VD, related to her daughter that a deformed baby would be the inevitable outcome of sleeping with more than one man.

The biology mistress had pointed with a stick at a cross-section of the male penis on one of those glossy, laminated wallcharts, and her final words were: 'I know I usually encourage you to experiment, but this time – don't.'

Our mothers had mostly married in white, with clear consciences, in their mid-twenties. They had been inhibited by their ignorance, and the invisible strings of their parents' moral values. And society's rules were crystal clear. No one wanted secondhand goods. Perhaps if you sat on a man's lap you might have a baby, along with the shame and ignominy which would ruin your whole life. What, though, was to hold *us* back, from delightfully exploring our bodies with boys, when we knew it would be all right if you didn't go all the way? Our mothers never discussed the practical problems of 'snogging' with boys. They just loaded the responsibility on to us, as it had been dropped on to them, but unfortunately it was not so easy to tell right from wrong as it had been in the thirties when progressive ideas were the preserve of isolated minority groups, the very rich or the intelligentsia; when many people's encounters with the opposite sex took place under the auspices of the church. We had also met at church hall hops, organized by the local vicar, but some of us took the bait and escaped the trap, in the growing atmosphere of secularization in society. When the Bishop of Woolwich attempted to bridge the gap, in 1963, with *Honest to God*, all he really achieved was the legitimizing of agnosticism and atheism by recognizing them.

Pop music was also counselling rebellion. Cliff (approved of by many parents) had broadcast a message in 1962: 'Mummy says No,/Daddy says No,/If we didn't go ahead/In spite of what they said,/Might as well give up man,/Might as well be dead.' It's true that Noel Coward brought out a song for our parents called 'Let's Misbehave', but the emphasis is on being naughty, whereas Cliff's aggressive assertion was that we were right and parents were wrong. The wavelength we had tuned into was telling us to go ahead, have fun, let go and enjoy the present – 'live, love, while the flame is strong,/'Cos we may not be the young ones very long'.

The boys were also listening. Did our mothers ever get into the situations we had to handle? I met a public schoolboy when I was 16. My mother encouraged me to accept the invitation to go for tea. His mother carried in the tray, no doubt eyeing my dark Inca tan stockings, slinky shift, backcombed hair, black eyeliner. The moment she withdrew, I didn't even have time to raise the cup to my white lips. I remember fighting for air between his lunging, groping assaults and pleading 'talk to me'. He dropped me at the end of the holidays and no doubt his parents were relieved that he had escaped such a vamp. Had I led him on by the way I dressed? Was I sending out 'come on' messages our mothers had trapped inside their girdles, in the way that he also was loosing his real response? Luckily, it was too clumsy on his part and too unconscious on mine to get anywhere.

The single memento I have of him, an old Elvis LP, gives me a clue: a near contemporary, whose hot breath, wet tongue and dirty fingernails I might have recognized, blamed it all on two song writers:

Leiber and Stoller's songs were potent because they teased our longing with such sly precision . . . We were nice kids studying hard . . . and . . . Presley was the original bad guy . . . It was even rumoured that he didn't wear any underwear at all when he sang.

Did Leiber and Stoller imagine us listening to the radio with lights out . . . rehearsing how to jimmy a Maidenform bra with thumb and forefinger? . . . Rock and roll alone spoke kindly to our appetites and answered our craving for sensation . . . rock and roll . . . made connections with the body. When Elvis crooned Leiber and Stoller's 'Don't' and 'Love Me' he wasn't issuing an invitation to the waltz. Leiber and Stoller knew . . . it was flesh we craved . . . Conquest was our only concern . . . we talked endlessly about aphrodisiacs . . .

(from 'Loosening Up the Libido', John Lahr, *New Society* 10.4.80)

It was hard to even confide in girlfriends about how far to let them go. Two girls who were very close did have a checklist, where number two stood for hand on top of bra, number three underneath, on up to the unmentionable number ten, but they never got much further than three or four because they never went out with any one boy for long enough. You didn't want to appear a prude, but you didn't want the other label either. One girl found out that her ex-boyfriend kept a notebook to record how far he had got with each girl on a star rating, and circulated it round the grammar school. There was no moral beltline for the boys, but we were terrified of getting a reputation because it was synonymous with being used rather than liked, a deterrent much more powerful than our parents' censure.

One thing about exposing your body was that you were making yourself vulnerable to criticism of your small breasts or tatty bra. We didn't tend to assault the boys in the way they tried to roam over us. But when the Beatles released 'Please Please Me' in 1963 the innuendo was there. At the medical before 'O' levels, the rumour went around that the doctor could tell by looking at your nipples whether you were a virgin. Some dark horses visibly blanched, but going all the way was still utterly unthinkable for most of us. The penalties were too great. Our parents warned us, obliquely: 'They never mentioned sex itself, only that I had to be in by ten o'clock. But if anyone was heard to have got pregnant, how terrible, how bad, although nothing was ever said about how you got like that.'

Shirley: 'My mother had told me the facts of life and why to keep away from strangers, when I was about eight. But although she taught me to think for myself, she never gave me any counselling about sex. She would just say things when she was angry, if I had come in late from a party – "You needn't bring your baby bundles back here" – it used to worry me a lot.'

It did happen to one girl, who had to withdraw before taking 'O' levels. It was hushed up, though. In those days you were sent away to a mother and baby home, run by nuns, until the evidence of your disgrace had been adopted. It was something that was expected to happen at the secondary modern, though, not to High School girls.

Hilary: 'At home I was inhibited from participating as fully as I might have done in the social life. My mother seemed very fearful that I might get into trouble, in some way, so my father used to collect me at ten o'clock from parties, which was very embarrassing. I think my mother was so keen for me to have the chances of a career that she had missed, that she didn't want me to muck it all up by doing something silly.'

5 What Shall I Be?

1963–65 educational aims – high hopes and fears of failure – 'careers for girls' – stepping off at sixteen – staying on in the sixth – first cracks in the generation gap – lost innocence and the luck of the withdrawal method

> *Shall I be a nurse*
> *But not without a purse*
> *Or shall I be a teacher?*
> *But I'm not a very good speaker.*
> *Or shall I be a model?*
> *But the trouble is I wogel.*
> *Or shall I be a queen?*
> *To go upon the screen.*
> (Maureen Dennis, 11, from
> *School Leavers*, Thelma Veness,
> 1962)

What career chances did our mothers not want us to spoil? We were getting the education they had been denied, but what was it for? The popular saying of the fifties and sixties went: 'Educate a man and you educate an individual; educate a woman and you educate a future family.' Yet our mothers hadn't had a grammar school education because it was assumed to be a waste. A good education didn't matter for a woman because, like Sandra's mother, she would get married. Were we getting a grammar school education because it was assumed we would do something besides getting married?

The 1944 Education Act, which granted free secondary schooling to all and grammar school places to those who proved themselves suited for an academic education, was seen as a major step on the path towards social equality of opportunity, because it allowed working-class children to compete for white-collar jobs and university places. This breakthrough for working-class children attracted a lot of attention; the girls who also flooded in for the first time for the opportunity of secondary education joined them almost unnoticed.

If education had been more closely linked to future adult roles, this might not have been so. The 1944 Education Act, which instituted the 11-plus, had managed to crystallize three rather contradictory nineteenth-century arguments about the aims of education: as an end in itself, to enrich the mind; as the right of all citizens to be literate and numerate; as the necessity of providing an industrial society with a skilled disciplined workforce, by its threefold provision of secondary education, at grammar school, technical high school or secondary modern.

Traditionally, grammar school education prepared the ruling classes to take their place in one of the professions – the church, the law or teaching. Secondary modern education, with its emphasis upon basic literacy and manual skills, fitted a child to join the workers. This value-loaded implication, that a child was being shunted towards a particular place in the social hierarchy, was evaded by stressing that the 11-plus was a measure of a child's suitability for the different types of secondary education on offer. In the haste to emphasize 'parity of esteem' at secondary level, grammar school education came simply to represent to our parents an 'opportunity', a better start in the race for a place at the head of the queue for white-collar work in a middle-class aspiring community. Our teachers also, judging by their obsession with GCEs, saw education as an indefinite points system, rather than a direct preparation for adult life.

Any leftover doubts about wasting a grammar school education upon a girl who would only get married were dispersed by the rationalization of the inestimable value of an educated mother. But when we were little, however much time we spent tucking dolls up in bed, playing mothers and fathers, quite a few of us knew exactly what we wanted to be when we grew up, and the answer was never a housewife and a mother. Julie had just had a wonderful pair of new shoes when she was set a composition at junior school, entitled 'What I want to be when I grow up'. She wanted to be a shoe shop assistant. Her twin sister's ambitions were grander, she told me: 'Janet was going to be an opera singer, wear lipstick and live next door to the theatre.'

Sandra, whose earliest memories are of living with her head-master grandfather, says she used to lead the little ones off into a field, sit them down in a circle and read to them. Marjorie, who played schools with dolls and little exercise books, was also going to be a teacher. Others planned to be doctors, nurses, explorers, pilots. At 5 Catherine knew exactly what she wanted to be – an astronomer: 'I had a tiny telescope and I thought astronomers sat underneath and said "Oh, how pretty".'

Such early ambitions were of course star-gazing, based on an attractive image, a whim rather than a realistic assessment of a job for which we might not have the talent, the temperament or, of course, the opportunity. At 5, you don't notice that very few women become explorers, astronomers, doctors or, for that matter, opera singers. But it was significant that we did want to be something.

At 5 I was just as certain as Catherine what I was going to be. I pirouetted on the front lawn while my mother patiently sewed layers of pink net on to a satin bodice for the infants' dancing display. Later on, when I was much more shy, the ambition switched to one I didn't have to test while the mothers sat at the back and watched. Twirling a one-and-threepenny Woolworth's sapphire ring on my finger, I confided in my aunt that I was going to be an actress. I wasn't stagestruck, I assured her. I really meant it.

The budding actress was still there, when my mother and I walked down to the interview with the headmistress, before I started at the High School. The single-storey building with large pivot-hung windows lay at the bottom of a long gravel drive which curved around a vast expanse of green hockey field. I was even more overawed when we were ushered in to the presence of the headmistress herself, a tall, gaunt woman with spectacles and a wispy bun, who asked what career I had in mind. This was the question she put to all of us at this introductory interview and it was the first time we had to put our ambitious dreams to the acid test of reality.

I instinctively protected my fantasy balloon from her piercing scrutiny, hid the actress behind a more acceptable answer. My favourite occupation was reading, I fancied being surrounded by books to read, so I told her I wanted to be a librarian – and received the nod of approval.

If any of us were stuck for an answer, being more vacuous about such a faraway object as leaving school, the headmistress helped out. Her girls became teachers, or, if they couldn't manage that, nurses. Marjorie's naive fantasy about marking books was suddenly transported into the realms of reality: 'She said straight away, "Right, that's seven years with us and three years at college" and my mother said "Ten years! Good heavens!" but she reassured her that it would pass very quickly, and it did.'

In retrospect that time may have passed quickly, but the next five years were actually dragged down by the requirements of the GCE 'O' level syllabus, all the things we had to learn every day, the books, the tests, the homework. In the third form we were streamed into three classes according to our measured ability and made the choice between a concentration upon arts or science subjects. Most of us opted for the subjects we happened to succeed in, because that made them more enjoyable: a simple process of natural selection, but one which shattered some ambitious dreams. We had all tasted success when we got the new school uniform, and now, as the skirt turned shiny where you sat on it and the cuffs and collar of your shirt got frayed, some of us were having to face failure.

Until the third form I did well in English. I upped my ambition from librarian to journalist. I saw myself joining the local paper at 16 and working my way to Fleet Street. But then a new English mistress arrived and marked me down at the end of the year examinations to fourteenth. Paralysed by humiliation and ashamed of my presumption I flinched, turned my back. I didn't want to be a journalist any more.

I was apparently exhibiting a classic female response to failure. Studies of girls' under-achievement argue that girls shrink from challenge, lower their sights earlier than boys

because they equate success with luck and failure with lack of
ability, whereas boys react the other way round. If, instead
of assuming that the first teacher had simply favoured me, I
could have blamed the second teacher's blindness to my brilli-
ance, I would have been better armed to prove her wrong.
Boys are better able to combat failure simply because they
externalize it. In a way, I did try harder, not so much to prove
myself but from sheer terror of failure, much like my mother's.
Fear of drowning kept me bobbing up among the upper marks
from then on, but the ambition I had previously proudly sailed
was furled, waterlogged, submerged. In pushing us to fulfil our
potential, the teachers tended to neglect our need for positive
encouragement to want to succeed.

Gillian remembers sitting in front of the headmistress saying
she wanted to be a doctor, when she first went to the High
School: 'Biology was the only subject I did well in, but that
ambition had gone out of the window by the second year. I'm
not a very academic person, I never used to concentrate much
on my homework. In a way, it was easier to just give up, because
they expected so much of us. I was more interested in going to
Guides or the youth club than stopping in doing my homework.'

If girls lack staying power when the going gets tough, perhaps it is partly because they are encouraged to abandon dis-
plays of initiative when they start going out with boys. Whether
we went to youth club dances, or sat in coffee bars, played the
sultry temptress or lingered bashfully in hand-held tête-à-tête,
we were beginning to learn the rules of the game which still
depended upon the boys taking the initiative. At school if you
stuck your hand up and you had the right answer, you got the
reward. At home if you wanted something, you learnt how to
ask for it. With boys, it was all subterfuge.

I once wangled a date with the boy across the road by sending
him a valentine. The other method was to indicate interest
through the grapevine of mutual friends, but after the first date,
if he'd casually left you at the gate, you had to spend the following week in mounting agony, unable to concentrate on your
homework – every time the phone rang it might be him. The
antidote was passive resignation, counselled in the agony
columns by Evelyn Home, who advised sitting at home 'serenely

certain' that if he really wanted you he would batter the living-room wall down to get at you.

The penalty for stepping out of line would be the agonizing 'see you around' left ringing in your ears. We could never play it straight, because the ball was always in their court. You could only counterattack cavalier, cliffhanging treatment by being coy, playing hard to get, pretending you didn't care. These tactics, when transferred to the classroom, were fatal. The tendency to withdraw immured you from the pain of public rejection, but it also prevented you from developing tough skin like boys had to, the self-assertion with which to laugh off defeat and try again.

The trouble was, as Catherine discovered when she gave up the idea of becoming an astronomer after discovering they did a bit more than stare at the sky – 'and maths was never my strong point' – there was little else to replace it, if you didn't see your-self as a nurse or a teacher. Some of our fathers had quite definite ideas about what we could do when we left school, but our mothers, who had never got much further than thwarted dreams and resentment at their brothers' preferential treatment, were much vaguer. They simply wanted us to get on, be happy, do what we wanted to do, in ways that were as ill-defined and unresolved as their own hopes had been, torn up before they could be tailored to reality. And our teachers were too intent on pushing us through the examination system as far as we could go to bother about giving us careers guidance, although there were some careers novels in the school library.

Apart from the Sue Barton books about nursing, there was a Bodley Head series, 'Careers for Girls', published in the mid-fifties: *Valerie Fashion Model; Air Hostess Ann; Pam Stevens Secretary; Jill Kennedy Telephonist; Sheila Burton Dental Assistant.* I only read the glamorous ones, but they were all romantic. Every girl starts off freshfaced and enthusiastic, determined not to be sucked into marriage, but somehow her progress is impeded by romance. Although she has become a television announcer, Clare's final triumph, in *Clare in Television*, comes when the producer asks her to marry him. *Judith Teaches* and *Margaret Becomes a Doctor* (published in 1957) were the only stories which combined the idea of marriage with a woman continuing her career, featuring normal women, neither capitulating nor swearing celibacy, even though they do tend to be the ones having to compromise:

> 'You know, Donald, I've been wondering what sort of work I should do. When I was staying with Uncle Robert, I saw quite a lot of infant and school clinics and I'd been thinking I would rather like to go into Public Health. And now it seems just the answer. I'd be free in the evenings to get your meals. If we're both GPs it would be box and cox all the time and we might never see each other.
>
> 'And when we have children, later on,' Margaret added, 'I can resign from my job while they're young . . . – but later on I'll work again. I don't think a doctor has a right to waste her training.'

In the mid-sixties, however, the Bodley Head decided to dodge the thorny problem of career versus homes and husbands and non-existent promotion prospects and confined itself to practical non-fiction titles on catering and domestic science, beauty, fashion, travel; the options hadn't changed. Discounting the glamorous jobs, the choice narrowed down to teaching, nursing or office work, mostly subservient to marriage. The boys at the grammar school probably had just as little actual careers guidance, but they knew from the start that they would have to shape their own lives, and if they didn't watch out they might end up having to do something they didn't like. The pressure on them was to make positive, decisive choices, whereas we could cushion ourselves with the hope that the future would take care of itself.

And the boys had role models of working adults all around them with which to identify. As one girl said, 'the only image I had of women's prospects was teachers – otherwise you became a mother and stopped at home'. How many working women could we see, if we eliminated the nurses, teachers, secretaries and cleaners? When we were little, playing explorers, we hadn't noticed that there were many jobs that only men did. Later on, the space vacated by the explorer remained empty, partly because girls weren't encouraged to think in terms of work as a means of achievement or self-expression; partly because the choice against which one had to match one's own inclinations and enthusiasms was so limited. All this was only very vaguely sensed at the time, swept away in the rush towards 'O' levels.

At some stage in the fifth form we were all called into the main hall to listen to a lady in a wide-brimmed hat from the Youth Employment Office, who had come to give us a talk about careers. I have no idea what she said because I didn't listen. I'd toyed with the idea of going into hotel management because I fancied living in grand surroundings, but had decided to stay on and take 'A' levels because all my friends were staying on, because you were expected to stay on if you were good enough and because it meant that you could put off making the decision about what you were going to do with your life.

The talk was aimed at those who were about to leave school, but they didn't listen either – it all seemed so boring. Those who were about to step off the academic conveyor belt at 16 looked forward to leaving because their interests lay outside the school gates. You were expected to stay on if you were good enough; by inference, therefore, you were weeded out as the failures if you left, even though it was good to see the back of a repressive system which had no room for your own talents. Girls who were leaving looked forward to having money in their pockets, wearing high heels, make-up, not having to fasten berets on the back of their backcombing with a battery of grips.

In the absence of any clear ideas of their own on what they wanted to do, they accepted the limited choices which were open to them. Sheila's first choice had been nursing, but she wasn't the studious type. She then fancied hairdressing, but there weren't any apprenticeships going locally and it was hard to find anything out about it because it wasn't considered a suitable job for a high school girl. 'It just seemed the obvious thing to do,' Sheila says, 'to go to secretarial college.'

Barbara hadn't got a clue when she was asked what *she* wanted to do at the Youth Employment Office. They suggested a secretarial course, so that was what she did. Most girls went straight into routine office work or took secretarial or catering courses at technical college. Julie was a bit more ambitious: 'I visualized myself working in an office, but at something interesting, not shorthand/typing like my mother had done. I was good at maths, which was probably why I went into banking. I thought it was a cut above the ordinary.'

One girl, determined to satisfy her early ambition to become a domestic science teacher, stayed down in the fifth form to take 'O' levels again: 'But the effort of repeating a boring syllabus all over again finished me as far as academic work was concerned. I left and took the only course open to me, or that was what it felt like at the time, a year's secretarial training, and I quite enjoyed it; it was much more stimulating than school.'

Two girls, who'd grown up with very strong ambitions, chose to step off the academic conveyor belt because they found school and the sixth form syllabus too narrow and stifling. Andrea's father had been a St John Ambulance instructor, so there were always first aid and anatomy books in the house: 'I wanted to be a doctor, not a nurse. My mother had been bright at school and wanted something more for me, but there was no scene when I changed my mind.' Andrea had done badly in a physics exam, and stubbornly decided to turn her back on school. She got a job straight away as a lab technician.

Sylvia's earliest ambition had been to be something professional, like a doctor or a lawyer: 'I wanted to go to Oxford, perhaps because they didn't like women very much. I thought I was a new breed and they'd have to make way for people like me. My father had given me ambition, because he'd wanted to do something like that. Even now, I could kick myself, because I didn't, but I was unsettled at that age, I wanted to live a bit. My father didn't speak to me for three months when I left school. The headmistress was annoyed, but no one at school pressurized me to stay. It was so refreshing to meet people who had done things. I became an industrial chemist, which involved a lot of practical skills, so I thought I'd do equally well taking my training on the job.'

The official story that filtered through to the rest of us, after Sylvia's defection, was that studying had been too much of a strain for her. Similarly, when another girl left to go into staff management it was looked down upon. A high school girl didn't tangle with the male-dominated world of commerce and technology. Without really realizing it, our teachers were pushing us to accept the limitations they'd had forced upon them.

A small dose of opposition could serve as a stimulating innoculation against this pressure to conform. Deirdre happened to see a film at the cinema about girls doing mechanical engineering, which appealed to her immediately: 'The physics mistress helped me find out more, but all the others were dead against it. If I ever got anything wrong in applied maths, the mistress used to say, "You'll never make a mechanical engineer." I used to get furious. Afterwards, the maths mistress told me they'd all thought I wouldn't survive the course. They thought it was wrong for a girl to go in for that sort of thing. But I hadn't been impressed by typical girls' careers. There was nothing adventurous, nothing to inspire you.'

Quiet, shy Eileen had begun to read a lot of exciting articles in newspapers about computers, and applied to IBM to sponsor her to go to university to study computer science: 'After he interviewed me, their representative wrote a very nice letter saying what a tough world it was and how he didn't think I was cut out for it. Well, that really settled the matter, I was determined that was what I wanted to do.'

Viv was spurred on by the preferential treatment she felt her brother got: 'I always did better than him at school, to prove I was as good as he was. At one time I used to cry myself to sleep, thinking I was adopted, because he always came first.' She decided to follow in her grandfather's footsteps and become a pharmacist. 'I wanted to go one step further than he had, and open my own shop. It was entirely my own idea, at school they only encouraged you in what they felt fitting. If we'd had guidance, I would probably have gone into computers.'

In 1961 the sixth form had suddenly doubled in size and went on growing. More of us had stayed on to take 'A' levels partly because there were so many of us, and partly because it was an indulgence to daughters that most fathers now felt they could afford. One girl had been coerced into leaving because her mother was convinced that it would be a waste of time and money for her to stay on, but the more dominant, subtle social pressure now was not to stand in bright children's way.

And those of us without any strong sense of what we wanted to do were content to carry on in a dream state of indecision about our futures. Compared with the work prospects offered by a provincial town, school was an oasis of stimulation in a stultifying desert. Locked in that intimidating building, nevertheless, our minds were being tuned and primed, travelling around the world, back in time, communicating in foreign languages, conducting experiments, making calculations. We were trapped at a desk, but we could still gaze out of the window, fantasize our futures. Our mothers' lives were neatly hemmed into reality, a world where the daily routine was of running round after other people or facing solitary confinement. If you were late for school you had to run through that world of silent houses, deserted gardens with washing flapping disconsolately in the wind, down the accusingly empty expanse of the driveway before invading the animated world of the classroom. The town centre looked as if the streets had been cleared by some early warning siren which only married women and old age pensioners hadn't heard.

In the vacuum that lay beyond school, however, we were slowly drifting towards the only two options that seemed open to us. Applying for teacher training was, for some, a definite compromise. Karen, after wanting to be a pilot from the age of 5, found out that the RAF didn't, after all, train women recruits to fly: 'I didn't want to end up in a flight control office, pushing other people's planes round the sky. I liked the idea of speed, being in control of a machine. I also liked glamour, so I thought I'd do drama at teacher training college, because my mother impressed on me that I needed a career.'

Glenda, however, knew exactly why she wanted to be a teacher: 'I wanted to help people to enjoy maths, like I did. People still cringe when I say I taught maths, but isn't it a nice feeling to achieve something that's perfect, a right answer?'

Glenda planned to take a degree before training to be a teacher. If you were good enough to aim for university, that was what you did. It was seen as an end in itself, we were never encouraged to look beyond it; so it solved the problem of trying to fit yourself into a specific career. With a degree, the world would be at your feet. I decided to go because all my friends were going, and because becoming a student began to look much more attractive than going out to work.

A group of us had visited a friend's elder brother, now at

university. We must have looked incredibly gauche, standing there in the students' union, smartly dressed up, beside the sprawling, nonchalant students in their sweaters and jeans, in the middle of intense conversation over black coffee and a cloud of French cigarette smoke. I couldn't imagine myself beyond this nirvana. It would change me so much. I had to get there too. I hadn't taken Latin 'O' level, which was necessary at that time for a languages course, so I shut my eyes and jabbed with a pin among a list of the arts subjects I was eligible to take. I applied for a sociology degree because that was where the pin fell, and it sounded exciting and trendy. The teachers kept assuming I had applied for French or English because we were all expected simply to follow our best subject to the end of the line.

The grant system took us there, although the means test did require the better off parents to fork out. My father was reluctant but social pressure prevailed. University began to look more and more like an escape from the increasing tensions at home, which was probably why my father was unwilling to underwrite me to go. I was the cause of so many rows.

Rebellious heroines and repressed daughters figure in literature in every age, but for some of the daughters of the mid-sixties the collision with parents was head-on. Mothers who had wanted their daughters to have the education they'd been denied found themselves constantly questioned. We argued more cleverly than they could. Fathers resented being contradicted. When I was 11 or 12, I supported my father's conservative political views. But when election time came up again, I was in the sixth form and we held a mock election in which I voted Labour. The school also formed a debating society. There was a lot going on to debate.

To those of us who responded to the new ideas in the mass media, our parents' values appeared shallow, hypocritical. The Beatles may have been out of reach, but they became our spokesmen because they talked our language and for some reason the grown-ups listened. Their honesty cut through all the hypocrisy we were beginning to see in our parents' world. But with the uncompromising idealism of the young, we were capable of judging our heroes just as harshly. A friend of mine wrote me a letter, describing a dream she had had, that John

Lennon kissed her: 'I kept saying what about your wife? Isn't it terrible that John really is married. I can't believe it though I know it's true. But doesn't it show how false it all is, those things he said about girls he liked and dated and everything, and none of it was true. The character he has drawn of himself must be all a sham. I don't know how he dare show his face again. I can't express the queer feeling I get when I think of him as married.'

Whether it was by sporting a CND badge, seeing Dylan when he toured in 1964, or wearing black eyeliner and going to coffee bars ('You do go straight in, don't you?' my mother asked anxiously, fearing her friends might see me), we were echoing Dylan's message in 'The Times They are a '-Changin' '. We didn't have much opportunity to join the marches, even less to vote against our parents' conservatism, but there was one area of parental authority which some of us would challenge and defy.

There had always been girls who became sexually experienced before marriage, but it was very much a guilty secret, a private tryst between engaged couples, because a girl who slept with more than one man became a slag. Women's magazine agony columnists therefore unanimously counselled the defence of virginity at all cost. He'd lose his respect for you if you gave in, and if he really loved you, he'd wait until you were married. The assumption was that women didn't have uncontrollable feelings.

But what was my friend who dreamt about John Lennon describing when she wrote: 'When I woke up I was sweating. He was wearing fab clothes, a Beatle jacket and a grey and greeny blue diamond pattern sweater shirt. Every time I see John Lennon I go all queer, and when I hear "Twist and Shout" I can hardly stand. I'm enclosing the pic that made me dream of him. If you stare at it long enough you'll be surprised what you dream.'

And what about Beatlemania? I had joined the fan club quite early on (member no. 1042) and flew to school the morning free tickets arrived for their appearance on 'Juke Box Jury' and a concert afterwards at the Empire, Liverpool. But my friends at home watching the television saw and heard more than I did. From a balcony seat overlooking four tiny puppets, the sensible sixth former covered her ears and screamed. It was utterly irrational, but it was a safe outlet, for something.

I've tried to think back to when it was that I decided to fly in the face of Evelyn Home; when was it that I decided that virginity didn't matter that much, that sex wasn't awful and wicked, and that the kind of boy who was hypocritical enough to want sexual experience for himself and still expect to marry a virgin (who couldn't compare his performance with anyone else) wouldn't be the kind of boy I wanted to marry? Part of the answer lies in the fact that I never really thought any of those things, I was never required to articulate my morality. There was simply a very, very slow, subtle process, a wind of change blowing through society's conventions, which carried a few of us along with it.

Publicly the process manifested itself as an argument between the adults over the provocative behaviour of some members of our generation. This sometimes hysterical concern, heightened by the media, lent authority to rather childishly irreverent attitudes and behaviour. In 1964 a book called *Generation X* circulated round the sixth form room. We were fascinated to read this collection of interviews with young people, that our age group's thoughts could be taken so seriously as to appear in print:

Old people are ridiculous, anyway, so phoney, everything they do is false.

Mother says never give in to a boy because he won't respect you, you'll only end up a tart . . But Sheila at school slept with her boyfriend and everyone looked up to her, there's a sort of mystique to it.

Royston Ellis, beat poet: 'Adult sex means furtive bunkups in hired rooms, the marriage bed, the divorce court and babies. Teen sex is for kicks.'

Canon Bentley: 'The sins of spiritual pride, self-complacency, jealousy, self-righteousness and hatred are much worse than sexual immorality.'

If only the rules weren't so quaint and silly.

Some undergraduates sleep with their girlfriends . . . not because they are being rebels or seeking kicks but because they argue that conventional morals are unnatural and outdated.

Sex is a vital element which should be faced with less hypocrisy
. . . . I find my parents humdrum and I feel I've grown out of their
ways and the ones of small-town existence. I don't think any two
people can really get on together in a state of permanent legal
bondage. My ideal of a woman comes from poetry and films and
is therefore unreal and rather infantile. Blame it on education.

Why don't they face up to the realities they're always telling
us to do . . . for example, they should issue contraceptives on the
National Health . . .

Shocking yet prophetic statements like the last added fuel to
the fire of adult horror that other parents had nurtured spoilt
savages, likely to corrupt their own innocent children. Peter
Laurie published *Teenage Revolution* in 1965 partly to counter-
balance the sensationalism that implied all teenagers were
immoral, sex-mad. He claimed that the country's six million
teenagers were really much more conventional. In explaining
the generational clash he likened parents to settlers, teenagers
to explorers. Parents, who have exchanged freedom for security,
have a vested interest in avoiding anything which threatens
their stability, new ideas which might expose the folly of old
decisions. Teenagers, on the other hand, travel light, ranging
round for the best place to put down roots, receptive to fresh
ideas because their attitudes have not become fixed.

To put it simply, we were less shockable than our parents.
One of us remembers her mother couldn't take anything
slightly suggestive on the television: 'If a bedroom scene came
on, she'd say "Oh, let's see what's on the other side" and jump
up and switch it over.'

Our parents' stance lost its force as it lost its face. Their coy
prejudices seemed narrowminded and petty compared with
the assurance of the new, enlightened approach to sexual
morality put forward by Dr Alex Comfort, author of *Sex and
Society*, who claimed that not hurting others and not producing
unwanted children were the only moral virtues which should
be taught. The implied irrelevance of virginity was unthinkable
for a generation bound by chastity and abstinence during much
of their sexual maturity.

It is hard to imagine today, but anyone living in sin in the
mid-sixties either had to pretend they were married or keep a

very low profile. Twiggy claimed publicly that she lived at home, while sharing a flat in Kensington with her boyfriend. These anti-establishment figures appealed to a romantic notion of idealized love that did not need strings to bind it: 'If Dave ever asked me, I'd live with him in Montmartre. But I know it would upset my parents if I did anything like that. I wonder how we'll all end up? It's queer to imagine,' one friend had written in 1963. We could think such things, but not yet link them with the reality of our lives.

While the passing nature of our relationships with boys renewed the plaster on the principle of protecting our virginity, for some of us the bricks and mortar of belief in it were being quietly dismantled. The barrier was paperthin, but no one had yet got close enough to lean the weight of their persuasion against it. By not yet actually practising what we preached, some of us admitted sexual feelings in the same way as we had responded to pop stars too far away to threaten to seduce us. Our bravado belied our innocence. The friend who, in 1964, wrote the letter I could not read out to my mother, had decorated it with the word 'sex' with a heart round it. I could never have explained that she really only meant the vague, excited ferment she felt when she fancied someone, partly because she wrote in the same letter 'vive le Pill'.

Our generation was growing up with the knowledge that somewhere out there existed a contraceptive which promised you would be able to get away with it, in the way only men had been able before. Rumours circulated about daughters who took their mothers' pills and substituted aspirin: the unsuspecting mother got pregnant while her daughter got away with it. It was ludicrous to anyone who'd ever seen a contraceptive pill to mistake it for an aspirin, but we didn't know; it made them appear more accessible. Having expressed an abstract willingness for the experience of sex, we were still held back by the fear of pregnancy, although some of us, in more steady relationships, would dare to overcome that fear.

Peter Laurie hastened to point out, in *Teenage Revolution*, that despite all the sensational stories of headmistresses complaining there were no virgins in their sixth forms, what was remarkable was the restraint of the young, given the opportunities they had and the encouragement. Michael Schofield, another investigator, published a survey in 1965 which showed that only one sixth of girls between 17 and 19 had ever had sexual intercourse, mostly in the home of a parent, with someone they had known for a long time.

By the time we were 18 many of us had settled down with steady boyfriends. For a small number of us, the understanding that a long-term relationship brings dismantled the barricade that put them on one side grabbing and us fending off on the other. The conclusion was inevitable, given the ingredients of mutual attraction, trust, freedom, and the message on the grapevine. The Kinks, ever upfront when it came to sexual innuendo, sang to us:

> *Girl you really got me going*
> *You got me so I don't know what I'm doing . . .*
>
> *Girl I want to be with you all of the time*
> *All day and all of the night*
> *All day and all of the night . . .*

The Hollies promised they'd be true to us, Concrete and Clay swore that we'd be in love eternally . . . It wasn't much more scandalous than had been done by engaged couples many times before. The difference was that we were doing it younger, because we were more physically mature, had more opportunity and media encouragement, along with a strange parental complicity. In such a dangerous atmosphere, they obstinately chose to trust us: 'They let us watch the old television in the front room . . . His mum used to bring us a cup of tea sometimes, but she always coughed very loudly as she was coming through the hall.'

Parents suspected glowing cheeks, or telephone conversations they overheard, but they never confronted us directly: 'Mum overheard me saying to Nigel, "Oh, it's all right, you needn't worry" and he bought me a box of chocolates, which was unheard of. I could tell what she was thinking. She worried about it for ages, struggling with herself. But she couldn't bring herself to broach the subject.'

The existing gulf of misunderstanding made room for the

added deception. The clandestine intimacy, the risk drew the couple closer together, towards marriage. They had drifted too far from parents' moral values to experience much guilt: 'When she had calmed down from calling me a whore and a prostitute, she simply said very conspiratorially, "No one need know", meaning I could pretend it never happened, and it wouldn't ruin my marriage prospects. She made me swear on the Bible we wouldn't do it again, but we did, because I'd stopped believing in God at that age, and I didn't think it was wrong – we loved one another.'

Parents who found out couldn't do very much. One girl's brothers discussed going to beat up her boyfriend but they never did, probably because although it still wasn't done to have premarital sex it certainly wasn't done to beat up the boyfriend and lock up the daughter. In a strange way, though, you needed parents' disapproval, like a kind of fireguard, as if you sensed that your position was too volatile to be stable or safe. I resented my own parents' repressive, puritanical attitudes but I was shocked when a friend told me her mother had discovered her in bed with her boyfriend one Sunday morning – the church service had been cancelled – and all she did was offer them a cup of tea. To my mind that was *carte blanche* to become promiscuous.

Most girls who slept with boyfriends did so because they were in love and anticipated getting married, and the two went together. You weren't necessarily planning to get married straight away, simply playing russian roulette: sex was the gun aimed at your own course in life, knowing the bullet of marriage and a family was in one of its chambers. 'Every time I told him my period had come, he'd stagger about in mock relief, but our way of avoiding pregnancy wasn't terribly efficient or responsible. He thought you couldn't get pregnant the first time. I didn't think that was right, but I went along with what he said. After that we relied on the withdrawal and rhythm methods. We didn't ever seriously consider what would happen if I did get pregnant, while I was still at school. We couldn't think beyond the horror, and then the relief.'

At the same time as planning your own future, you were lobbing a hand grenade at it. The relationship somehow encouraged an insular attitude, not minding what happened so long as you could be together. Love was too immediate and too powerful. Or perhaps some of us *had* looked ahead, beyond the lists of prizes in the school magazine, to the pages of engagements, marriages and births that followed. This, after all, had been the rationalization for our education. Did we have a sneaking suspicion that the teachers were grooming us as academic racehorses with no particular race in mind because they knew we would simply be put out to stud? Why not sink into it now, with the one you loved, instead of being separated, furtive, unable to spend the night together?

Perhaps the perpetual threat of pregnancy conditioned such a fated attitude. You resigned yourself every time your period was late, and half-relinquished yourself to the fantasy of fruitfulness. As it turned out, fate took a strange hand in our affairs. It was the ones who risked most, who were going away to college who got away with it, while those who'd been defeated in some way in their own ambitions fell pregnant, had their futures sewn up and sealed at home. One girl had wanted to go to university to do languages, but the teachers didn't think she was good enough. She halfheartedly started a secretarial course with languages, but never finished it because she had to get married. She now admits that in a way, all she had wanted was marriage and children 'when the career seemed gone.' She had three practical alternatives: keep the baby, have it adopted, get married. 'You just didn't consider abortion. We got married. It seemed the right thing to do.'

The summer we all left school, Anne's periods stopped. 'For two and a half months, I was convinced I was pregnant. In a way I didn't take it very seriously, perhaps because there were no adults to confide in. I just used to laugh nervously whenever Sonny and Cher came on the juke box, singing "I got you babe"!

'I started university still thinking I was pregnant. I didn't join any of the societies, because I thought I would have to leave at Christmas. Part of me didn't mind. I'd wanted to go, but I didn't have any career plans, and I was miserable away from my boyfriend. We were planning to get married. I missed him so much, in a way it didn't matter. It turned out, though, that I wasn't pregnant. My life would have been totally different if I had been. I would have stayed behind. We would have stayed together. As it was, the relationship broke up in my second year, because of the strains of being separated, growing apart. I remember waking up the morning after we finished, suddenly realizing my future was no longer mapped out. There was this big question mark over it again, because I didn't know who I was going to marry.'

1965–68   working girls and weddings – off to college – Robbins report – student freedom and equality – staging the sexual revolution – abortion and the pill – fending for yourself

> *I think I'm gonna be sad*
> *I think it's today, yeh,*
> *The girl that's driving me mad,*
> *Is going away.*
>
> *She's got a ticket to ride*
> *She's got a ticket to ride*
> *She's got a ticket to ride*
> *And she don't care*
> ('Ticket to Ride,' The Beatles, 1965)

My parents insisted that schooldays were the best days of one's life and I sighed with impatience, under the self-inflicted penance of my bulging satchel. We'd stayed on in the sixth form because we were good enough to take 'A' levels and try for university or college, and now we had to prove it. The offers that began dribbling in from UCCA (the new centralized administration for handling the flood of university applications) excited even the most diffidently unambitious upper sixth formers. But as time went on we were also tussling with the temptation to put off revision with its horrible reminder of everything you didn't know.

Back in the 1950s Jo Grimond had deplored the 'useless snobbery of the exam system' and pointed out that what young people want to do is go out and enjoy themselves. Herman's Hermits agreed, dismissing their ignorance of geography, trigonometry, algebra or what a slide rule was for: it would be a wonderful world if we could simply be together. And in May 1965, when the exams really did loom up, Venus answered Sandie Shaw's plea. It was all right for Sandie Shaw to meet him every night at eight and not get home till late, but Viv had been offered a place to do pharmacy. It meant so much to her that she lost her voice at the interview. Being popular, one of the crowd, also meant a lot, and everyone seemed to be pairing off with boyfriends. Then, just before the exams, she got off with someone too: 'I ended up having a row with him and we finished, probably because I knew I should have been working when I was seeing him, so I took it out on him. I felt such a failure when the results came out.'

In the revision heatwave, freedom shimmers just out of reach. And yet the longed-for end of the exams is always an anti-climax, as dull and disappointing as the weather. To refresh my memory of that chilly July in 1965 when I finally left school, I revisited the offices of the local paper, still in the High Street of the sprawling redbrick town where I went to school.

Not yet transferred on to microfiche, the back copies were kept in heavy ledgers piled in a small attic room. Fifteen years seemed to have toughened their pages, or was newsprint thicker in those days? Only then did it strike me how long ago the mid-sixties were.

The sixties revival, and its influence on fashion, has given that time a deceptive closeness. It is easy to forget that the world we stepped out into with our nerve-endings so alive was such a foreign country where things were done so differently. For me, a child of the sixties whose tastes formed and gelled then, it took the yellowing process of light on paper to convince me that I was gazing at history, a part of my history. It was the headlines that startled me most: US PLANES POUND VIETNAM TARGETS. Not some local council scandal but the international war story that was to dominate world consciousness for the next ten years. The inside pages were choked with our mothers' voluntary activities, cosy figures, solidly dressed. A young man leaned protectively over a young woman, advertising a building society. The Sits Vac offered men's jobs with prospects and pension schemes, whereas women's jobs stressed instant pay or short hours.

On 9 July 1965 Ronald Biggs snatched the headlines by escaping from Wandsworth prison. They were still looking for him on the 15th, when we escaped from that walled-in prison known as school. Leaving empty desks, clutching hollow promises inked on the school photograph, finer feelings had already been crushed among the pencil shavings as we fastened satchels and began to go our separate ways, striped dresses spread out along the drive, in the middle of a cloudy weekday afternoon.

Perhaps I began to appreciate what my parents had meant when I rushed up to my bedroom, pulling off the cotton dress for the last time. Perhaps, beside the messy dressing-table littered with grips, rollers and panstick, my first taste of freedom was an odd, disjointed sense of anticlimax and unease, rather than euphoria. School is, after all, the perfect incubator for dreams because you never have to test them out.

When Julie left school in 1963, she wanted something 'a cut above the ordinary', so she aimed to work in a bank. Starting work, however, meant confronting real life, where mistakes matter because they cost money. Julie hardly ate for the first week, her mother had to push her out of the door every morning. But she survived and began to enjoy working as a remittance clerk. Then they moved her on to the accounting machines. Like my mother, she was terrified of making a mistake where money was involved. Like my mother, she looked around for an escape route. But unlike my mother she couldn't retreat into domesticity. Teacher training college was the only alternative she could think of, but in the process of applying she survived the ordeal at work, and from then on took everything in her stride. Confidence carried her forward to the counter.

Most of the girls who left school when Julie did went into routine office work and if you joined as a clerk, you stayed a clerk. However indispensable a secretary you were, you would never be in line for your boss's job. Working carried the limited cachet of spending money of your own, but denied the ultimate independence that most people seek, of running your own life (rarely to be achieved under your parents' roof, however late they let you stay out at night). The most you could do was stockpile pillowcases and pastry cutters, tokens of the self-determined life you were powerless to gain for yourself. Why did you put up with this enforced poverty, as hobbling as bound feet? The simple answer is that, like bound feet, the process is initiated imperceptibly as you are growing up and you adjust to it because you know no other.

When he was 6, my brother enquired anxiously of our parents whether he should start saving for his furniture. Pedalling carefree on my tricycle, I never asked questions like that. I knew one day a man would provide me with a home of my own. When I left primary school to move to the midlands, my friends all signed messages in my little red autograph book. Sandra Wells immortalized herself with: 'Mary now/Mary ever/ Ingham now/But not forever' which I had no reason to doubt, just as I accepted the logic of: 'Romeo and Juliet/In a restaurant they met/They had no money to pay their debt/So Romeo'd what Juli-ate', contributed by Angela at the next school I arrived at in 1958.

And in 1965 nothing much had changed. All around you couples met, went out together and he paid because she earned so much less and most of it went on looking nice enough to be taken out. A woman's career didn't matter because it would be so shortlived. Ten years before they became illegal, advertisements left no doubt who would get the job:

> there is always room for high calibre young men . . . to become members of our engineering, sales and marketing teams
>
> excellent career opportunity for young chartered accountant. His work will be varied and interesting and offers full scope for initiative.
>
> opportunity for . . . young journalist . . . to rise quickly in status and salary for man willing to work hard
>
> (*Daily Telegraph*, July, 1965)

The same newspaper advertises for women hairdressers, typists, secretaries and clerks. Mme Yvette Vaucher hit the headlines that month when she conquered Everest, because women rarely made it to the top in any sphere of achievement. Theoretically there was nothing to prevent Julie taking the banking exams to make a career of it, instead of simply moving round different departments for the nine years she spent in the job. Some determined girls did, but the banks themselves reassured male applicants that there would be a fifty/fifty chance for them of becoming a manager, because the majority of recruits were girls who never aimed that far. You accepted immersion in a colourful sea of fellow females, below a mountain range of men in dark suits, because it never occurred to you to identify with the odd stalwarts who tried to climb higher.

However much girls who had not yet met Mr Right claim they were not consciously anticipating marriage in those days, it was such an assumed inevitability for a woman that her working life would be cut short by marriage at some point. And as every gardener knows, if you nip out the tip of the bud the plant will send out shoots sideways. Thus Julie looked not for money and success, but for fulfilment in the variety of her work. She did not need to take on worrying responsibility, trap herself on a career ladder, yet she could look forward to the rewards of material affluence, because fate would provide it.

You could look forward to being grown up in the same way that you daydreamed at school, without having to struggle to realize it yourself. The wedding, conferring the status denied you at work and symbolizing the freedom of your full sexual nature, became the focus of your ambitions. Sheila: 'After I met Greg, all I was interested in was getting married. I always wanted a home of my own, it meant a lot to me. I'd started my bottom drawer when I was sixteen. We had a fantastic white wedding, it was the best day of my life. The photograph album plays "Here Comes the Bride" while you're looking at the pictures. The nails aren't false, they're mine. I've always bitten them, but I held off for six months, just so they would be beautiful for the wedding.'

And the husband bestowed the status you were powerless to achieve for yourself. He would not simply be a wages clerk. He would be something impressive, even if, at 15, that meant having a scooter and being 18, which was what made Gillian fall for Rob, because 'he wasn't on my level, he was a bit above it'.

There were, however, some possibilities for personal advancement within the limited fields open to women, and school-friends who managed to find out about them went after them eagerly. Caroline: 'I was doing a secretarial course when I found out about a scheme which really attracted me. You joined the firm's headquarters as a trainee secretary and moved round the other depots in the country, building up a terrific knowledge and eventually ending up in a super-secretarial position. It petered out, after about nine months, mainly because the man who initiated the scheme left. Perhaps if it had gone through and I'd ended up with a really good job I wouldn't have got married when I did. I was never anti domestic life, but I suppose I might have been had I got the sort of job I originally set out for.'

Lyn, who had left school to join Marks & Spencer as a staff management trainee, looked forward to becoming a personnel manager. She enjoyed the training, travelling round the country over the next two years and attending college courses, at one of which she met her husband-to-be, Mick. They got engaged, planning to marry in three years time, when he graduated: 'Unfortunately, the M & S reaction was very negative. I was told they didn't encourage women in the training programme to marry, as they would no longer be as mobile as the firm required. I don't think anyone would dare to say that to a woman today! That decided us to get married sooner, and we went to live where Mick was finishing his degree, and I found a job as a dental nurse/receptionist.'

The dilemma was much the same as our mothers', and the trouble was, from the employer's point of view, that sponsorship meant expensive investment in an unreliable employee with divided loyalties because of the demands of her private life. But there was one girl whose company sponsorship had been turned down who didn't drop back into line for the marriage market. Eileen, who'd been turned down by IBM as not tough enough for a career in computers, took a degree in computer science all the same. Along with the two dozen of us who went on from the sixth form to college and university, Eileen was trained at the expense of the taxpayer and ratepayer.

In theory women had been perfectly free to take university degrees since the 1890s (bar Oxbridge, with a longer history of male exclusiveness than the fourteen Victorian redbrick universities). In practice, when our mothers were at school in the thirties, university remained impossibly out of reach. Most girls had to forgo the education necessary for matriculation until the 1944 Education Act, which suddenly exposed this wastage of potential university material. Then in 1949 (as part of the postwar Labour government's equality of opportunity policy) local authorities became responsible for awarding a grant to anyone who won a place at university or college.

It still cost more than sending your daughter out to work; the means test element only added to the parental final word on the subject. My elder sister, who passed her school certificate with distinction, longed to go to university, but was firmly propelled towards secretarial college. However, in the late fifties, parents were becoming more indulgent towards their daughters, because they could afford to be. On 20 July 1957 the Conservative Prime Minister, Harold Macmillan, said in a speech at Bedford, 'Indeed, let's be frank about it, some of our people have never had it so good.' This casual remark passed, misquoted slightly, into the language, because it struck the chord of the times.

As more children stayed on in the sixth form and went on to college and university, female students increased faster, proportionately, than males. The total number of higher education students (full-time) in the mid-fifties was 55,000 men and 28,000 women. By the mid-sixties it had risen to 112,000 men and 68,000 women.

> The early 1960s were years of intense debate about the future shape and extent of higher education. During this period, there was considerable growth in the secondary school population, as the immediate postwar 'bulge' in the birth rate passed through and as the trend for sixteen-year-olds to stay on at school gathered momentum.
>
> (*Loughborough: From College to University*, M. L. Cantor &
> G. F. Matthews, 1977)

The force of our numbers, the tidal wave that had swept through all facilities since we were born, and the increasing number of pounds in our parents' pockets, led to concern about what would happen when we arrived to deluge the doors of universities and colleges, all over the country.

The government had appointed a committee in 1961, headed

by Lord Robbins, to investigate present patterns and future needs for higher education. Between 1961 and 1965 seven plate-glass universities sprouted in a sea of mud, just in time for us to wade through it to get to their lectures. Colleges of advanced technology were upgraded, like Loughborough, to university status. One of them, in recording the 1962 intake of 561 students, had added that 'alas' only eight were women. Why the sudden concern about women, which Deirdre had also noticed, when she applied to do mechanical engineering?

Since the 1950s the brain drain to the US had been a topic of increasing concern, and a White Paper on the subject of technical education (1956) had pointed out the small numbers of women in technological professions: 'Their hopes are naturally bent on marriage, and they fear perhaps – although there is much experience to prove them wrong – that by aiming at a certificate they may miss a husband.' Once again looking for some untapped labour supply, the government had hit on women, only this time it was trained minds they wanted, not cheap labour. In 1963, when we were either leaving school or staying on to do 'A' levels, the Robbins report came out, bemoaning the high wastage of girls, showing that their 'O' level achievements equalled boys'; fewer girls gained three 'A' level passes simply because fewer stayed on to take them. The report concluded:

> The tendency towards early marriage . . . may well be connected . . . We should greatly welcome a tendency for more girls to stay on at school if only from the national point of making better use of what must be the greatest source of unused talent at a time when there is an immediate shortage of teachers and of many other types of qualified person . . . Means must be found to attract more of the ablest students of technology. In particular, it is desirable to encourage more girls to read applied science. At present few girls in this country seem to be attracted [to these careers] and the contrast with some other countries, notably the Scandinavian, is very striking . . . The prospect of early marriage leads girls capable of working in the professions to leave school before they have entered the sixth form.

The report deplored girls being lured straight towards marriage, without really acknowledging how understandable this was. Working for 'A' levels demands application and will power, for which only the promise of probable success or direct personal benefit makes the effort worthwhile. Few girls who found studying an effort were tempted with the prospect of an interesting career to spur them on. Julie had already made up her mind to leave school and was applying for jobs in banks, when the 'O' level results came out. She had assumed that she wouldn't get the five subjects necessary to go on and take 'A' level. To her surprise she did, but didn't change her mind, because she had had enough of studying. She didn't think in terms of 'A' level subjects entitling her to higher pay or easier promotion, because girls didn't – and weren't encouraged – to think about promotion. The assumption that you would leave work at some point in your twenties was very deeply entrenched.

Why did the rest of us bother to go on to college and university? Perhaps academic ability also endows you with obstinate singlemindedness to follow your own budding ambition, however indeterminate, rather than succumb to the dead wood of women's job options. I was only aware of wanting freedom; I could see the way work moulded you, strapping you into its routine commitment. The summer that the Beatles film 'Help!' was released, I had my first job, as a chalet maid at a Butlin's holiday camp. It was there that the envelope arrived, containing the flimsy slip of paper with my 'A' level resuts. My friend and I felt so anxious about it that we each read the other's, to discover that we were both on our way to the most formative, influential period of our lives, she to Leeds University, me to Liverpool.

Bravely striking separate paths was easier because it wasn't so final. You were leaving home, cutting the apron strings without slicing the wedding cake, but you would be back among familiar faces at Christmas and at weekends. Many of us were going steady, but that simply influenced us to plan our own path to coincide as far as possible with his, rather than abandoning it to follow him. If you wavered about going, your parents were behind you spurring you on, instead of counselling contentment to stay at home with him. Glenda's fiancé was a policeman: 'He'd never known a girl who wanted to do a degree and all the things I'd got in mind. He couldn't understand why I wanted to go away and yet still marry him. Things were quite stormy between us before I left. Feelings are so strong at that age. But my parents knew I'd always wanted to go to university. They'd done everything they could to help and encourage me. I don't think I could have faced the ructions at home if I'd given it up. As it was, they used to pull a face if we went out during the week when I should have been doing my homework. I can remember wishing I could simply fail the exams and get a job in a bank. I wouldn't have minded it being taken out of my hands like that, but with it being up to me, I couldn't let myself down, and it was what I'd always wanted. And we're both really glad now that I went.'

Even those who didn't get in to university had begun to cut their ambitious teeth. Shirley had always been aware of her working-class background at school: 'But all the time I had this feeling, I'll show them one day. The headmistress told me I wasn't university material, which made me more determined than ever, so I decided to resit one 'A' level and did some student teaching in the meantime. When I got into university, I was quite a different person. I went armed with fresh confidence and also this determination that people weren't going to stand in my way; that was all behind me.'

You could make a new start at university, just as we had when we passed the 11-plus. But this time, naively wearing the college scarf, we were there together, boys and girls alike. Universities still discriminated in their job hierarchies, and girls weren't expected to talk much in tutorials, but we were all rated together on paper, and insulated from the prejudices of the outside world, as Deirdre discovered when she arrived at Loughborough to study mechanical engineering: 'When I went for interviews, all the colleges wanted girls on their courses, to show they were up with the trend. There were seventy-five of us on the course when I got there, and only two girls! I'd worked at the local Coal Board the summer before I started, where I met people who'd got a prejudice against women doing that sort of job. They think you're weird, and they haven't got much confidence in your ability. Some of them were quite rude, actually, saying things like "You'd better not do that, I'll do it". They accepted you if you could prove that you could do it, but I always thought that was wrong, that a girl had to prove herself first.

'And of course the law stated that a woman couldn't work down a mine. So they used to criticize me because I couldn't see what the actual job was like, I was too much on the clean side. It was a bit of a handicap, but I felt it was just something they picked on . . . At the start, with people being so strange about it, I did begin to wonder if I was doing the right thing. But once I got to college and found the boys and the lecturers were perfectly all right, and I was doing as well as the boys, I thought why worry?'

Deirdre had stumbled across a strange anomaly between the academic and the outside world. Over the past twenty years, Professor Downs at Loughborough University claims never to have encountered active discrimination against women, and his views are upheld by the Engineering Industry Training Board. Perhaps this reflects the tendency for self-assertive girls to make it as far as college to do applied science, compared with rather introverted boys, but the prejudice Deirdre met in 1965 formed part of the natural fallout from women's and men's roles and the way their interests differ(ed) in society at large, to which the universities were largely immune. The resistence of medical schools to women students (a quota system operated right up until the implementation of the Sex Discrimination Act) reflected the power that the professions wielded (unlike other male-dominated occupations) over selection for membership and training: its working practitioners could exercise their prejudice in a way that Deirdre's critical colleagues couldn't.

The rest of us didn't even stop to think about the concession of equality at university; we had never met patronizing prejudice. And the process extended beyond lectures to the all-encompassing experience of student life itself. Not only were we sharing the same status, with the same hurdles to jump, the same importance attributed to the work we did (or didn't) do, we had the same money to spend. You could hardly expect your boyfriend to reach into his back pocket to pay for your halfpint when you knew you had as much as he did in your purse. You paid your own way, and you were on a much more equal footing in other ways also. In my hall of residence girls had to make their own beds, whereas men were considered incapable, but the cleaners cleaned our rooms for us, and when we had finished the meals cooked and served for us, we pushed the plates away, just like men did. However, there was one important respect in which our treatment differed from that of the boys and that was the university's attitude to our moral welfare, which reflected society's entrenched double standard.

Early female academics earned the label of 'blue-stockings' because in the struggle for equal educational opportunities they not only had to devote more effort to their studies; they had to keep themselves above reproach morally. A similar attitude prevailed, half a century later, when I arrived at Liverpool University. Male students lived where they pleased, or could find room; girls had to stay in halls of residence or lodgings until their third year. The university claimed simply to be acting *in loco parentis*, fulfilling its legal responsibility to us as minors, but judging from the rules, parents did not care what their sons did or where they were.

In my first year, I lived in the hall nicknamed 'the Convent'. The atmosphere was very much like a boarding school, where thin-lipped tutors addressed us formally and entertained us to genteel conversation, sipping sherry while they knitted. The signing-in book sat on a table in the entrance hall and every evening you had to sign it by 10.30 p.m. A late pass required a good reason, and normally wasn't issued later than midnight, unless it was for a twenty-first birthday party. Needless to say, there were a large number of those.

Visitors of the opposite sex were only sanctioned on certain days of the week, between certain daylight hours. At those times all doors were firmly bolted, to ensure that any male's arrival (and departure) was carefully monitored. Dreadful warnings circulated about what happened to those who broke the rules. During my first year two second year students were fetched back from an all-night party, one of them suspended for a term and the other sent down, because she had premeditated staying the night by saying she was going home for the weekend. Generations of girls had accepted this blatant injustice, whereby boys were assumed to be capable of running their own lives and girls were not. My generation, however, had become accustomed to a measure of freedom at home which made the rules appear childishly repressive. Our rational minds recognized the irrational assumption that sin only broke out between certain hours (some colleges enforced a rule that you had to keep your door open when entertaining, which stimulated a trade in specially crushed waste bins for door props, guaranteed only two inches thick), and that your boyfriend could seduce you in his room every night of the week if he so wished, as long as you were home by 10.30 p.m.

By the end of the summer term we had triumphed, partly because the new fashion for building student villages made these rules impossible to enforce:

> One unforeseen effect of the student village accommodation was a general relaxation in the regulations regarding students in halls. It was no longer possible to . . . limit visits to rooms by students of the opposite sex. At first, attempts to apply the old rule led to some difficulties but it was soon realized that behaviour largely had to be left to students' common sense and in general this worked very well.
>
> (L. M. Cantor & G. F. Matthews, *op. cit.*)

Other university governing bodies were less complacent, possibly because they had more female students to worry about. Attitudes often varied between individual wardens, one saying, 'I won't have immorality in my hall' (*Residence and Student Life*, Joan Brothers and Stephen Hatch, 1971) while another assumed a moral example, leaving the students to determine their own behaviour. Some expressed a certain amount of *laissez-faire* doubt:

> I don't know whether sexual intercourse between teenagers should be worried about, or perhaps you should accept it as something which takes place. I'm a bit of a puritan, I suppose. I have found it possible to persuade most students that there are . . . standards which you have to adopt if society is going to survive.
>
> (Brothers & Hatch, *ibid.*)

Vicky's boyfriend was caught leaving her room by the college security officer. Summoned to the principal's office, Vicky took the wind out of their sails by announcing that she had already told her parents and by admitting her guilt: 'I think she realized that honesty was above sexual morality and so I got away with it, even though I told her that the bloke wasn't serious. I needed the physical side of it and my steady boyfriend was miles away.'

Many of our generation of female students were left to struggle to find a functional personal morality of our own in a society that seemed increasingly to condone slack moral boundaries. Shortly before we had left home for college and university in 1965, a dramatized version of Nell Dunn's novel *Up the Junction*, about the daring sex-lives of London girls, was shown on television. My boyfriend wrote, after seeing it: 'It makes you want to chuck it all and go and live down there, it's a gas. Still, it'll be great at university, *if* I get there – I've just got to.'

And on 13 November 1965 Kenneth Tynan made broadcasting history by remarking on a television programme called BBC3: 'I doubt if there are any rational people to whom the word "fuck" would be particularly diabolical, revolting, or totally forbidden. I think,' he continued, 'that anything that can be printed or said can also be seen.' He was being interviewed on the subject of representing intercourse on stage, and while the BBC switchboard jammed with complaints, Jonathan Miller and George Melly applauded him with a telegram.

In the same month of that year Jean Shrimpton appeared in public in a skirt four inches above the knee. I too wore my first miniskirt that autumn, away from my mother's critical eye. I still had the same Marks & Spencer skirt I had worn (knee-length with a ruffled blouse and my confirmation cardigan) at my first church hall dance, at 15. I turned the hem up, to all of two inches above the knee, and I remember battling up the hill towards the students union in a strong breeze, exposing a lot more than two inches of thigh.

Rigged out more daringly than the flappers of the twenties, we were also sailing much closer to the wind. Whereas they had merely tussled in the backs of motor cars, we found ourselves, having accepted the invitation back for coffee, perched on the edge of a single bed. In May of 1965 the managing director of Slumberland had proudly announced a special student bed, designed to 'withstand very hard wear'. Whatever he meant, it was a prophetic statement. Student rooms all over the country were to become the battle/testing/playgrounds for the determination of the New Morality. This was real, not a television play – and neither party had the help of a script.

In the old days of the Chastity Rule, it was simple. No respectable girl risked relinquishing her virginity until she had a ring on her finger. The man, on the other hand, was free to 'test' every girl he met, loving and leaving the willing ones, until the pure vision of his dreams appeared. Despite public cluckings and tuttings about schoolgirl sex, a large proportion, probably the majority, of our age-group of girls who went away to university and college were still virgins. But among those were some who regarded that state as an awkward, unsophisticated encumbrance, to be lost as soon as possible; some who anticipated the probability, given what had filtered down to us about student life, of starting to sleep with a steady boyfriend once we got there, because a mature relationship now extended that far; and others who still firmly believed in chastity before marriage, and did not think that anything would happen to dissuade them – not all of them were right.

Once you got there, you ran the gauntlet not simply of persuasive young men, but something our mothers never encountered – encouraging young women. Losing your virginity had become for some a status symbol. 'I was always out of line,' says Karen. 'Lots of girls had this idea that sex was the greatest invention since Bacardi and coke, all part of Saturday night out – "Oh, you don't know what you're missing" – they were all trying to persuade me to find someone to do it with. They just couldn't understand my attitude, which was that as long as I can say no, why say yes? The whole idea of going into a physical relationship, to my mind, was that you couldn't resist it, so that if you can say no, you might as well. I was out of step in that respect with my college friends.'

University life had quite a revolutionary effect upon the hitherto coolly-ordered quality of the lives of other, more impressionable girls. One, who'd always worked hard at school, and remained relatively innocent, found herself neglecting her work when left to discipline herself and floundering also in other respects. She wrote distractedly to a friend:

'Going out with Tony is wonderful, but the trouble is, the sort of life I've led up to now hardly fits in with the one Tony has always been used to. He says he doesn't expect anything from me ('I ain't trying to make you give anything you never gave before') but if I even try to object to anything, he says I don't care about him, and am not trying to make our relationship work. You see, I don't know how far you can go without any risk of getting preggers. I can hardly ask Tony, and I should feel a right fool having to talk to any of the others about it. I'm a nervous wreck, most of the time, dreading midnight, because he'll refuse to leave. My position as far as village rules are concerned doesn't affect him in the slightest. To hell with the rules, but how can I risk getting chucked out in my first term? I've already been caught once, emerging from the men's block at 7.30 a.m. I've never smoked so many ciggies or eaten the skin around my nails so much in my life.'

Some of us had stepped outside the clearcut guidelines our mothers followed, when they stalled any discussion of the subject by referring to right and wrong. The boys broke the rules without really realizing that that was what they were doing. They were prone to perpetuate an exploitative, superficial one–night stand approach to sex, if a girl gave in too easily. What she innocently assumed to be a more open, physically honest overture to a relationship, he treated as a passing conquest, unlike the slow-growing intimacy with sweethearts at home. College girls were so much fruit, ripe for picking, to be discarded, unfeelingly and insensitively once appetite was satisfied. In *Sex and Society* Alex Comfort suggested:

> boys, who in our culture are more sexually aggressive [should be given] some rudimentary insight into the way girls' responses differ from their own . . . For a girl, every act of penetration . . . is an invasion of her body by forces outside herself. She can never feel exactly the same towards a man who has 'known' her thus, even if only once – many boys are staggered by the change in her attitude which one act of intercourse can bring about, and her intensity may scare them off.

He added that women are not weaker, only more vulnerable to a sense of rejection, because socially they have to be passive, dependent. Anatomically, sex *does* happen inside a woman's very being, whereas for a man it is something peripheral, external and therefore perhaps more externalized. But it could also be argued that women were responding to the new permissiveness in its most positive sense, and meeting men who used it negatively, unthinkingly, according to the old chauvinistic rules, which were almost totally repressively passive on the girl's part. You were expected to restrain initial advances, and then gradually resist less and less to a boy's wandering caresses. But that was a formula which fitted garden gate gropings and sofa snoggings rather than the aforementioned single bed. The vicinity of wrathful parents and the prospect of a long walk home were enough to dull the keenest appetite; but what about when they became pressing on their own territory and the onus was on the girl to stalk out primly and go home alone? Badly articulated protests that she didn't know him very well (the only way she could express what felt 'wrong' about the situation) sounded feeble and ineffectual in the alcohol-blurred gloom into which she had allowed herself to be led.

When some of us now wrily confess that we 'used to get into a bit of a pickle' with boyfriends at college, or 'my parents kept a tight rein on me at school, so I wouldn't do anything foolish. Instead I made all my mistakes at university' what we mean is that we got into situations we couldn't handle. How could mothers have understood what it felt like to fall asleep in the comforting romantic warmth and alien fascination of someone else's bed, only to wake up among rucked-up sheets, pricked by a tangle of blankets as well as one's conscience? They were never serenaded with the Dylan lines: 'If you got to go, go now,/ Or else you gotta stay all night.'

Those with boyfriends at home to whom they could be faithful were spared a lot of the agonies of finding some sophisticated reason for fending off amorous advances. The ones who remained faithful and carried on to marry the boy at home were the ones who went home at weekends, who had engineered a place at a college not too far away. Some got engaged, a useful strategy to keep up Saturday night morale. You got together with other engaged girls. Otherwise if, like me, you tired of staying in on Saturday night with a piece of toast, the relationship invariably foundered.

When I first arrived at university my boyfriend did not write to me for four whole days. I endured this agony by going to bed early so that the next postal delivery might reprieve me sooner. That year I fitted Alex Comfort's description of women. I was the vulnerable, clinging vine. If I could have wriggled out, I would have done, but it wasn't like giving in your notice at a job; you had to pay back the grant, admit defeat. In the second year I found my feet and a circle of friends, going to parties, getting off with boys, having fun. Now, when my boyfriend at home started jealous rows, *I* was the one to react with indifference; when he suggested we got engaged, *I* felt the panic of claustrophobia.

Other boyfriends sat at home while their girlfriends went off and had fun, a rather intolerable reversion of the normal state of affairs. Angela had been going out with Dave since she was 14 and expected they would get married. So did he. Angela: 'At first I came home every weekend, and then less and less, until he finally realized I had someone else. I hurt him so much, I don't think he ever dreamt it would happen. I always felt rotten about it, but it's a good job, because I don't think we would still be together.'

Vicky and Brian's relationship began to crack when he got a place at college miles away, and they hadn't got enough money to see one another very often. Vicky: 'You can't be apart and doing completely different things for long before you become different people. When he took me back to college in September, I'd already made the decision that it wasn't going to work. He was trying to keep it alive, he didn't want to lose it. But when I saw him walking towards his car and saw it turn the corner, I thought I'm never going to see him again, and I didn't.'

Hilary's relationship with Tim broke down for similar reasons: 'He wanted to marry me and I felt the same, but I think at that stage it was more because I wanted to escape from home. I'd never been able to be myself, really, until I left home, and then he started getting jealous, so I had to get out. I'd had freedom to meet new people, form new relationships, it was a new horizon, another life, a second chance. At college I wanted glamorous things, the life on television you think exists somewhere . . .'

Once we'd found our feet, it was fun to flirt. My diary in that second year at university records me feeling 'crazily happy' when I got off with someone and then, a week later, 'wanting to push him away'. 1966 was the year that the tables were turned. It was the summer of swinging London and the dollybird, who knew her own mind and the power of her attractiveness, swinging down the street in much shorter skirts, now that tights were on sale.

The difference, however, between the boyfriend at home and the one at university was that the first relationship was underpinned, if you were sleeping together, by the assumption that you would get married. The second was not necessarily so committed, on either side. How was it that girls allowed themselves to run such risks, and how great were they?

In 1966 if you were unmarried it was still almost impossible, unless you lived in London, to get the pill or the diaphragm. Contraception was largely a man's responsibility and perhaps, over something that wasn't a direct threat to him, he could afford to be more confident than circumstances permitted. The longer you got away with it, the more recklessly optimistic you were. One couple stopped associating sex and babies until, of course, the inevitable happened. Another girl went to see the student health service doctor. She wasn't pregnant, as she'd feared, but the woman railed against her that she was sick of hearing girls' fears about VD, whether they were pregnant, if their boyfriend was sleeping with someone else . . . 'I was stunned, because my boyfriend and I really loved one another. But she never said anything to me about contraception. She just let me get up and walk out of the surgery. I suppose it was inevitable that I would get pregnant in the end. We were so ignorant and naive, I suppose. We just accepted the risk instead of trying to be responsible, find out the best method to use.'

When the nagging fears in the back of a girl's mind did become a horrible reality, how did she handle the discovery that she really was pregnant? One girl's boyfriend had been gaily giving her pills, telling her they were contraceptives. He then fixed up a backstreet abortion for her, in 1966. It seemed the only alternative. She felt she just had to get rid of it and couldn't afford to pay the £100 for a proper abortion. They scraped up the necessary £40 between them and both were too naive to realize what she was in for, planning to go out dancing in the evening.

She spent 24 hours in terrible pain, lying on newspaper in a grubby deserted flat in a terraced street somewhere in London. The doctor had used a saline injection to induce labour, and then gone away and left her, so she was all alone when the pains started. She had to go into hospital afterwards, where the nurses were really nasty to her: 'I didn't want my boyfriend to come near me after that, and for a long time afterwards, if I slept with someone, I used my body as a sort of shield. They could have that, but they couldn't touch me. I'd get up and waltz out afterwards, just like they did, only before they did it. The abortion was the changing point of my life. It's the only thing my parents don't know about me. It gave me this insight into the difference between your mind and your body. To have your body doing something your mind doesn't want is very hard to accept. Yet I was able to talk about it totally dispassionately, afterwards, because it had happened to my body, not to me. I hated my body because it had done this to me, plus men as well, because it was all their fault.'

Before the 1967 Abortion Act, induced abortion was illegal, under an 1861 Act, which still applies to criminal abortions. But the Infant's Life (Preservation) Act 1929 allowed termination of pregnancy if the physical or mental health of the mother was gravely threatened. An elastic interpretation of this law enabled some terminations under the National Health Service – if, for example, a psychiatrist felt you were unfit to go through the pregnancy – and a lot of fairly lucrative private clinics in London to flourish.

For anyone living at home in a provincial town like ours, both these courses of action were hopelessly out of reach. Your choices were to have it adopted; keep it, as an unmarried mother – not a very enviable option, as it ruined your marriage prospects – or hastily get married. This was the most usual way out, since the couple would be thinking of getting married anyway.

At university, however, girls chose different paths out of their dilemma. One shared a room in her first year with two other girls. All three found themselves pregnant at the end of their second year: 'We each chose a different way of handling it. Ironically, the girl who'd had a burning ambition to become a doctor left and got married. The other girl decided to go through with it and have the baby adopted. She managed to get a year off, which was difficult in those days, because you were usually sent down if you were pregnant. But the department head covered it up so the authorities never knew. She carried on with the course after the baby was born, and kept it, and ultimately married the father. Whereas I paid £150 and had a private abortion in a clinic in London.

'I couldn't face seeing our family doctor, so I went to his partner, who confirmed that I was pregnant, but he just let me walk out of the surgery, with no advice except that there was nothing I could do about it. But I trailed round a list of Harley Street addresses. Dressed in jeans with a rucksack, it must have been obvious what I was there for, among all the women in fur coats. I got nowhere, because you need a letter of referral from a GP, until one gynaecologist's partner sold me one which he scribbled on a piece of paper, without even examining me, and charged me ten guineas.

'The gynaecologist sent me to a sweet little old lady psychiatrist who was very deaf. Have you ever tried telling someone who's deaf that you're very depressed? She charged another ten guineas for a very long letter and I was booked into a nursing home in St John's Wood, where I had to take one hundred and fifty guineas in cash and sign a form saying I was over 21 – which I wasn't.

'My boyfriend got half the money from his parents, but I had to borrow my half and pay it back with money I got when I was 21. Everyone was fantastic at the nursing home, though, really kind and nice. And when I woke up after the operation, I couldn't believe I wasn't trapped by that nagging worry any longer. I was lucky, they kept me in for three days. Some girls paid as much as I did to climb up onto the operating table themselves, seeing all the blood spattered round, and be dragged back to bed, and got up the next morning to go home, because the bed was needed for the next. I didn't feel at all guilty – the relief was so much greater, having escaped from the terrible scene at home and having to leave university, lose all my freedom. But I remember seeing my boyfriend again at the beginning of term and my legs buckled and I had to sit down. The gynaecologist put me straight on the pill, which she'd apparently helped to pioneer. I took it, even though I didn't have a boyfriend – we'd split up just before I found out I was pregnant – and the last thing I wanted was sex. All I knew was that I wanted to be sure I never got into that situation again.'

Concern about the increasing number of backstreet and dubiously legal private clinic abortions, and the rise in the illegitimacy rate, contributed to the passing of the 1967 Abortion Act, which made abortion more easily accessible under the National Health Service. But the pill was still officially not given to single girls. There were now, however, one or two sympathetic GPs, mostly women, mostly in large provincial towns and cities, to whom all the girls trouped and as long as you told them what they wanted to hear, that you were engaged, you got what you wanted. You ran all your boyfriends into one, to make the relationship sound more stable.

Our generation was learning to play the system to get what it wanted, a reflection of our growing sense of our own power since leaving home. 1965 was significantly the year the first draft card was burned. And in Britain a large part of the New Establishment supported such rebellious behaviour. Shockingly outspoken celebrities of the day were courted by the prime minister, Harold Wilson; the Beatles had been awarded the OBE even though John had made the famous comment about being more popular than Jesus. What had begun as an energetic surge in popular music around 1964 had become an exciting new cultural movement, extending to fashion and the arts.

The passing of the Homosexuality Bill in 1967 underlined the new liberal attitudes towards individual freedom of expression. But an increasingly articulate student population were still not satisfied with the hypocrisies in the adult society they had joined. The 1967–8 academic year was dramatized by the militant demonstrations at the LSE and the Sorbonne. At Liverpool the organizers of a sit-in to divert Princess Alexandra's car around slums owned by the university were sent down.

The children who'd been given the best their parents could afford were throwing it away. In the summer of 1967 the fragrance of the Californian hippie movement, rejecting all materialism, wafted over to these shores, bringing 'If You're Going to San Francisco' to the top of the charts and a three-day festival of the flower children to Woburn Abbey, although the

Duchess of Bedford swore blind she thought it was going to be a flower show . . .

The pastoral antics of the flower children may have been confined to a mind-blown minority, but the spontaneous freedom and irresponsibility they reflected were mirrored in our own lives. At home in the holidays, neighbours accosted me with the accusation 'Not engaged yet?' and offered their condolences. Whenever I wrote home complaining about working hard, my mother would reply 'Give it all up – I know you just want to get married and have babies.' But I was immune from her persuasion – there was so much still to explore . . .

At the beginning of my final year I moved into an unfurnished flat with two girlfriends. Now I really knew what Virginia Woolf meant by a room of one's own and £500 a year (except that I had to live on £360). I could decorate it how I wanted, come and go as I pleased. It confirmed and protected me, it was mine. These were the first true stirrings of emancipation, learning to cook, for yourself, not as a way to a man's heart; cleaning up, because you wanted your own place to be tidy, but not slaving over it, because there were better things to do.

Janet agrees, that the freedom of living in a shared flat was crucially important: 'Six of us went into a flat together and I really enjoyed that, we all had our own lives. We didn't have parents hanging over us and without that experience I know I would have been more like my sister, who's always had mum round the corner. She missed out not going to college, on mixing with your own age group, seeing things from other people's point of view, standing on your own feet. It's certainly given me a much broader outlook on life. I was bone idle at home, but in a flat I jolly well had to feed myself, be responsible for my money. It's a good starting ground for men as well, so they don't go straight from a mother doing everything to a wife taking over where mother left off.' Male contemporaries did move into flats of their own, and were forced to make gestures towards looking after themselves, even if their grubby, neglected kitchens littered with festering milk bottles showed that they weren't much good at it.

I ought to be able to say at this point that we were all fiercely self-determining, but in 1968 I wrote in my diary: 'Oh God, why am I not married and happy with two kids? Why am I aimlessly wasting away?' The trouble was that the £360 a year was about to come to an end, but no one had told me what happened next. One teacher at school had admitted that she went to university to find a husband, and I think I had probably automatically assumed I would be bound to meet someone in whose shadow I could follow.

I toyed with the idea of market research, and had an interview with an advertising company which was a disaster, mainly because I believed that being clever and attractive and having a degree would put the world at my feet. Underneath that naive confidence I was exactly like my mother, frightened of a competitive world in which I would have to prove myself. I clung to my boyfriend and confided, in May 1968, to my diary: 'I see life stretching before me – endless hurdles too high for me to jump. Unless you could be there, lifting me over . . .' and after the exams, 'I now feel as if I've just been born, thrust out into the world, with no one to say you'll be all right.'

In melodramatic undergraduate style that sensation I experienced fleetingly, climbing out of my school uniform three years before, returned with its full force. Somehow I'd let myself drift off-course, by playing at life like we played at looking after ourselves, at relationships, at politics, at work, because students inhabited a privileged world cushioned from the draughty one ordinary people lived in. I had happily cut loose from the claustrophobic inevitability of getting married, but it never struck me that there was a price for that freedom – deciding what I wanted to do with my life. I'd failed to find a husband at university because I hadn't been actively looking for one. But buried deep in my psyche was the hatchet of all those expectations, assumptions, rationalizations that had accompanied the privilege of my education. You got to the end of the conveyor belt and the man and the family were waiting. They knew the way.

On degree day I watched all those people cross the platform, receive the scroll of paper, shake hands and pass out of my life forever. I also had the first big break-up row with my boyfriend. I had reached the terminus and no one had come to collect me.

teenage marriage and the Feminine Mystique – carving careers and new conventions – 1970, a turning point for all women – moving towards marriage – 'I'm a bit anti-women's lib' – discrimination, an enemy in disguise

In 1968, when my diary confession confirmed my mother's conviction that my real ambition was to get married and have babies, Gillian had already effortlessly claimed everything I clutched at. She had married in 1966 and, at 21, was anticipating the arrival of her second child. While I dithered before a blank page which could only be covered when I knew where to begin, Gillian's life was being comfortingly mapped out on the grid of the happily-ever-after: 'I was a stock control clerk. They never told me what promotion prospects there were, but I suppose I didn't see much future in my job because I got married. We had a marvellous white wedding, and a week in a caravan at Filey. I felt I should have been waited on on my honeymoon, at least, but finances didn't allow it. Funnily enough, when I gave my notice in, six months later, when I was having Simon, they offered me a better job! But of course I couldn't take it. We were hard up when we first married, those first four years.'

If she hadn't been in such a hurry, she could have had a more luxurious honeymoon, and they wouldn't have been so hard up if they'd waited before starting a family, but Gillian wasn't alone in hurtling headlong into wedlock at the earliest opportunity. The average age for a woman to marry had been steadily falling since the late fifties, mainly tugged down by the eagerness with which early school-leavers became teenage brides. Earlier sexual maturity, the permissive society and teenage affluence were all blamed and blameworthy, but these were no rebels. They faithfully copied the blueprint of their mothers' lives because it was the only way of enjoying a guilt-free sex life and achieving grown-up status.

However much marriage was viewed as an equal partnership, the giving away a quaint ritual, the distinct division of labour remained: the two were joined together and their daily lives immediately fell apart like the halves of a sliced melon. Teen-age marriages were generally deplored, not because they diminished the length and effect of a working girl's single freedom, however, so much as that their eagerness to leave home precipitated these girls into a lifelong emotional commitment at such a tender age.

The trouble was that home and husband came as a double gift-wrapped package: you married for the one as much as for the other. The shut-in reality of a boring underpaid job merely heightened the romance of escape into marriage. But, as Gillian discovered on her honeymoon, Cinderella's former skills come in very handy in the sequel to the fairytale. The housewife is a strange superimposition of both reels of the Cinderella story, run concurrently. The hardworking housewife-cum-lady-of-leisure swanning round the shops sprouted from the social developments at the beginning of this century which swelled the ranks of the middle classes. The expansion of white-collar work encouraged the decline of domestic servants along with the status of employment in the home: factories and offices were far more egalitarian, convivial workplaces. The middle-class wife was abandoned to play her own one-woman band, a mutation of social hostess, efficient housekeeper and un-paid skivvy, handcreaming away the evidence that it was she who scrubbed the floor. My great-grandmother was one of the first victims of this levelling among women, when she paid someone to come and clean the front step, in spite of the fact that she spent all day cleaning on the other side of it.

The technological innovations of labour-saving devices and modern, easy-to-run homes played fairy godmother to our mothers' generation while we were growing up. We were not schooled in housecraft methods like our mothers; when Gillian married there was no recognized standard of efficiency against

which a housewife could measure her efforts. If she was conscientious enough, household chores could consume all the
hours between the split-shift duties of meal provision. And yet
her life could also be enviable, carefree, semi-leisured, because
she worked her hours to suit. Never having to fidget under the
eagle eye of a critical boss, fight your way to work on time; safe
in the knowledge you were lovingly supported – who wouldn't
exchange a few hours of manual work for that?

Yet since the war young wives had been carrying on going
out to work, shouldering the drudgery of housework while
relinquishing its rewards. Running a home became their
primary responsibility when they married, probably their first
taste of responsibility of any sort, but it was up to each how she
interpreted the part. Margaret went back to work when her son
was 2 because she was bored and restless at home all day and
couldn't sleep at night. More and more mothers were returning to work after their children had gone to school. Was it
fair that some stayed at home with what was obviously now
only a part-time job, while others took on two jobs and were
run off their feet? When 'the bulge' was born, only 18 per
cent of married women were going out to work, but this
figure had doubled by the time we grew up to join them and
the vexed question of what part paid work could or should play
in the life of the married woman had begun to interfere on the
wavelength transmitting the story that ended happily ever after.

The woman who combined marriage with a fulfilling career
was still the exception; most women expected to embrace their
role in the home wholeheartedly, judging by the way they let
go the strings of their single working lives. So why take up
part-time poorly paid jobs, unless the dream or the princely
provider hadn't come up to scratch? Housewives in advertisements showing off spindryers or spooning instant nourishment
into clamouring mouths didn't look as if they went out to work;
but then they didn't look as if they did much around the house
either. Perhaps, ironically, wives were going to work to afford to
keep up with the advertiser's image of what they should be, the
only measuring stick a generation of untrained homemakers
had, and in the process utterly failing to exude the conscientious, contented glow of their cardboard cutout counterparts.

Three years before Gillian succumbed to it, five years before I secretly clung to it, an American contemporary of our mothers identified the softsell on the image of the happy housewife in the book she had been writing while we were all growing up. In *The Feminine Mystique* Betty Friedan yanked the plug on the romantic glow spotlighting the image of the charming hostess, attractive wife, loving mother, proud homemaker and exposed what housewifery had become – a dreary, insular existence fed by vicariously living through the activities of others, servile slavery chained by emotional blackmail. She presented the modern American housewife caught on a treadmill of the unremitting regularity of her intermittent commitments, bound because she did them for love, a currency not acceptable outside her own front door. Here was a book which quoted ordinary housewives, led them to articulate what it was really like after they'd shaken off the confetti, to find the shreds of the advertiser's image.

Betty Friedan exposed housewifery as unremunerative and particularly unrewarding for the educated woman. She saw education as the key to this prison because it offered women a first step to finding something really worth doing, apart from the washing up. She urged every woman to adopt a three-phase lifeplan, so that she could rejoin the working world when her children no longer needed her at home. The idea was that instead of seeing life in two phases, as our mothers had done when they gave up work and settled down to have a family, a woman should anticipate the probability of returning to work when her children were no longer so dependent upon her. She should therefore acquire work experience or training in the early working period in some field to which she could then return, instead of having to start all over again.

Betty Friedan's message may have been revolutionary in 1963, but it was not new. As long before as 1956 two British sociologists had produced a more sanguine treatment of the same theme, entitled *Women's Two Roles* (A. Myrdal and V. Klein), in which they had argued that just as the patriarchal family with dominant, protective husband and coddled, submissive wife was an anachronism in the latter half of the twentieth century, so society could no longer support a leisured class of indolent 'ladies', whose social isolation and lack of self-esteem often triggered appalling emotional crises when their sole *raison d'être*, the family, had grown up. They suggested that women and men should learn to share their respective roles, extolling the Swedish practice of teaching housecrafts to boys, and a three-phase lifeplan for women, much like Betty Friedan's; working hours should become more flexible to allow for the demands of domesticity; equal partnership in the home was the only ideal compatible with prevailing democratic ideology. The second edition of the book, published in 1968, required almost no revision, having so uncannily pre-empted Betty Friedan, if in a much less emotive manner.

By 1968 Betty Friedan had attracted thousands of disgruntled American housewives to join NOW (the National Organization of Women, formed in 1966 to fight discrimination which denied women equal opportunities with men). But women like Gillian were too far from academia and women like me too far from domesticity for the message to penetrate our consciousnesses. The difference between Gillian and myself (rather a large one, as it was to turn out) was that she had already turned to phase two and I had not.

The trouble with the two-phase lifeplan was that the second phase eclipsed the first. Before you met him, the anticipation of allowing for your husband's status and career movements and after you met him the overwhelming temptation to abandon all thoughts of yourself as a separate being – since his life was already more sharply etched than your own – made it impossible to look beyond marriage until it was upon you. By this time it was too late. Some of us, however, managed to contrive to carry out the three-phase plan, juggling a career and marriage, without dropping one.

Liz, Glenda and Kath had all qualified at training college or university, still holding the hand of their schooldays sweethearts. This clever contortion had been contrived by a combination of choices usually upended in teenage girls' lives: dedicating themselves to studying rather than being lured by student social life. Their careers were constrained by the necessity of applying for a job back home where their fiancés worked, but they accomplished this without much difficulty, largely because of the career they had chosen, although Glenda did have some last-minute doubts about going into teaching: 'But when I looked around for alternative careers, there weren't any, and it was a convenient career because you can go back after having a family which we expected to do. I'd work for four years, have a baby or two, and then go back.'

You'd been too independent at college to revert to living at home, so these women took on a career and marriage and the attendant responsibilities simultaneously. Luckily, Glenda's husband worked shifts, so it was easy for him to prepare the vegetables and put on the dinner, and justifiable as, for a time, she was earning more than he was. Liz and Kath, however, who got home in advance of their husbands' tired arrival, found themselves playing the conventional wife as well as the career woman, fitting in housework and shopping around school hours and at weekends with husbands helping out. Liz's problem was in persuading her mother, who never went out to work, that there were certain things she simply hadn't got time for: 'Whereas Brian quite happily turns his hand, and I feel he would do a lot more if my working hours were in keeping with his. The only job he hasn't tackled is the ironing, but he fills the washing machine up same as I would. I do think of the domestic jobs as mine, though, and Brian helping me out.'

Janet also got married straight from college to the boyfriend from home, but their marriage didn't fit so closely to the conventional pattern as Liz and Brian's. Getting engaged had forced Janet to modify her fantasies about working in Geneva after her interpreter/translator secretarial course, and she took a job with an exporting company: 'Dave was still a student when we got married, so it seemed the natural thing for me to support us and pay the rent. He had to do most of the housework or it wouldn't have been done at all. He's a dab hand with a duster and vacuum cleaner, but I've never seen him clean a loo. I suppose it's because I crack and do it first. The only thing that really bugged me during that year was having to go out to work while he lay asleep in bed, and I also envied his long holidays. It certainly helps you understand how a man feels when the boot's on the other foot. I'm sure that's why I don't rush to get up and give him breakfast now – which my mother thinks is a sin!'

Those student flat-sharing years had erased Janet's identification with the domestic role and need to control it, to allow the sensible role reversal that the situation required. Janet's problems were all associated with her work, taking the first job she was offered, feeling too indispensable to leave, and then having to, when her husband got his first teaching post in a town where the only job she could get was as a secretary, which she hated: 'My boss thought he could just order me about, but I got very bolshy with him. I hated the assumption that being a woman and a secretary landed you with jobs like answering the telephone, making tea, taking visitors in to the big chief's office, things it just wouldn't have done for a man to do, no matter how junior. It struck me that there were certain things that by being a man you avoided, because your position was automatically more elevated. On the other hand, if you were female, it was a foregone conclusion that you were a pretty thing that was useful to have around the office.' Janet began to wish she'd gone into teaching where it would be easier to work your way up the ladder. Part of her problem had been underrating herself initially and then allowing her sympathetic nature to sway her self-interest, but she had also chosen a field where it was all too easy for the way to executive level to be blocked by a typewriter on the desk in front of you.

For most of the rest of us, leaving college and university in the late sixties, the future was not nearly so clearcut and neatly assembled nor its smooth running so easily assured as the combination of career choice and marriage that had dovetailed in Liz, Kath and Glenda's adult lives. Some of us had planned ahead, but the rest were blindly swept along, unwilling or unable to reach out and steady ourselves before the conveyor belt tipped us off. I suffered from the socially-transmitted disease of conditioned helplessness to which my shyness made me particularly susceptible. I had been relieved that being a girl I would never have to get into fights, and growing up as a woman I was deluded into the belief that staying inside a safe world would be a solution to my lack of self-assertion.

The trouble was that the university's parental rein had been comforting but slack. The grant, the student union melting pot of familiarity and excitement, the easy termtime timetable had buoyed me up while I free-floated out of my depth. With a handshake and a scroll of paper the university had pulled out the stopper and deflated the aircushion. Discarding my school uniform in my bedroom at home was a mere dress rehearsal for what I now faced, in the summer of 1968, alone in an attic flat. Then, in 1965, I'd been certain of the future – a place at university and the man I was going to marry. Now both had been left behind. I was at last facing adult life, free and on my own – and I longed to be rescued from the awful responsibility.

As a small child I had often lain awake after a nightmare and banished the horrible images from my mind by planning the refurbishment of my dolls' house. In the same way I now found myself seduced by the comforting idea of staying at home, on the decorative, familiar side of life, everything the rebel in me had formerly disdained. The never-ending tasks my mother had been tied to now seemed a small price for the prospect of someone covering you from the crossfire for life, especially as I had got used to doing these things for myself anyway.

There was no job I wanted to do; work took away your freedom, whereas living happily ever after promised the dilettante student lifestyle, the same opportunity for free-expression that had always attracted me to arts subjects at school. I didn't imagine ahead, to parties where I would be embarrassed when people asked what I did, apart from being Jon's wife, or dull days feeling bored and trapped in the house, envying busy career women and yet lacking all self-confidence; or nights alone in the double bed after a divorce which left me stranded in the marital home with two children to look after. The creation and care of a family seemed so all-encompassing that it was impossible to imagine the breakfast scene when you were 40, with your husband poring over some important agenda, and you desperately wishing you'd done something with your life. My daydreams never travelled that far towards reality, and neither did those of a friend who also awaited the knight in shining armour, even at the eleventh hour. Susan: 'I went to graduation ball covered in fake tan in a green silk dress, and I thought I looked fantastic and even then, I still thought I'm bound to meet somebody . . . I'd applied to do teacher training, but I didn't believe I would actually teach in the end. It was just something to fill in a year. I still thought somebody would come along and rescue me.'

Others, however, had strengthened their ambitions at university rather than just drifting through the course. Anita, for whom the summit of success while at school had merely extended to being an MP's secretary, found herself, while doing English honours, editing the student magazine and reverting to her childhood dream of becoming a writer, and started applying for jobs in journalism. Jane's stagestruck adolescence had found an outlet in drama at university – she wanted to find her way into the theatre. Deirdre was set to become a mechanical engineer, and Yvonne who had always vaguely planned to be a scientist, contemplated the real-life possibilities: 'I felt as a woman I'd have a reasonable chance of being a hospital physicist, and I fancied doing research, if I had the talent. That was what I did, taking a teaching diploma while writing up my thesis, because I thought that would come in handy, although I went into a job as a medical physicist.'

Eileen was taking a four-year sandwich course in applied mathematics to become a scientific computer programmer at the end of it. Pat had changed courses at university in favour of politics and economics, and then a business traineeship, which would lead her into economic research and marketing, as one of a handful of women executives with a large brewery empire.

Pauline, who disdained the commercial world, took a teaching diploma. What else could you do with an English degree? Half of those of us who'd gone on to higher education had gone straight to teacher training college. Most of the rest, armed with degrees and art college diplomas, went the same way. For some it was a lukewarm acceptance of the only option that presented itself, something to do until we discovered what it was we really wanted to be. Hilary saw teaching as a passport to foreign places. Shirley, who'd enjoyed student teaching before university, had intended to use her degree to go on to better things: 'But I never got round to seeing the careers officer. I was too busy on my thesis. I'd filled in the form for a post-graduate teaching certificate as a failsafe, so at the end of the year I took the place I was offered.'

I, meanwhile, found a job in Chester, promising at the interview to move there, but never did. I clung to my nice little flat in Liverpool, to the ever-diminishing circle of friends there and to my boyfriend – in the reverse order of course. I had succumbed, until I found something I really wanted to do, to social work, the profession our lecturers had warned us against, because we wouldn't meet any men. It was true, which was probably why I hung on to my boyfriend. Stouter souls than I were striking a path on their own, neither pulled back under the protection of parents, nor blindly following boyfriends, however insecure they felt. Deirdre left a crowd of college friends to start an engineering job in Coventry, where she didn't know anyone: 'But it was a matter of making your own life, where you got a job. I deliberately avoided going back to the Coal Board, in my home town, because it was more important to make a fresh start somewhere I'd be accepted as a professional equal.'

Catherine went to work in Sheffield, because she liked the atmosphere of the city. Life was lonely at first, centred around work, which was also a struggle: 'I had a hell of a first year in teaching, but I was lucky to have a very good Head of Department, who literally dragged me through it. By 1969, I was beginning to feel I was in the right job, and really enjoyed contact with the children.'

Much to her surprise, Hilary also found herself enjoying teaching: 'It got me out of myself, gave me confidence, and away from the boyfriend I'd been hanging on to, simply because I was lonely. When I found a new boyfriend, I realized I'd changed a bit. I always used to get sucked into their world to escape from myself, but I found myself putting him in his place when he kept trying to make me more sophisticated. I thought I was all right as I was.'

Even I had begun to enjoy, after the initial terror of it all, the responsibility of an interesting and varied job where I could use my own judgement. And, dragging myself to work after an upset with my boyfriend, I would miraculously come to life by the end of a working day. I was still crushed, however, when he left me. I know that man first stepped on the moon in the summer of 1969, not because I have always kept abreast of current affairs, but because that was what my friends were watching on the television when I fell in on them in floods of tears. My decision to move to old friends in Manchester to find a new job was the action of the drowner, not the explorer.

I was, however, developing independence, if only by default. I shared a rented unfurnished flat with a girlfriend and felt quite proud to be self-supporting. My brother was also renting a flat, in London. He went home once a month, the boot of his car stuffed with dirty washing. My mother expected me to share her sympathy at his having to fend for himself. I could not quite see why she wasn't equally impressed by my greater independence – I never brought washing home. But then, as she pointed out, I was a girl.

The sixties had seen us through school and college and now as that decade drew to a close, we were out at work, becoming self-sufficient and self-confident, although I, for one, was despairing of meeting any eligible men. This sudden celibacy forced upon me in my early twenties was not simply the result of having been spoilt for choice at university and starved of it in the female-dominated profession I had entered, although that must have exacerbated the situation. A statistical survey called *Population*, by Professor R. K. Kelsall (1967) – which might have been among the final year setbooks I never read – could have offered me the dubious comfort that my predicament was not entirely my own fault. It concerned itself with

. . . the special case of the babies in the 'bulge' years of 1946 and 1947 reaching marriageable ages. It is obvious that, as a result of the additional births of these years, more girls will be entering the young marriageable age group in the early 1960s than have hitherto been doing so . . . traditionally, in this country young women tend to marry young men who are on average nearly three years older than they are. Consequently when the first of the 'bulge' girls reach marriageable ages, the number of such young men available will be smaller than that of their female counterparts of three years younger because these young men were born before the 'bulge' occurred. And this deficiency of bridegrooms the traditional amount older . . . could be substantial.

A few years later, when the 'bulge' boys begin to think of marrying, they are likely to find a corresponding shortage of brides the traditional amount *younger* than themselves . . . It is hard to predict . . . the outcome of this complex situation . . . but it could well disturb traditional patterns of marriage ages at least for a time.

Professor Kelsall was as little acquainted with the workings of our minds as we were with the fruits of his. The fact that marriage statistics would shortly begin to bear out his predictions was only partly the result of the unbalanced game of pelmanism the sexes of my generation were forced to play.

What I confessed to my diary in 1968 I would never have told my closest friend. I had passed the 22 milestone for marriage not simply because my boyfriend had not married me but because relationships were no longer necessarily on those terms. The cossetted, pampered younger generation, that had never suffered the moral obligations felt by its parents, had no use for their restrictive customs: getting engaged and married, accumulating mortgages and sets of relations you didn't get on with. Marriage had officially gone out of fashion in 1967 (according to an article in *Nova*, the daring new magazine for the modern woman, which carried advertisements for black satin sheets). *Nova* dictated that the fashion was to live in sin, although that was the parental label for what you did. To the younger generation it was simply a matter of moving in and living together, having already been well steeped in the sin.

It was simply a natural extension of what you'd naughtily indulged in at university, but you were freed from having to creep round corridors at dead of night or toss and turn in a tangle of sweaty covers on a single bed. It was more exciting and romantic than marriage, which still loomed ahead if you planned to have babies together, because that was when it got bedevilled with official red tape, social stigmas that showed.

The number of illegitimate births and shotgun marriages (brides pregnant on their wedding day) began to decline from the late sixties onwards. You didn't need marriage to get away from home, or out of trouble. You were out of range of parental standards of respectability. Your friends positively encouraged the voluntary, honest commitment these informal liaisons idealized. And though this pattern of setting up home together included many of the advantages of married life and a good many of the traditional role customs (playing at being grown up again) they were woven much more loosely into the fabric of such unconventionally conjoined lives. Maureen: 'We enjoyed home-making when we moved in together. I sewed the curtains and Nick built the wardrobe. I cooked and cleaned and shopped, that was part of being a woman, but I didn't clean very often and we tended to eat out because we were more interested in going out than staying at home. I did take pride in taking his clothes to the launderette because it was a way of saying I'm a grown woman too, I live with a man. I would iron his shirts with delight, because it symbolized that he belonged to me, but we felt like equals, although I was looking after him in this woman way. My parents didn't come very often; when they did I just tidied his things away and he went out and I pretended I lived on my own. They never commented on the double bed – they were masters at closing their eyes to what they didn't want to see.'

This bravado was, however, practised at some cost. Freedom from parental criticism also cut you off from their caring wisdom and support. You really had to go it alone, trapped on one side of the generation gap. The girl who kept on a bedsit as an alibi while living with her boyfriend and dreaded the weekly phone call home to parents, in case during the week they had found out, had to grow up very fast. Security spread between friends (in whom you confided) and work (which confirmed you) as well as the man in your life, who leant on the latest fashion in not letting you lean on him.

Back home, however, provincial life went on very much as it had always done, with the right and wrong sides of the blanket clearly labelled by our parents' generation. Premarital sex took place (if at all) outside the comfort of the bedroom. Young women lived at home until they married. The sensational sixties were coming to a close, but here, where scandalous behaviour varied in inverse proportion to anonymity, the old rules held sway.

In 1970 Julie, who had been going out to work since she was

16, left home to get married. At 23 she had become a grown-up woman: 'When I was first married, it was a game, playing house. You like to show what a good housewife you are. Steve sat back and behaved, jokily, as if I was on trial. I didn't know much about cooking, I'd only ever helped mum out occasionally, and we didn't learn much at school, did we? I used to do the works, really go to town, but as time went on, I did think it was a bit unfair that I did it all, while Steve sat down and read the paper. It depressed me sometimes, getting home tired at night and seeing the breakfast pots waiting and the bed not made.'

The novelty of playing the part had worn off, but Julie was stuck with the role. The breadwinner/homemaker division of labour had seemed fair for our parents, one of whom was at home all day while the other was out at work, but now that married women carried on working fulltime, surely there was a case for sharing the household chores? Julie discovered at work that other husbands did help out, 'but Steve thought it was my responsibility, because his mother had waited on him and his father hand and foot.'

The new decade marked a turning point in Julie's life. We didn't know it then, but it was a turning point for every woman of our generation. The average age of marriage for women had been steadily falling for over ten years until in 1970 it was 23, the age at which Julie got married. But in 1970 the trend suddenly began to go into reverse, because with our generation women began putting off marriage. The year 1970 also marked a turning point for every woman in this country, of which most were equally ignorant. In 1970 Britain's first national conference of women's liberation groups was held, attracting six hundred participants.

Like most of the events of that year, its roots were in the previous decade. News of the women's liberation movement had begun to waft over the Atlantic, mainly sensational press stories fanning the flames of burning bras. But they sparked off an issue closer to home, that of the Ford women's strike for equal pay in 1968, and the fiftieth anniversary of women's suffrage in Britain, neatly following on from Human Rights Year (1967), when the issue of sex discrimination was first raised in Parliament. By 1969 most major British cities had sprouted women's groups.

But it remained a minority obsession. Just as Mrs Pankhurst's 'argument of the broken windowpane' had attracted hostile and uncomprehending publicity, echoed by ordinary women like my grandmother, too busy to understand what the fuss was all about, most suburban housewives, my peers at home among them, dismissed 'women's lib' as extremist nonsense. Bra-burning *was* an unfortunate, outdated symbol, ridiculously inflated by the press. The fashion for pointed, uplifted padding was disappearing in favour of a softline, more natural look or, if you passed the two-pencil test (put them under your breast and they don't stay there) no bra at all. Many women failed it, and felt the need of their bra.

Roll-ons had rolled off more easily with the advent of tights in 1966, making suspenders redundant. The typical sixties attractive young woman wore her clothes to please herself and to confirm the power of her attractiveness. The mini-skirt was a gesture of defiant, flaunting unattainability – here it is, but you can only look – and then when women dressed up in trouser suits and maxi-coats and midis they couldn't even do that. Contrary to the New Look and its interpreters, long skirts were a sign of our liberation, not a constriction of it. What could women's lib do for us?

1970 also saw the publication of a book which sought to enlighten us. Germaine Greer professed not to be a radical feminist, nor representative of the women's movement, but she became its spokeswoman in people's minds, mainly because of the publicity accompanying her book, its strange bodystock-ing cover haunting bookshops everywhere. Her persuasively argued thesis explained our passivity, in spite of our demon-strably equal capacities, as a direct result of our sexual re-pression. I always meant to read *The Female Eunuch* but never did (until recently), possibly because I could not identify with the implications of its title. Pauline heard Germaine Greer dis-cussing it on the radio and her intellectual appetite for any new argument led her to buy the book. Reading it opened her eyes to her own repressed sexuality, she admits, but the rest of it merely confirmed what she had always assumed to be true.

She was the only one of us who read the book when it came out.

We were far too busy living our lives. Those who had been carving out careers were also moving towards marriage, but it was more of a merging of two paths than a takeover bid in a flurry of romantic over-expectation. Hilary and Barry were just friends at first 'but it sort of grew. I liked the fact that he let me be myself, so I put off going to work abroad.'

It was sometimes hard to recognize Mr Right when you'd been looking for a prince on a pedestal, however. Susan had always imagined getting married at 24 'until I *was* 24, and I suddenly thought "aagh! I haven't even met him yet!" I had, but I didn't know it. Kevin used to come round and take me out occasionally, but I was still looking for someone tall, dark and handsome. It took ages for the penny to drop.'

Catherine found that she could hardly see someone she worked with through rose-tinted spectacles, especially considering the accident that brought them together: 'One of my class was sick all over the new maths teacher's classroom floor. I felt honour bound to help in the clearing up operation. Things sort of "came on" after that. Simon and I got engaged and were married in 1975.'

If you'd been living together, marriage was more of a practical development of an existing commitment than the momentous event that would change your life: 'I knew it would come out sooner or later because we lived near parents of children I taught at school, and it seemed silly to be pretending to live apart, keeping both our flats on, and I suppose I started getting conventional . . .'

Parents were coming round to the new morality: 'My mother began making up both beds in the spare room for us. My father was quite shocked, but she waved the objection aside. "I've been thinking about that time I told you about," she said, turning to me, "when we turned down a double room on holiday before we were married. I've only just realized how stupid we were." '

Shirley and John were always a bit worried about how much their parents knew about their relationship, particularly Shirley's mother: 'But it was she who suggested it would be

cheaper if we lived together and I thought heavens, it's my
mother saying that! That was in 1971, and we got married a
year later. I remember being frightened about the finality of
marriage, the commitment, losing my freedom. But we did
everything together and I knew I couldn't stay unmarried forever. I was 25. We went to fifteen weddings that year.'

Those of my school year who had passed through the higher
education system mostly married in their mid to late twenties,
combining an established career with domestic responsibilities,
but with a difference. Susan, who had always longed for a nest,
and took up teaching as a stopgap before Mr Right came along
and rescued her, found to her surprise that she felt more of a
teacher than a housewife, with no inclination to stay at home:
'Kevin does tend to come in and ask what's for tea, but if I'm
with my adult literacy student, he'll get his own. The man I'm
helping to read feels very uncomfortable when that happens!
I tend to do more in the house because I work shorter hours,
but I don't like housework. Kevin's mother used to wait on
him, but he has changed because of me, and because he lived on
his own for several years, whereas men who marry straight
from home never start household jobs. We found a mouse
upstairs in the spare room and realized that neither of us had
cleaned in there for months. I don't mind ironing, but I can't
stand cleaning or washing. I came home once and found him
doing the washing. He thought he was being marvellous, but
he wasn't doing it properly!

'It's funny, in the back of my mind, I still think someone's
going to come along and rescue me. Yet when I went to the
interview for my present job I was bursting with confidence. I
always paid my turn when we went out and still do, and I do find
it irksome relying on him to give me cash because I can't get to
a bank. On the other hand, if we entertain, I tend to hide in
the kitchen because I'm no good at smalltalk. I'm a bit anti-
women's lib, I don't know why. I read *The Female Eunuch* and
I thought it was terrible. I'm very middle of the road. It's too
extreme.'

Susan, talking in 1977, when she was 30, could not be said to
be the stereotypical housewife nor the liberated lady, but her
attitude towards the women's movement does betray a

characteristic complacency of believing in equality yet disowning those struggling to further it.

It seemed by 1977, the year that we were all 30, that the women's movement had made great strides. In 1970 Margaret Thatcher had not expected a woman to have gained any top-ranking cabinet post by the end of the decade, and yet in 1975 she became leader of the Conservative Party. At the end of 1975 the Sex Discrimination and Equal Pay Acts came into force, along with the setting up of the Equal Opportunities Commission; and the Employment Protection Act of the same year introduced paid maternity leave and the right to return to work within twenty-nine weeks of childbirth.

These advances necessitated the revision of *Women's Rights*, a handbook first published in 1974, jointly written by Anna Coote and Tess Gill. But when the second edition emerged in 1977 journalist Anna Coote cynically rejected the maternity leave provisions as useless to most women; pointed out the massive loophole in the Equal Pay Act because it left most women workers untouched, bemoaned the persistent attitude of the DHSS and the Inland Revenue of treating women as male dependents, and concluded by saying that one thing had changed:

> Now [the women's movement] is terribly respectable. Only a handful of Tory backwoodsmen bother to rail against it. Perhaps that is because it has failed, after all its apparent success, to disturb one hair upon the head of the dominant male.
>
> (*Guardian*, 22.8.77)

Increasingly, in the late seventies, activists for women's rights were beginning to feel that women had let them down. They had lifted the lid of social convention under which women had been simmering for so long and exposed, assisted by the increase in divorce and single parenthood, the personal poverty of many women, hitherto masked by their husbands' affluence. Refuges for battered women let out secrets long held in the family cupboard and all sorts of discrepancies between the sexes and their respective status were exposed to the glare of the women's rights campaign.

Yet women themselves continued wiping up after men,

accepting poorly paid jobs, swallowing the Cinderella myth. And as Anna Coote herself had written about the first edition of *Women's Rights*: 'new laws don't bring social change', but only favourable conditions. 'Women will get nowhere unless they organize and fight for themselves.' By the end of the seventies, the happy band of sisters fighting our Agincourt for us, closing every breach with their campaigning rhetoric, began running out of breath. Men, sensing their advantage, resumed their dominant attitude, banging doors in women's faces, grabbing seats in front of us, yet still dismissing us as weak and ineffectual, ganging up to exclude us from real opportunities for equal status.

Or so Suzanne Lowry claimed (*Observer*, 3.8.80), bemoaning the plight of the worn-out, unsupported feminist agitator, the first target, apparently, of this male backlash. In *The Guilt Cage* (published earlier in 1980) she asked what ten years of feminism had done to the 'grass-skirts of Britain', and why did it still seem so difficult for women to give up their lot as housewives and strive for a more independent life?

When I set out on a similar, less professional, research project in 1977, trying to reconcile my mother's image of me with the one I confronted in the bathroom of a shared flat, one of the first people I managed to interview was Gillian, who had married in 1966. Her husband had become a successful businessman, both her children were at school now and she was still a housewife. Gillian sat, casually swinging her legs, on top of a highly polished table and described her daily life, running voluntary youth activities, going shopping in town, ironing in front of the Monday film on television: 'You sit back some days and think what am I doing? I'm going nowhere, but fortunately my life is rather full . . . although it seems very small, very limited, when I start to talk about it. You live from day to day, don't you? I like not having to keep to a timetable, and I do have a lot of control in the house. It's my territory. After all, we live here, females do, all day and every day.

'My husband doesn't ever cook, unless I'm ill and if I'm inconsiderate enough to be ill on a weekday, he'll see to the children. I don't feel I've missed out on anything by putting my husband and children first. I gave up work many years ago, so

I can't see my situation from the point of view of someone who's got a job, but I would imagine they would think I was missing out on the company and extra money. I'm fortunate, I don't need that.'

Meeting my peers who had left school at 16 only seemed to confirm the conclusion that the women's movement has had little effect at grassroots level. Few of them had moved far, either psychologically or physically, from where they grew up. Despite their grammar school education most had been content with second-rate jobs with no prospects, settled upon after little apparent consideration or choice, as a prelude to marriage.

Yet job opportunities were so restricted it is hardly surprising they saw themselves primarily as wives and mothers, roles which gave them better opportunities to express themselves, although the preoccupations of their daily routine encouraged a rather shortsighted view of the future: their reality was firmly fixed in this middle phase of housekeeping and childrearing; the early one too unremarkable and the future one too indistinct.

How could they remain immune from new opportunities and wider horizons opening up? The easy answer is the simple one, that many of these women established the pattern of their adult lives (and therefore their opinions and beliefs) before any enlightened alternative for women had seeped outside academic circles for those who didn't become academics themselves.

As newlyweds they responded energetically to the novelty of copying conventional roles, with helping husbands if they were lucky, and the promise that the double burden was only temporary. They left work, like their mothers, and settled down to bringing up the family and looking after their homes. Husband and wife slid into their respective roles, she having forgotten that, long ago, she wanted to be a doctor or a hairdresser. The consolation prize was complete domestic control and contentment. Margaret: 'So long as you produce a meal in the evening and keep the house reasonably OK, your day's your own. It's a great life to have somebody to keep you. I don't think much of personal possessions, so I don't crave them.'

There is a price for not responding to the challenge of becoming more independent. One housewife (who only learnt to drive by using the family allowance) explained that her husband wouldn't babysit one night for her to go to an evening class. Similarly, mild-tempered Julie gave up complaining about her husband and settled for the satisfaction of her role: 'If I went back to work, I doubt if Steve would be any different. He can make tea and toast, he's not helpless, and when I had a threatened miscarriage, he did the washing! Mind you, it was only a matter of pressing a few knobs and hanging it on the line – which he did all wrong, of course. If I'm ill, I have to tell him what to do in easy stages. But I wouldn't like a man hanging round me in the kitchen, interfering. I like to get on with it myself.'

Relationships do tend to harden into role patterns – hence the maxim start out the way you mean to go on. Both sides have to be willing to change. Nagging wives lack the power to state their case openly because their husbands refuse to acknowledge it. And everyone knows what husbands with nagging wives do . . . The women's movement has problems which the labour movement never had to contend with – few of its members slept with their oppressors.

As Virginia Novarra points out, in *Women's Work, Men's Work* (1980):

> Women are unique among oppressed classes in that they mix with their oppressors on intimate terms in marriage and sexual relations . . . Campaigns for legal change are . . . far less taxing than the daily application of feminist principles to one's own life and relationships . . .

If a journalist friend of mine, committed to women's rights, had to hiss into the telephone, 'There's eggs and cheese in the fridge' when her man rang her at the office demanding 'Where's my tea?', what hope has there been for those of us cemented into traditional marriages for the past ten years?

Also, in its early years, the message of the women's movement was far too radical for women to relate it to their own problems. American housewives responded to NOW because it simply called for sharing the burden of keeping house and childrearing, as well as their support. However NOW also attracted a type of woman who wasn't a housewife, who was young, intelligent and left-wing, who had joined the civil rights movement and discovered, while making the tea for her male comrades, the spectre of sexism in the midst of such self-satisfied egalitarian ideals. Her anger against this hypocrisy was more vehement, her background in revolutionary politics made her more impatient. By the end of 1968 this vociferous young offshoot was calling itself women's liberation, condemning male-dominated capitalism, campaigning for abortion and test-tube babies because motherhood was the means by which men enslaved women.

It was this radical branch of the movement which crossed the Atlantic, to be dubbed 'women's lib', rather than its milder parent organization. In *Woman's Estate* (1971) Juliet Mitchell suggests that anti-Vietnam activists imported the women's movement to Britain when they came over to London to campaign against the war. Wherever it came from it preached revolution. Germaine Greer exhorted women to be irresponsible, even promiscuous, to set up shared group living to revitalize family life. Juliet Mitchell blamed the family for perpetuating women's socio-economic powerlessness, and urged them to join consciousness-raising groups. But these works, weighted in the language of politically immersed academics, tended to preach to the converted and, by their dismissal of traditional female skills (home-baked bread a 'hopeless last-ditch stand against the drudgery of housework', which itself was 'best reduced by mechanizing and socializing it' – Sheila Rowbotham, *Woman's Consciousness, Man's World*, 1973) alienated many women. Ann Oakley (*Housewife*, 1974) claimed that housework could not be satisfying because it did not supply earned recognition, thus totally discounting women like Cherry: 'Sometimes I think, Oh God, I've got to do this, but I don't find it a terrible chore, and I enjoy cooking. It's creative, jollying up day-to-day things. I know it's old-fashioned, but I see it as a labour of love. Andrew is out there slogging away for us and I'm doing my bit on the home front. It's not the way I used to think, but when you actually get into the situation where he's out at work all day, well you don't feel the drudge, you don't feel put upon.'

Housewives *are* totally dependent upon their husbands financially; waiting on people and cleaning up after them *is* a servile occupation; and feeding, because it is a messy activity pursued every few hours if the life force is to be maintained, *does* effectively interfere with concentration upon any other project, representing life bondage for the caravan honeymooner and married woman cabinet minister alike. But why should sitting all day in a stuffy office be a superior occupation? Those whose early work experience did not confirm their sense of self, whose efforts contribute to their most precious relationships and the partnership they call marriage, do not necessarily see themselves oppressed by their world-weary husbands. If anything, they are more content than their mothers, having had a good education but simply failed to make the grade for a good job.

For most of the seventies the real concerns of the women's movement were inaccessible to ordinary housewives, who weren't readers of *The Times* or the *Guardian*. *Spare Rib*, launched in 1972, insisted upon a strict feminist stance; its shoestring budget and limited circulation kept it off provincial newsstands. The image of 'women's lib' remained that put forward by the popular press of man-hating, unfeminine extremists, and the movement itself did little to reach ordinary women to refute this. In 1977, when I first started interviewing, I did not dare mention the movement, such was its image. But the reluctance of many of my generation of women to respond to the challenge of the women's movement isn't simply a matter of the mixture of conditioning, chances and choices our lives represent, blended by the times we lived through. It is something to do with the options we faced during the critical periods of early adult life.

Probably the most difficult and dangerous time of an individual's life is that for which they long at school – the first taste of adult freedom. The conflict felt during this time is described by Gail Sheehy (*Passages*, 1974) as the 'merger/seeker' conflict. We feel the pull between the need to merge back into safety and security and the impulse to grasp at life, 'seek' our own potential for growth. The way we resolve this conflict determines the identity we create among friends, with the opposite sex and at work, forming the bedrock of beliefs and attitudes which carries us along a path in our twenties.

The 'seeker' in those of my school group who left school at 16 met an offputting blank or a brick wall, as far as work was concerned. Only in their social and emotional lives could they extend themselves, but then they were able to resolve the seeker/ merger conflict in a way not open to men. Marriage offered instant grown-up status without the threatening demands of independence, but it confined both parties to the adult status determined by the division of roles in conventional marriage. The man, whatever his earning capacity, never learnt to look after himself, but Gail Sheehy claims that helplessness in the home is less crippling than missing out on successful work experience in the formation of a stable personality, because it encourages the individual to develop the confidence to function in the outside world.

One teenage mother, Margaret, burnt up all the energy of her twenties juggling work with her domestic responsibilities. Only at 30 did she catch up with her neglected self-development. For the first time she made conscious decisions about her own life, took 'A' levels and a degree, and learnt to drive. But she didn't feel the need to establish financial independence.

In the absence of Mr Right other women who left school at 16 carried on living at home. Moving into their mid-twenties, however, they began to crave more freedom, some sort of challenge, as if they had begun to stiffen crouching for so long under the lintel of lowlevel job opportunities. Cherry had chosen a secretarial course as the only alternative open to her when she left school. By the time she was 24 she had a good job as a secretary to a sales director, but: 'You get to thinking deep down, I could be doing more than this. I was enjoying the job and having a lot of fun, but my friends who were teachers influenced me to apply for teacher training, and I wanted the stimulation of the course, the chance to move away from home.'

At this crucial moment in her life Cherry's boyfriend asked her to go to Australia with him. Who wouldn't have chosen the chance to stay together and travel rather than a career she wasn't sure of? Cherry now feels little of the ambitious urge she felt then, being content with the freedom of being a housewife: 'I keep thinking I *ought* to do something. Margaret tells me I should, because I was better than her at school . . . but

I'm happy reading lots of books, just sitting at home . . . I'm lazy I suppose really . . .'

What about those of us who managed to follow up real career opportunities without missing out on marriage? Those who married straight from college had kept the boyfriend back home at the expense of exploring greater independence at college. Their marriages followed the conventional pattern although more loosely, because their domestic role did not assume first place in their lives; they did not need domestic power and control. Liz: 'Women's lib hasn't affected me much. Except that I don't see domestic chores as wholly my responsibility and that's something I grew up with all along . . . I've never been in a position of being kept, so I can't say what I would feel about it . . .' Their dual responsibilities force them to play supermum, streamlining housework and shopping. Kath shops all in one go once a fortnight. 'If I run out of things, I send the kids to the corner shop. I do the cleaning on Saturday morning and they help, and I bake bread on Sundays, which I find very relaxing.'

Domestic chores are unquestionably Kath's responsibility, yet her continuing to mastermind home affairs is more of a function of their conventional role relationship (he is the major breadwinner, working longer hours, coming home tired) than a symptom of her need to control the domestic sphere or identify with housework as her area of expertise, or making her feel more like a woman. Similarly those women who married in their late twenties assume the major part of cooking and housework because their working hours are shorter than their husbands' rather than because they identify with the role of the housewife.

When Pat and Martin got married, Pat drafted long lists of 'who does what when, etc.', but it didn't work out, partly because Martin's studying takes up most of his spare time. 'I resent spending mine doing housework,' Pat says, 'so I only do it when I'm in the mood. I hate to admit that sometimes I quite enjoy it and have to stop myself getting annoyed if Martin wants to take over the hoovering! He does a lot about the house but rarely any cooking and *never* washing or ironing. I'll expect him to do a bit more when his studying is over.'

Karen, an art teacher, prefers crafts and amateur dramatics to the 'necessary evils' of cleaning and cooking and readily admits to not being houseproud: 'Derek does do things around the house, but if the place is untidy I feel it reflects on me, because even women who claim it's a joint responsibility still say things like "She never seems to do such-and-such a thing". That might occur to me, but I would correct myself before voicing it. All the same, I still automatically think when I go into a house where something's not been done, Good, here's someone like me, she doesn't necessarily see why she should do it.'

Karen is conscious of never wanting to accept the limitations, as she sees them, of being a housewife, the way it narrows a woman's horizons. 'If all you've got to achieve is housework, you adjust to it. It's no good people saying you can use the freedom to do other things. If your sights have sunk so low, how can you raise them?' Yet she confesses: 'Derek will sort out the washing and start it off, but I think every man and woman needs something to confirm their sexual identity. Me doing the ironing makes me more of a woman and him more of a man because he doesn't have to do it. It's a minor thing, but it's important.'

Pat says she enjoys doing the messy household tasks most, like collecting the rubbish, unblocking the sink, or doing the washing, but adds: 'Do other people have this sort of split personality? I can get a lot of satisfaction out of doing these things sometimes, whereas at other times I rebel at the feeling that I "have" to do them. We have been conditioned to think that we are somehow failures if we don't keep the bath sparkling and wash up straight after a meal. Stupid really – why should it matter and why should it be the woman's responsibility? Sometimes I feel I should let some things slide to the point where Martin decides to do them himself.'

It would be surprising if we weren't a crazy paving of new attitudes overgrown by old ones, considering the times we have lived through. Laundering seems to be the most sensitive domestic area. Washing is a time-consuming skill which Susan hates, but was reluctant to delegate to her husband, just as he did not want to admit he would have to learn how to do it properly. Julie's automatic washing machine dispensed with the element of expertise, but her husband failed when it came to hanging the washing out – he did it all wrong. Margaret's husband helps, but he 'can't iron'. Liz's husband does the washing quite easily but hasn't yet tackled ironing. Karen positively enjoys ironing as part of the sexual tension of separate roles. At the other end of the scale Janet enormously resents every shirt she irons, and Shirley guiltily bundles her ironing into the spindryer when her mother-in-law is due.

Laundering still requires skill and expertise, but unlike cooking (the other domestic craft remaining an art rather than a simple manual task) little inherent creative satisfaction attaches to it, unless, like Pat, you enjoy the mess. The satisfaction women do derive from washing and ironing is tangled up in their need to assume power and control, confirmed by expertise, and their need to identify with being a woman. Those of us who shared flats and fended for ourselves tend only to be touched by our conditioning about a woman's role when we are caring for a husband's clothes, although one woman has even doused that intimacy down to a fiddly and irritating task to be resented.

Women who polish their self-image out at work do tend to be less concerned to expend elbow grease at home. And it is easier to hand over the apron if you aren't also parting with your identity. Deirdre: 'It's only fair when you're both working that you share the household chores as well and my husband thought so too. If one is doing a job, you let them get on with it. It only irritates, doesn't it, if you say I wouldn't do that, I'd do it so-and-so.'

Catherine found her job too demanding to hog the housework as well: 'Simon learned how to use the washer and the vac very soon after we married. I was spending two hours travelling each day and he didn't get so much marking, so we split the chores down the middle. We did the washing together on Friday nights.'

These women, individuals with individual idiosyncrasies, are not necessarily representative of any other women. Shared opportunities and common impulses may have shaped their lives, but none of them conforms to any stereotype. However much Susan hides behind her sex-role when it suits her shy self, she's not prepared to be the little woman at home, although she'll never quite overcome the seductive power of that idea while she was growing up. She chooses the mix of options that suits her best. If, in doing so, she reneges on her responsibility towards less fortunate women, she does so because most people's priorities are personal rather than political. Political commitment is minimal, unless an issue concerns you closely. However much we may have sympathized with women's rights issues, only one of my school group became directly involved with the women's movement and she was a journalist furthering her career.

There is another 'catch 22' reason for the apparent apathy of most women in response to the women's movement, accepting the gains it makes but not fighting to further it themselves. It appears from our experience that the level of one's consciousness corresponds with the contours of the easy passage one has had as far along the path as one has been freely able to go. You cannot see obstacles you haven't yet met, or those which are so large you walk around them.

Most of us chose a career in teaching, which not only offered the option of returning to work after having a family and fitting in part-time domestic commitments while at work, but was paid equally with men and offered equal status, a continuation of the equality we had enjoyed all the way along the line from school through college and university.

Germaine Greer, however, in *The Female Eunuch* castigated teaching as a second-rate ghetto for intelligent women, preventing them discovering and developing their own potential. She was right in that we were shunted towards teaching because what vague ideas we had of our own aptitudes only became concrete if they happened to concur with the one career opening our teachers saw ahead of us. Opting to go into teaching was either a happy coincidence of personal preference and possibility or, as more of us experienced it, the result of shepherding towards a very narrow opening into a pen full of other sheep.

But this was not a dilemma confined to our sex. The over-cultivated sensibilities of the male arts graduate are equally unsuited to a crudely technological and commercial world. One contemporary writer, discussing the status of teaching, likened higher education to 'a peculiarly inbreeding . . . machine that manufactures its own spare parts'. Those who went into teaching found enough satisfaction in it, once their confidence was established, not to feel they had missed out on opportunities of a different career. Pauline, who had doubts, opted out for a short time, but long enough to decide that she really did want to be a teacher, and Yvonne, who found medical physics boring, turned to her teaching qualification to find a much more stimulating job as a polytechnic lecturer.

Of course it is impossible to assess whether women like Glenda (who had doubts about going into teaching) would have been happier elsewhere, had other options been more readily available. People do not readily relate such abstractions to the reality of their lives, yet here surely, in lack of equal opportunity (in terms of encouragement towards a wider range of careers) is where the most blatant sexual inequalities exist.

The real issue the second wave of the women's movement had to face during the 1970s was not equal pay for equal work, which had been conceded in principle twenty-five years previously, and simply needed resurrecting and restating. As one (male) contributor to the *Sunday Times* commented (1.2.70): 'The women's dilemma is not so much equal pay as gross and systematic lack of opportunity.'

And as Norman Shrapnel, in his book *The Seventies* (1980), rightly claimed it was the decade of the discriminators. The trouble is that sexual discrimination, unlike the two previous monsters the women's movement has battled with (the vote and equal pay), is a subtle and shadowy creature, given to slow poisoning of its victims rather than outright attack. Like the poor, because it has always been with us, it has, until recently, been curiously difficult to see. In 1967 Harold Wilson, then prime minister, actually confessed ignorance of any sexual discrimination about which there could be legislation.

When we were forced, after college and university, into choosing between a very limited selection of options, it did not really strike us that we were being discriminated against, partly because we shared with male graduates a disdain of commerce and industry, and partly because you only recognize discrimination if you are unreasonably obstructed from something you desire to do. People only sense patronizing attitudes if they feel entitled to a worthier estimation of themselves. But you only develop self-worth through confidence-building experiences and nurture your desires with positive encouragement. Many of us abandoned early ambitions because the dream could not be translated into real terms, and those who stepped straight from school into the male-dominated working world accepted their place in it in the same way that they accepted the valuation put on their work by their superiors.

Janet was able to recognize office chauvinism and the way women are kept in their place because she put herself in a position beneath her knowledge of her own self-worth and was old enough to feel confident of the self-image she had formed. Similarly, my first encounter with office chauvinism (having been protected in the false environment of the female-dominated career of social work for so long) was when I was pinched at the photocopying machine by a fat ugly man. I pinched him back, because I was old enough and confident enough to feel a sense of outrage and a desire for retaliation.

Those of my school year who went into teaching continued blithely, retaining an innate sense of equality which they brought to their relationships with men, but did not need to test in their professional relationships because for various reasons they did not climb high enough on the ladder to feel the cold draught of male prejudice. Because this was their choice, they did not see ways in which they would have been restricted from climbing higher.

Kath was too busy running a home and looking after two children on top of working full-time to be able to take on more responsibility at work: 'I wouldn't put myself in a position where I was doing a job with hours as long as my husband's. I suppose I would like to be head of department one day. The reason I changed from teaching science to remedial work is that I haven't got a degree and in secondary schools that means you're only ever going to be a lackey in a science department. I couldn't think of going back and doing 'A' levels and a degree, not until the children are much older.'

Vicky, however, had always had a burning ambition to have her own studio to do pottery. It drove her forward, to return to her home town to teach in order to buy her own house, which was a strange thing for a single woman to do in those days: 'My headmaster was convinced I was having orgies every night, he couldn't accept that I simply wanted to be independent, have a place of my own.' Marriage hadn't turned up in Vicky's life to deflect her from the need she felt, in her mid-twenties, to consolidate some of her achievements. The self-assertion she developed led her up against an obstacle she might otherwise not have noticed: 'I like the school I teach in, but I get frustrated with it, because our headmaster is a woman-hater, so any attempt by a woman to get ahead is just thwarted, no matter how good she is. He lets us get a little way, so we won't moan too much, but if there's a choice between a man and a woman, he always takes the man.

'At the staff meeting most of the other women don't bother to get involved, because they sense that they've got no decision-making powers anyway. If you throw out an idea they dismiss it, but one man (whose wife goes out to work and who has three teenage daughters to put him right) tends to say well, what about Vicky's idea, and coming from him, that's different. But my ideas are never accepted from me, which in some ways is more frustrating than not getting promotion, and it might drive me out of teaching in the end.'

Only those of us who've gathered the confidence to follow our own noses and stray over the borderline ever feel the electric fences of discriminatory attitudes by which women are restrained from fully participating in the men's world. Many married women workers, catching up with housework, shopping and cooking, and gaining satisfaction from this role, do not demand enough from their jobs to discover the restrictions upon them. Pauline drifted into teaching, like so many, and then opted out because she had doubts about whether it was what she really wanted to do. A boring administrative job decided her, but she had to come back into teaching at a lower level: 'That made me work harder to make up the lost ground, and I suppose I became ambitious in the process. I decided I wanted to be at least senior mistress, if not headmistress.' Getting married didn't deter her – 'we shared most of the chores, after a little "discussion" on the subject, because my husband had always lived at home. He was very reasonable, and I'd long got over the excitement of going out to buy cleaning powder for the floor of the first flat I lived in.'

Eventually Pauline paid someone to come and clean. She had become head of department by this time. 'I fought back when I met male chauvinism at work. Some men tried to treat me in a patronizing way but I was pretty sharp back. I never backed down. I met a lot of it at work, mainly among the older men, but luckily the first school I taught in was mostly women. By the time I encountered male chauvinism I'd got some status and my views were respected, I had enough power to fight them back, whereas I wouldn't have had the confidence as a junior teacher.'

Confidence, that urge that encourages us to reach beyond our grasp, seems to be something nurtured rather than natural. Shirley was given the opportunity to develop confidence; and in the process became ambitious and assertive: 'In my first job they gave me the responsibility for geography in the upper forms, which had been a man's job before I came along . . . and I turned it from a nondescript department to the one that got most GCEs. The whole of those six years was a big ego trip for me. When I realized I was succeeding, it just gave me the confidence to go on and on and I became one of the inner core of decision-makers in the school. I was the working-class kid made good. If only my father had lived to see me . . .'

Pat switched careers several times in her twenties, before finding a satisfying career in town and country planning. One of the jobs she left after a couple of years was as marketing services manager with a brewery firm. 'I met a lot of the "What's a pretty girl like you doing in a man's world like this?/I prefer women without brains/supine" attitude and a lot of the "Gosh you must be clever/can I lay you?" (i.e., liberated/economically independent equals promiscuous) and also the patronizing – and sometimes totally ignoring – attitudes.' At the time (1972) Pat didn't know how to handle this. 'It was all new to me, I *was* rather naive, and no doubt in some instances deserved it. It made it difficult that only a few people treated me normally.'

It seems that one can only recognize and deal with restrictive discrimination when one has gathered enough momentum of self-confidence in one's work to leap such obstacles, rather than be deflected by them. When Valerie joined the bank, she was planning to be one of the first lady bank managers 'but they never asked me at the interview if I wanted to make a career of it. I think they automatically assumed that every girl was going to get married.'

Valerie stayed for twelve years, loved it and progressed quite rapidly. She worked in foreign exchange, and security where none of the other girls did, alongside younger men who earned less than she did: 'I think all the opportunities were there if I'd wanted. I could have taken the banking exams. It's funny that I didn't. I think I just was tired of exams at school and the bank's advice was that it wasn't necessary for a woman. I was the first to advance that far, and after me it inspired other girls. I never found any obstacles in my way.'

Valerie couldn't see the obstacles, that however far she progressed on a day-to-day level up the ladder, she would never make a manager because for that you needed to pass those exams they told her she didn't need . . . The most striking example of discrimination against women is the number holding top jobs, which has actually declined since the mid-seventies, even though more and more women are going out to work. But discrimination is very difficult to fight because there is no obvious front upon which to pitch the battle as there was for the two previous victories for the women's movement. Women only seem to recognize restrictions and discriminatory attitudes when they have to a certain extent risen above them. Despite favourable legislation, discrimination is hard to eradicate because women's lack of opportunity at work tends to encourage them to lower their aspirations and turn towards the sphere in which they can freely express a positive evaluation of themselves.

It is this other option which enables women to ignore low work status, and which in the past alienated them from those campaigning on their behalf at work, who tended to belittle homecrafts. Recently, however, feminist writers have been rediscovering Betty Friedan's reformist argument for full equal participation of both partners in all family responsibility, first mooted by the authors of *Women's Two Roles*, twenty-five years ago.

> Men and women cannot be equal partners outside the home if they are not equal inside it . . . why do we talk about 'under-achievement' of women in public life . . . rather than about the under-achievement of men in the home?

Ann Oakley (*New Society*, 23.8.80) goes on to ask:

> why the encouragement of women's participation in the masculine public world was chosen as the correct way of promoting sex equality. One reason why women should become like men is that if men become like women (by doing more domestic work for instance) men's status is threatened rather than women's raised.

Hitherto, men and women have always had 'separate positive valuations of their own spheres'. However, the equal pay debate, based on the argument for remuneration according to individual effort rather than acknowledgement of responsibility (real or hypothetical) to support others, had the effect of carrying men out further on the tide of empire-building self-aggrandisement, leaving women stranded paddling in the low-paid shallows of pin-money prospects because their traditional fields of expertise did not call for a 'living wage'. Men who fought in the earlier part of this century for enough to support their families are, if you like, overpaid to the same degree that women are underpaid.

The only real justification for dividing the financial rewards of going out to work more equally between men and women in a more effective sense by giving them equal encouragement to compete for better paid jobs, is that, unfortunately, the position of the dependent, homebound wife is increasingly an anachronism in a society where pragmatic self-interest is the only defence against the erosion of trust, loyalty and respect. The struggle for women's rights has been a struggle for the right to be self-supporting and self-fulfilled and therefore able to enter into a relationship with a man on equal terms. The woman who finds herself dependent for her standard of living upon the indulgence of a male patron almost inevitably falls under pressure to comply with the conditions of his patronage, a victim to his patronizing attitude. *He*, after all, who pays the piper, calls the tune.

Of course most conventional marriages do not appear in this light, because the man and woman are drawn together by mutual love and affection rather than the motives which dictate the terms between employer and employed. In this way the bargaining position of women has always been masked by the compensations of marriage and masculine protection, which in the traditional role relationship shield us from the harsher realities of life, so that we may more lavishly succour him with the support to face them. Many women in happy marriages cannot see the need for others to campaign for all these basic freedoms.

However, at an Action Day for Women held in November 1980 in London to try to establish women's priorities, and in which prostitutes, housewives, politicians and lesbians all aired their views, one of the organizations present was the Married Women's Association, pledged to the benefit to the family of equal financial partnership and mutual responsibility and respect of the value of the contribution of both parties in the home. Their slogan is very simple, that the happily married should support the rights of the unhappily married. Everything is beautiful in the garden of trust inhabited by the married woman until her relationship breaks down.

Like it or not, marriage is much more of a tenuous commitment today. Divorce reforms in the seventies have been criticized as a Casanova's charter, whereby a middle-aged man can run off with a younger woman. Official statistics appear to uphold this fear, but simply to assume that a man trades his wife in when he needs a newer model is surely too much of a condemnation of the opposite sex. Perhaps it should be seen as a symptom of a relationship in which both parties grow further apart mentally and socially because their worlds are so separate, the wife being the loser because she is the dependent, socially isolated one.

Wendy, whose marriage broke down, has had a hard struggle with two children, at 30, training for a new career, but it has been worth it to gain the independence which she would not relinquish easily: 'I've formed my own identity now, and I would want someone with the same interests as me. I'd get married again, yes, to the right person. I'm a lot more cautious now. I've got a lot of friends and freedom. We are much more of a family now, me and the children. When I look back on my marriage, I was a drudge, really.'

Karen's first marriage seemed so strong that she allowed herself to become dependent, giving up her family and her job to fly to Africa with her husband – but two years later it was all over. She was back at home, had had a baby and was back at work, because her husband died suddenly: 'I made the mistake of becoming far too dependent in my marriage and although he was forced away, it still has the same effect. You're on your own. My grandmother and mother had always insisted that a career was important, you never knew what might happen and they were right. Going back to work was the only thing that saved me, and I met my second husband there.

'I think, because of my experience, it's a terrible mistake to be dependent upon anyone for anything. It's all very well saying you must be emotionally interdependent for it to be any good, but I don't believe that's true. You have got to hang on to everything that's your own, because it's you, and after all it's you who is loving and being loved for what you are. It can so easily be removed, all the props go and you can so easily fall flat on your face. Maybe this is what people like.'

In 1970 there were 70,575 divorces in Britain. In 1976 the number had doubled. Increasingly, according to the president of the High Court Family Division, couples are living together outside marriage for simple financial reasons, or because they distrust marriage, or it does not matter any more.

This, more than anything else, is the overwhelming argument in favour of encouraging women to strive for independence outside the home. Girls can no longer be brought up believing in the myth of happily ever after, something that will save them from facing the responsibilities and realities of life, because none of us can be certain of that any more. Things have changed, even over the last few years, since we were all 30. Gillian, whom I quoted at the beginning of this chapter, has been through a divorce: 'My outlook has changed, I'm not the same person. I have a superb relationship, but we don't want to get married, we'd rather live together. I'm very independent, I have to earn my own living, which I enjoy. Looking back, my life was so restricted, but I didn't realize it. Now I meet such a lot of people. It takes courage, though, to break out, especially if you haven't worked for twelve years.'

Women are beginning to realize that they have to arm themselves against the uncertainties of modern life, like Margaret learning to drive. But until more of the happily married recognize their vulnerability in this respect, it will continue to be the unhappily married who strive for greater independence, whose consciousnesses suddenly clear when the romantic mist surrounding their marriage disperses. They are then, more often than not, left with the challenge of shouldering both roles, playing supermum, but at least realizing their forgotten ambitions, like Sylvia, who trained to be a teacher when her marriage started going wrong, and was able to take over the mortgage when she finally got divorced: 'To all intents and purposes, I'm completely independent. I've got my own four-bedroomed detached house, a good teaching job. But I do find it difficult making decisions, not having someone to back you up. Consulting people only brings about more problems. There's no negotiation. If Rod and I were under the same roof, we'd have two or three days to communicate, agree or disagree. I don't have any help with the housework. It's hectic, but I'm pretty organized. I enjoy doing what I want, when I want, with whoever I want – and that's the bit that compensates for all the rest.'

One thing Sylvia feels she lacks is a name of her own, which bothers her 'because I'd like to think I'd got a name that described me as a person in my own right. Obviously I could revert to my maiden name, but I'm a different person now. Being divorced isn't the same as being single.'

spinsters or single sophisticates – the counter culture – creating alternative sex-roles – security in singleness – 1977 – where did we go wrong? – the sexual revolution, its victims and beneficiaries – coasting on co-operative lifestyles – after 30, the fertility countdown

> Some have more need than others to camouflage their deepest emotions and conceal their private sorrows. This is especially true, perhaps of women who . . . are living on their own . . . They often feel more vulnerable and may go to elaborate lengths to protect themselves. This applies equally to women who are alone by choice, as some undoubtedly are.
>
> (*Woman Alone*, George Scott and Leslie Smith, 1971)

Was this the image, ten years ago, of the single woman, vulnerable and over-defensive, even that rare specimen who had chosen to be on her own? Has anything changed, after a decade of women's liberation?

Certainly the single woman today can camouflage her single status, although officialdom is still reluctant to print 'Ms' on forms as an alternative to 'Mrs' or 'Miss'. However, just as 'Mrs' can mask a self-supporting woman separated from her husband, 'Miss' doesn't necessarily mean what it used to either.

Once upon a time, when the Cinderella fairytale was much more of a fact of life, only glamorous filmstars dared cling to their single status and the youthgiving properties of the 'Miss' label. Now, more and more women are remaining legally 'Misses' by not automatically binding their liaisons with marriage vows. *Statistics of Education*, published each year by the Department of Education and Science, no longer give separate figures for married women teachers because marital status is so difficult to define in a society with a high divorce rate and a toleration of cohabitation. 'Miss' is much more misleading than it was when we addressed the teachers at school.

Then 'Miss' stood for missing out – on romance, passion, sexual excitement and fulfilment, a nice home, children, the daily warmth of companionship with a loving man. Its compensations were harder to define. We glossed over the fact that they travelled, read books and did all the things our mothers hadn't. Even though they were professional women earning a reasonable salary, with demanding, interesting jobs, singleness denied them access to the physical pleasures of life, which to our mind was akin to entering a nunnery. And as they had taken no vows of chastity, they must be single because they had failed to attract a man. Their personal lives were so far removed from us that nothing ever swayed us from this belief.

Some of us, though, had spinster aunts, who crushed you to their wet kisses and fur collars when they came at Christmas and Easter because they would otherwise be alone. This was spinsterhood from the other end. Just as we could never imagine our teachers with parents, stooping to hug and kiss young relations, no more could we believe in the shadowy working lives of our aunts. The two sets of single women emerged alternately between holidays and termtime, like the Dutch couple on one of those toy houses that forecast the weather.

Spinster aunts only existed at holiday times, or when someone was ill, or had died. They often cared for grandparents, whose dimly-lit hallways they had never left. They were the guardians of the family bible, old photographs in silver frames, Grandma's trinkets . . . My mother never kept anything for long. She had treasured a scent bottle which had been my father's first present and in which the smell of Ashes of Roses still lingered, until I, playing hospitals, filled it up with water. By contrast my aunt's dressing-table re-assembles itself vividly before my eyes because it remained unchanged for years, rather like my aunt's ordered life. There was the embroidery-backed, silver-edged set of hairbrush, mirror and comb, the large, opaque china pot of powder with a bee on the lid, the lacy mats, the jar of glinting necklaces and jewellery cases of strings of pearls with marquesite fasteners, in their satiny hollows, and all the time in the background the large upright clock ticking away until it stopped the day Grandpa died.

After her sisters married, Auntie was left at home keeping house for my grandfather, but carrying on as a 'business girl' doing the same clerical job she had been trained for in 1928; so she never had the compensation of increasing status and responsibility at work. The penalty for remaining your father's responsibility was that you were there to care for him in his old age. He knew that, when he made scathing remarks about men you might have gone out with . . .

Auntie passed Jane Austen's 'bloom', but she made the most of Jean Brodie's 'prime'. In her forties, while her sisters were struggling to bring up families, Auntie went on holidays abroad. Once, when I was depressed, she gave me a photograph of herself, like a talisman, to keep. It was taken in the fifties, judging by the crimped hairdo and wideskirted spotted dress. Auntie squinted on a Spanish quayside, amid rubble where a tourist industry has since sprouted, one hand clutching dark glasses taken off for the photograph, the other rather awkwardly pushed into her pocket. The sun threw a strange shadow behind her, like a large bird about to take off, only fastened to the ground where Auntie's feet were planted, one in front of the other.

But Daddy got too frail to be left on his own. She called him that still, although my mother tended to refer to him as Grandpa, like we did. Auntie retired and took him to a bungalow by the sea. And then he died, and she was alone, almost an old woman herself. We still went for holidays, but it felt somehow heavy and claustrophobic there. I was always homesick for the lived-inness of home.

It has only been comparatively recently that I began to take an interest in my aunt. It grew with the understanding of how it felt to be an appendage to someone else's Christmas, the odd one out, or visiting parents and being sucked back into a child-like, vulnerable self. On one occasion my nephews and nieces started to smile at the suggestion that Auntie might have turned down offers of marriage. I leapt to her defence. The unfairness of the spinster image is that of the reject, whereas the single man, because the choice appeared to be his, earns the more dignified title of confirmed bachelor.

Yet against their dim, shuffling, tobacco-reeking male counterparts, spinster aunts blaze like beacons of eau-decologne'd sociability. Spending a few days in hospital, I was once forced into the company of a number of ageing women. I could not help noticing that the dozy, doddery senile ones were not necessarily the oldest, but were often the married ones. By comparison a retired headmistress and a nun in her eighties were much more lively and stimulating. The virtue of being single is that it does not allow you to rest on your laurels.

Auntie is still very active, interested in other people, partly because she isn't immured in the immediate companionship of a relationship; she cannot trade on emotional blackmail; she has to give affection to win it. I don't mean to imply that all elderly spinsters are wonderful, outgoing people and all grand-mothers are possessive, day-dreaming vegetables, but simply to redress the unkind image that attaches to the former and not the latter. My aunt isn't dried up and embittered, however much her restricted situation has encouraged that to happen. But I didn't spring to her defence solely out of admiration. I defended my aunt because I knew I might be defending my future self. Would great-nephews and nieces of mine, if I remain single, be saying that about me in twenty or thirty years time?

Perhaps my fears about my future status are unfounded. The rebirth of the fight for women's rights, facilitated by the over-oxygenated atmosphere of belief in basic human rights and equality of opportunity, has been about one of those basic rights, which, however idealized and difficult to put into prac-tice, enable one human being to confront another without feeling threatened or intimidated. The struggle for women's rights has been the struggle for the right to be self-supporting and self-fulfilled and therefore able to enter into a relationship with a man on equal terms. This can only be achieved if a woman can function adequately on her own, if necessary.

The rationale behind Germaine Greer's goading of us all into irresponsibility back in 1970, urging us to reject marriage, was her recognition of the over-dependence of women upon men. By the time *The Female Eunuch* was published, enough of our generation had already met its author's challenge, kicked over the sexual traces, for men to change their attitude towards female chastity because we acted collectively. Faced with all these 'nice girls' enjoying sex, men had to give up insisting that a woman be sexually unresponsive before marriage and a loving partner immediately following the ceremony. This is not to say that women should not be free to choose chastity, just as many of us did. But these women can now act according to their own conscience, rather than society's pressure, simply because enough of the irresponsible members of our generation tested that choice by going against it.

Similarly some of us risked living in sin, going out on a social and emotional limb with nothing of the status of the married woman to protect us. That collective action paved the way for women to be freer to choose marriage, which most of us have, opting for that institution that Germaine Greer in 1970 saw as so restricting. But those of us who took up careers after university or college did not have to sit at home with their parents, waiting for a man to offer them a home. Many of them had established themselves independently of their parents, even though it was much harder in those days for a single woman to get a mortgage. Today, one prominent building society, at least, claims to look favourably upon single women because although the single man's earning capacity is still potentially greater, the independent single woman is more likely to join forces with an equally solvent male if she does marry, and return to work more quickly if she has children, whereas the male single homebuyer may simply acquire a dependent wife and children. Today's single woman isn't necessarily unloved and frustrated. Those mirrors of footloose and fancyfree female souls, *Cosmopolitan, Over 21, Company* have killed off the sex-starved social failure with a new gutsy image. I was recently asked whether I was married. 'Choosey, eh?' was the response, when I replied.

Is that what we are? And if the man of our increasingly sophisticated choice does not turn up, will we have to assume that we have 'chosen' singleness in preference to the compromise of an unsatisfactory coupledom, admit that we are 'confirmed spinsters'? However much I now admire my aunt and sympathize more appreciatively with my schoolmistresses, I never imagined I would have that in common with them. When I gaily turned away from men who didn't measure up to my romantic requirements, when I scoffed at my mother's injunc-

tion to get married and have babies, I was merely putting off
that phase of my life. Did I accidentally do it too well?

This self-questioning prompted my research for this book,
tracing the women from my year at school to discover what they
had made of their lives compared to their mothers' and to mine.
And most of them had copied their mothers in one crucial
respect. I got so used to asking 'What is her name now?' when
I contacted parents until one mother answered, defensively,
'She's not married, but she's courting strong.' Several women
entered that category, nominally sharing my single status while
maintaining a committed relationship with a man. But while I
was busy rummaging in the past, they were busy succumbing:
Yvonne, whom I'd taken for the determinedly independent
career woman; Pat, whose chequered career pattern betrayed
a similar questing spirit to my own; and Vicky, the individual,
the artist who'd bought her own house. Vicky's first words when
we met on the library steps, where she was researching a work
project, were 'I'm married now'.

When I telephoned an old friend, now living in Paris, her
first question was 'Are you married?'. The starkest potential
difference between us had to be ironed out first, the thing that
would separate us much more than the ten years since we last
met. Of my own group of close schoolfriends, only one is
married; two are living with someone and two of us are still
single. I only managed to trace one other single woman, still
living at home, caught up in the same situation as my aunt.
Otherwise, what is it that distinguishes the single ones among us
from the rest? We certainly did not set out to be 'career girls' in
the single sense, but then neither did my aunt. The shy, plain,
studious ones at school, who never had boyfriends, are all
married now. What was it that set myself and my particular
friends apart from all the rest, and not simply my own friends,
but all the attractive, intelligent and eligible self-supporting
single women of my acquaintance? Somewhere our personal
histories must contain the seed of our dissent, the place where
our lives diverged from the pattern our classmates followed, in
order to meet up with the single women who surround us now,
friends, confidantes and informal family, the solo survivors of a
period of social turmoil just as violent as the one our aunts and

schoolmistresses lived through. Its violence, however, was not the senseless physical sort which disposed of their marriage partners, and it did not act so unselectively. Something in our behaviour singled us out, making us more susceptible to the social revolution taking place around us.

At school, if anything marked out me and my group of friends, it was our capacity to live in the fantasy world we devoured on the television and at the cinema and the theatre, in music and books. Everyone idolized a favourite pop star, but their feet didn't leave the ground quite like ours did. If any one characteristic marked me out, it was my loyalty to the friends who shared my dream self. I once ran away from a man I loved to one of my old friends. I chose my friends out of self-defence; they would never leave me and he might. But I also chose them because being with a man somehow defined me, tied down my future, whereas excitement and mystery hung over adventures with girlfriends.

It was only after university that I clung, so disastrously, to the boyfriend I was with. As Vicky commented, about recklessly finishing with one boyfriend before meeting the next, 'you always fear the gap', meaning the gap between men, the price you pay for being choosey. I couldn't face the gap because I couldn't face the threat of starting work on my own. Work was interesting but I needed a romantic *raison d'être*. Without that comforting blur, the fix of Saturday night, all colour drained from the face of my life.

Meanwhile my friend Jane had turned her back on her future husband for the sake of following her future career. Recruited as one of Granada's bright graduate girls, she had found a glamorous alternative to traditional women's careers as a television researcher on a current affairs programme, the snappy, independent career girl, glad to have left student days behind.

My job, by comparison, seemed a life sentence of responsibility, which forced you into company you had not chosen. For the first time I wasn't surrounded by my own age group, and without passionate involvement in my work, although I enjoyed it, I gazed back wistfully to the convivial camaraderie we had had as students. At work I could not dress as I chose.

I felt embarrassed if my friends caught me before I had changed into my clogs and long velvet skirt.

When my boyfriend and I split up, I moved to Manchester to live with an old girlfriend and tried to find an alternative career, but in the end unemployment dragged me down into demoralizing depression. I could not be a housekeeper as my mother had done when she ducked out of going to work, so I succumbed to social work again, all the time trying to crawl back into the womb of student social life. I joined sit-ins, squatting on endless miles of fitted carpet surrounded by coffee cups, sandwiches and strumming guitars. The pilgrimage to pop festivals also reassured me, but after huddling in a sleeping bag on a hillside near Bath listening to Country Joe and the Fish, Jefferson Airplane and Pink Floyd, it was harder than ever to re-appear at work on Monday.

Then I got a residential job, working with drug addicts. Moving into the cottage that went with the job and stripping layers of paint off its woodwork, I began to feel myself coming into relief, like the beading underneath. And gravitating to another job in London, in an advice centre run by young people in their mid-twenties like me, meshed me even more into that feeling. We sat up late, in a shared house, talking and playing guitars; this was mecca. It was here that my old friend Jane caught up with me again.

Jane had suddenly stopped taking taxis and buying *Vogue*, left her enviable job and spent a winter discussing life's paradoxes, her feet up over a stove in a Welsh cottage where they sent your unemployment benefit by post. In the spring she came to live with us in London. She brought with her the scent of patchouli, Indian cotton clothes to match my sweaty bedouin peasant dress, semi-vegetarian cooking with brown rice and tahini (new to me), the *I Ching* and a mystical outlook which complemented my own growing interest in the occult, sides of life which seemed to be ignored by the materialistic society we lived in.

When the charity I worked for was required to pay VAT in 1973, I volunteered for redundancy and joined Jane on the dole, no longer low status indolence slipping into depressive apathy but the opportunity for freedom of self-expression. Sara, another

arts graduate, also aimless and discontented, joined us briefly,
working as a temp typist, but soon disappeared to a cottage in
Wales to marry and have babies.

Neither Jane nor I were in a position to resort to our traditional role. Jane did take obsessionally to washing, cleaning and
clearing up the house in this indecisive period when her life
had slipped out of gear and stalled. But the very nature of what
we had begun to involve ourselves in cut off that avenue of
escape because it revealed it for what it was. The summer of
1973 marked the point of our departure from all the others of
our year at school because it was the summer we joined forces
with the spirit of the movement which had already become
known as the alternative society, the counter culture. While
our peers were all settling down, we had opted to carry on
exploring.

The counter culture sprang from the late sixties' student
unrest together with the 'hippie' rejection of the consumer
society among the children of the affluent in California, and
was so-called because it differed from teenage rebellions of the
early sixties. Then young people had been kicking against
authority rather than society itself. Here was a total rejection of
everything society offered in favour of more meaningful self-
expression, non-possessive co-operative relationships and a
frugal lifestyle. The explorers were learning to travel light.
Members of the counter culture tended towards an interest in
natural diet and eastern religion, socialist politics and social
work. But the most important shared ideal was the rejection of
authority in relationships and the search for personal dignity
rather than material wealth, which led them to reject conventional careers, in favour of the kind of casual manual jobs
we had done as students because they left your integrity intact.
While Jane and I were searching for our own direction in life,
we both resorted to cleaning jobs and shopwork; and the dole
also came in handy. The ultimate aim, however, was a creative
and viable form of self-support.

The counter culture was a wonderful mechanism for spreading new ideas because it worked from the inside out. It encouraged questioning of assumptions and demonstrated a
different outlook. For Jane and me it provided a means of

engineering a career switch which would otherwise, without indulgent male sponsorship, have been very difficult to undertake. But it also enabled us to work out an entirely different way of relating to the opposite sex. The counter culture provided an ideological umbrella under which all sorts of freethinkers 'doing their own thing' could flourish. The real drop-outs were only a tiny minority, but the alternative society was the biggest force of social change in the seventies and many of its values – wholefood, vegetarianism, yoga, meditation, alternative medicine, anti-nuclear energy – have slid into the most conventional households. Its ideals, openness and freedom of expression, were so simple, its effect upon society at large was like a stone thrown into a calm lake, its ripples disturbing the surface in everwidening circles.

But why had it appeared when it did? Sociologists, who had previously subscribed to the theory that generations were basically cohesive, had to admit that here was a breakaway movement of educated, privileged young people in their early twenties, and reached for the theories of Karl Mannheim and José Ortega y Gasset who had defined a generation as 'a particular type of sensibility' and therefore of vital importance as 'the pivot responsible for the movements of historical evolution'. Mannheim also linked generational consciousness to social change because members of a generation share a common historical environment, 'predisposing them for a characteristic type of historically relevant action'. If you think how many of your formative years are spent in the exclusive company of your generation, especially if you go on to higher education, that makes sense.

Mannheim also maintained that generations cluster around potent historical events and respond according to the problems thrown up by them. Frank Musgrove, in his study of the counter culture (*Ecstasy and Holiness*, 1974), claimed that the catalyst for the generational consciousness identified as the counter culture was its response to the growing problem of power in a society of apparently increasing personal freedom and affluence and yet at the same time of increasing restrictions and conformity.

The restless, middle-class intelligentsia was the generation which grew up with the Welfare State, wide-eyed to world issues via the television, the generation which crowded out schools and universities. The parasitical, cuckoo-egg mentality of the pioneers of the counter culture could only have hatched in the warm nest of NHS, NAB and the rational, liberal, permissive freethinking that accompanied our arrival at colleges and universities all over the country.

My generation came at the peak of a sudden population boom. The rapid increase in affluence which facilitated our education created the vital conditions of economic upheaval; our continuing further education together cemented even further our generational identity; the problem of authority in an atmosphere of declining deference was a perfect catalyst – the trigger-impulse for counter-culture values to develop – and the student's ability, at the expense of society, to stand back and criticize its conventions even further facilitated the conditions for social dislocation. And – without which, to my mind, the counter culture would never have had the staying power to survive its early days – our coming to sexual maturity coincided not simply with increasing affluence and greater educational opportunity, but with the rise of the permissive society, encouraged by the television age, which resulted in the 'sexual revolution'.

Participants in the sexual revolution, away at college or university, unwittingly took two steps on the path towards the creation of a viable alternative lifestyle. One of them was in acting behind parents' backs. You turned to your friends when you thought you were pregnant or were wondering whether to sleep with someone. Those who deceived parents most successfully were those who had expressed most dissent before leaving home, or who felt most secure among their peers. The thing was self-reinforcing: stepping outside their value-system alienated you; emotionally and physically you were closer to your peers.

Conventionally, a full, open sexual relationship demanded commitment to marriage and property, and therefore, by inference, work and the family. The sexual revolution encouraged short-term, spontaneous adult relationships. This experimentation – 'playing' at life – allowed some of our generation to believe that we could function very well, thank you, without all the restrictions on self-expression society demanded of those who craved to be grown up. Our alternative to teenage marriage did not precipitate mortgages, babies and the stereotyped sex-roles of our parents, burying us up to the neck in the social bonds which compel conformity. The radical, critical political stance which spread from America to arrive at the LSE and the Sorbonne, and various assorted sit-ins at universities up and down the country around 1968, was an important show of strength and solidarity, reinforcing a generational shared identity: those who participated in sit-ins, or sat at pop festivals, speak nostalgically of the sense of camaraderie they found there, but it was the sexual revolution that most fundamentally affected people's personal lives.

The old tricks by which previous generations had lured one another into commitment and responsibility – wily bride dragging reluctant bridegroom to the altar – were abandoned in favour of instant gratification with no strings. The ideal of unrestrained self-expression and non-possessive personal ties was heady and unrealistic but then perhaps most irresponsible behaviour is. Richard Neville choose the title *Playpower* for his celebration of the alternative society, and laid great emphasis upon physical pleasure combined with personal freedom and tolerance. At this point in the late sixties while we were students, the alternative society was still a game. But the most important element of that game was that it affected both sexes' integration into adult life.

Hedonistic pioneers of the alternative society, like Richard Neville, were not necessarily non-discriminatory against women – often quite the reverse. Women, by indulging in the sexual revolution, risked their reputation and their security, whereas men simply got what they wanted without the usual attendant fuss and blackmail, manipulation and persuasion. But the social equality between male and female students, and the idealistic notion of social relationships without dominating power structures and controlling games, laid the foundations for both sexes to kick against the roles they found themselves required to play when they entered the working world.

Just as male arts graduates tottered back from the brink of a life-sentence of conformist compromise within the confines of a short-back-and-sides and a dark suit, white shirt and sober tie because their women weren't pushing them towards it, so our generation of women, and the generation 'unit' that was most politically aware, recoiled from docile domesticity. Why nest-build when you're on the pill? They wanted to be free, and freedom spelled independence – paradoxically drawn towards the values their male counterparts were busy leaving behind. The thing that you most take for granted is most easily discarded. If the sexual revolution involved a massive leap in the mentalities of the girls involved, the creation of the alternative society depended upon just such a giant step in the opposite direction by the men. As Betty Friedan pointed out, women could retreat smugly, sensibilities intact, and let the man get on with it. We did not have to sell ourselves into a career structure for life, so it was easier to follow your man into the movement because it was not necessarily such an irrevocable step. A man, giving up the mortgage and the pension fund, could not anticipate someone creating security for him later on, when he might feel he needed it.

The counter culture split into two apparently opposed factions, the political radical types and the rather passive, peace-loving liberal, back-to-nature lovers. It was this latter group which moved much more into the area of 'feminine values'. If women who craved independence, took the pill, joined anti-abortion demos and fought for equality with men in a man's world were expressing their masculinity, men who went on the dole, refused to wield power, rejected inducements to compete for material wealth and status in favour of free time – valuing gentleness, sympathy, understanding and a return to 'natural living', home crafts and helping others – were exploring their femininity. The freedom from sex-role stereotyping allowed both sides leeway, to rebalance sex-roles closer to their pivotal point and resolve the dilemma of the severance between home and the family and the workplace, by attempting to revert to the crafts of the pre-industrial age.

The counter culture was a two-pronged attack upon the social conditions which had sucked our mothers and grandmothers back into the home, even after they had proved that they could contribute outside it. In the atmosphere of freethinking dissent, the women's movement was not merely asking a favour in return for letting sleeping dogs lie, like the suffragettes who had emphasized that their aim was not revolutionary. The modern women's liberation movement (thanks to education, the sexual revolution and the umbrella of the alternative society, which, in loosening the male/female bond, allowed women to step back and look the enemy between the eyes – partly because the enemy identified itself as the men in dark suits, the ones your man didn't go for much either) was able to exploit revolutionary politics and their own educated thought-processes against the irrational inequality and hypocrisy that riddled conventional society and the way it treated them. Some joined women's groups, took *Spare Rib*; others simply groped for their identities; the whole thing moved with the impetus of all true exploration – the search for the new and exciting, the desire to be fashionable and attuned to the latest trend.

When I first entered into non-demanding relationships with men, I was consciously fighting the desire for more security than that, in order to appear more 'cool' and sophisticated than I really was. The beginnings of the counter culture drew me in because I was anxious to show that I was among the avant-garde – the mountaineers who get their flag there first. As teenagers we expressed it in the way we dressed: the first to wear bleached jeans, fringed bell-bottoms with bells, and idolizing the Beatles before anyone else got to them. Going to see Bob Dylan on his second tour was as much for saying you'd been in the audience, as for sharing the ecstatic experience.

These first cracks in the generation gap, because your parents didn't approve of or understand your taste in clothes, music, idols or politics, widened at university where you could do as you liked. When I moved into my first student flat I was so excited that I could decorate the room the way I wanted, without worrying about sticking pins into parental wallpaper or putting a bed on the floor. I have stuck with my generation ever since.

Other girls tended to move more conventionally into marriage because they never found a room of their own. One girl had only known flats where she had to share a bedroom. Another succumbed to pressure to pair off because her friends were all married, leaving her on her own in a bedsitter. That didn't happen in my flat sharing. The shared, mixed household, where everyone had their own room and functioned as independent freefloating units of a whole, was not only fashionable, it offered escape from the odd-one-out solitude of celibacy. Sharing a house in London exposed me to a radical rethinking of the traditional role of a woman without my even really realizing it. Forced to think in terms of myself and *my* life without an avenue of retreat into domesticity, I recognized the unfairness of wasting time washing up for others who didn't reciprocate. You weren't nurturing your man, you were cleaning up after someone else's.

It forced a confrontation, on one occasion, between us and Marcus, who went out to work and assumed, as we were at home all day, that we could do his washing up. We pointed out that we didn't benefit from his money-making activities, so why should we support them? He agreed – he hadn't seen it that way before – and did his own washing up after that. My constant claim has always been that I was liberated by default, by force of circumstance rather than my own awareness of direct discrimination or inequality. And to a certain extent that is true; you only embrace a new idea when it becomes attractive, useful or supportive to you.

The beginnings of wanting my own identity had coincided with acquiring a room of my own. I felt the change strongly enough at the time to write a letter about it – a letter which I never sent: 'Perhaps it's the increased independence of living in the flat but my attitude to life has been mysteriously changing. I suppose it's the self-sufficiency I know has been so far lacking in me – or part of "growing up" – anyway, the revolution in my present attitude has quite surprised me. I can't really explain what it means, except that in banal mundane terms, I don't feel the need to "go out" any longer, I don't feel "alone", I don't live for the man I happen to have my eye on. Also, I think I'm going to "be" something, which is terribly important – I know you'd agree on that. Only a few things still sadden me. I've been thinking about Frank, because it has now become very real to me that it's gone for ever, and I suddenly felt frantically homesick for the time when we were at school and I was in love and everything was so good – nothing had been debased or destroyed in my life by any outside influences or, more important, inner ones – myself. Perhaps cooking Sunday dinner at the flat makes me nostalgic for the vague cosy concept "home" conjures up – 'cos I need someone to be cooking *for* and in those days I had someone. Nevertheless, I shall get over these self-centred indulgences of nostalgia – they're not all that important now – only if we had to leave the flat would it really start to matter.'

That was towards the end of 1967, before I'd ever heard of women's liberation, when the suffragette movement to my mind was another misty part of modern history they never got round to teaching at school. Every woman's ideal then was to have a man to look after; without the perspective of women's liberation or my own experience, I accepted the outside world for what it was.

These early intimations of independence, bolstered by the personal space I had newly acquired, later caved in under the weight of the inadequacies of my old self – the temptation to let my emotions sweep me off the ground, my lack of preparation and practice for managing my own life. I was forced, however, to test my self-sufficiency in 1969 and 1970, feeling isolated and alone as my friends paired off, until – although I never joined it – the women's movement came to save me. The power of the counter culture was that each small group tuned into the generational wavelength. Knowing that the women's movement was there, that it was radical and fashionable, held us up much more than we realized at the time because it contradicted all the messages of failure flashing round us – it was all right to be without a man.

I spent the 1971 census weekend staying with two girlfriends in a friend's bedsitter in London. We relished the fact that our relationship with this man was ambiguous and indefinable in society's terms. Where the questionnaire asked relationship to head of household, we wrote, 'just good friends'. That Saturday night we had sat in the King's Head and smiled and congratulated ourselves that we could enjoy female company on Saturday night. I think I needed that supportive moment more than my friends did. It broke the lifelong rule that had chained me to the man or the piece of toast. Up to then I had felt Chad

Varah's lone woman, although I hate to admit it, vulnerable and defensive, but here was a new identity which would return my self esteem – not Mrs 1970 with the gleaming household gadgets, nor Woman Alone struggling to get by – but Miss Independent who could have a good time being with her girlfriends on Saturday night.

When I started working on a small newspaper, acting out the ambition I'd swallowed at school, my sympathy with the women's movement was reinforced not by any feeling of being exploited at home but by chauvinistic attitudes I bumped into at work. In social work I had been protected from the pinch-me, pat-me-on-the-head persona of the female office worker. Discussing it all with my boss, who'd been a housewife in the sixties and was now divorced, helped me to articulate in my mind what was wrong with the way men behaved towards women. I remember rejoicing in the victory to achieve 'Ms' as an accepted form of address on one's passport. I had no desire to be judged on my marital status or lack of it. So I hadn't yet made a 'successful' relationship with a man, so what?

I had female friends with whom I shared something their men did not: the continuity of their growing sense of identity, aspirations. Concerning ourselves with women's rights didn't matter as much as spending our twenties doing what *we* wanted and, although it was much more of a struggle than it would have been had we been men, we hadn't succumbed to teaching or marriage and babies. We were taking ourselves seriously in a way we had never done at school.

I hardly ever read the literature of the women's movement in those days or lent my efforts to its causes. I never really dropped out and joined the counter culture. But I had stitched the pattern of my own life against the canvas of those two socio-political movements of the seventies. I had been dipped into one of the concentric circles irradiating from the minority group dissent of my generation, nosing its values gently into the mainstream of ordinary life.

I had begun to cultivate assertiveness, weeding out the irrelevancies of my shyness, because the woman's movement assured me that my own achievements counted. I appreciated the greater freedom I had in choosing my friends without worry-

ing what someone else thought of them, arranging my social life
without consulting another person, doing things instead of
hiding in the couple cocoon. The loose, co-operative lifestyle
gave us the freedom to pursue our own paths in this way and
yet also benefit from each other's company. Single women were
no longer social isolates, set apart from the opposite sex. I had
found a way of expressing my domestic self which did not
depend on yearning to cook a man's Sunday dinner. I did fall
into the habit (was it an accident?) of cooking on Sundays
when we all took turns, because I enjoyed walking down to the
local market on Sunday morning, and it rewarded me with that
cosy family feeling, regardless of the fact that I was dishing up
for a dozen unrelated people squashed around our kitchen
table.

My security in singleness came from the slow discovery that I
could be self-sufficient and survive the failure of the relationships that came and went. I could even criticize coupledom,
where separate identity suffocated under the blanket of insep-
arability. But then, just as I was feeling those things in my late
twenties, I began to be overtaken by the self-doubt and
questioning that set this book in motion.

A number of trigger impulses sparked off my sudden realization of a failing which overshadowed what I felt I'd achieved,
clustered around the fact that we were all approaching 30.
Looking at the identity I had created for myself, I had to admit
that it was as a single woman. In striving to bridge the gap, I
had never intended to fall down it; merely not to compromise
by staying with someone for the sake of security. I once glibly
suggested to a friend, torn in her feelings, that perhaps she
should spend some time on her own so that she could clarify her
mind. She replied with a shudder that if you learnt to survive on
your own, you would end up on your own. When I reached 30,
I began to realize what that meant. Singleness had been a
stopgap for too long to pretend that it was a temporary arrangement. This was me, what I was: a woman alone.

Shortly before my thirtieth birthday, I went on holiday to
India. We handed in our passports, as is customary, at each
hotel reception desk. Mine had not yet quite run out; it still
carried the picture of that doe-eyed 20-year-old – occupation

'student', marital status 'Miss'. At every hotel, the (male) management lectured me in well-meant, if over-paternalistic fashion. At first they quizzed me about my travelling companion. 'Your husband/father/brother/uncle?' At each nomination of a legitimate male protector, I shook my head, but refrained from elaborating on the platonic, non-blood tie, nature of our relationship for fear of some cultural misunderstanding of a relationship between a man and a woman of which these men had little conception. 'Next time you come to India,' they told me, 'you must come with a husband. A woman of your age should be married.'

In my own way, I agreed with them: I didn't want to be single all my life, even though I didn't need an old-fashioned protector. Perhaps, also, social pressures were beginning to reach me. A close friend went home for Christmas that year as usual, to be greeted by a neighbour with, 'Isn't it about time you brought a man back with you?' She rushed up to her old bedroom and sobbed, writing an impassioned entreaty to the man in her life explaining why she needed to get married. I had overcome that urge; I no longer craved the status of a married woman but that didn't protect me when friends started setting up home together, forcing me to recognize that I had failed to make a lasting, committed relationship with a man. And could I say that I had really created a viable alternative lifestyle within which it would be comfortable to remain, if Mr Right never turned up? Would the shelf loom as the carpet shifted?

It wasn't just the pairing off – Sharon with Jonathan, Ros going off to marry Philip – that exposed our lifestyle's thinness; we began to feel it ourselves, in the neglect of its shared spaces, the dirty worn settee, the living-room walls that badly needed decorating, the dirty cooker. Oh, we had our rooms but we were imprisoned in them. Our way of life had encouraged self-fulfilment at the expense of real relatedness. And that had begun to matter, more than freedom to do what you liked. The settler mentality was starting to surface.

Behind all the hip talk of love and peace and understanding, the proliferation of dogs on Californian campuses in the late sixties betrayed the underlying emotional starvation and insecurity, just as the lowest common denominator of our shared taste in decoration underlined the superficial, non-demanding functional relationship that doesn't go very deep. I began to crave the kind of attention with which the drama of real family life plumbs you into a sense of belonging. The settler instinct surfaced because I could no longer coast in the present, with the future as a parallel fantasy; the impending milestone told me that you clocked up the miles, whichever road you pedalled.

When I was 30 my brother and I helped my parents move into a tiny flat in a modern communal block. Later, in my brother's car, I confided that it had shaken me to the core. I'd gaily discarded mortgages and security because in the back of my mind I was still in my father's protection. It didn't matter if I lived in a semi-slum; there was still the home which reminded me of all the comforting protectiveness I'd grown up with and from which I'd felt free to roam.

Now that it wasn't there, I had to face the fact that throughout all the years in which I'd been paying rent, I'd been expecting that a man would come along and provide for me. The co-operative lifestyle had washed off some of my sex-role conditioning, but it hadn't wiped out those subconscious assumptions about adult life, simply because it had encouraged continuing to play, rather than grappling with life's larger issues. And however much the women's movement and the non-sexist nature of the counter culture had allowed me to establish an aura of self-sufficiency as a single unit, it couldn't protect me from myself and the knowledge, as I neared 30, that I had never meant still to be single. In my desire to be fashionably masculine in outlook, I'd never let myself acknowledge the inklings of feminine vulnerability. That year, 1977, was an all-time low. The women's movement had embraced the masculine in order to redress the balance but it had had the unfortunate effect of squashing certain urges among its adherents – and sitting on them hadn't made them go away.

The alternative society and the modern women's liberation movement had propelled me and my friends into becoming true pioneers of women's liberation and acting out its articles of faith: women who could not be accused of having fallen for the soft options of any part of our traditional role, whose lives were unrecognizable against our mothers', who shared domesticity equally with men, who were self-supporting and self-sufficient, competing with men in a man's world. It can hardly be surprising if, in hacking through that territory of hitherto unknown freedoms, we tore and scratched that which was closest to us – our personal relationships.

In 1977 we were forced to admit our vulnerability – that basically we needed and wanted a man. We had been covering up the kind of woman Joan Armatrading sang about in an album she released that year, who wanted her man to come home because she was afraid of living alone. We could no longer pretend that stalwart singleness, however appealing it had been in our mid-twenties, was an enviable proposition now. It wasn't that we wanted to capitulate into downtrodden dependent little *hausfraus*; we simply craved a loving, reciprocal relationship with a man. After all, the alternative was to reject them as obsolete, or deny our own desires, when there were still plenty of single men around. So why were we still single? If that was what we had really chosen, why was it so hard to bear – much harder than it seemed for our spinster teachers or maiden aunts? As my friend puts it: 'Those women were forced to repress everything. They didn't have the permissive years we had, to arouse them. But we're the victims and the beneficiaries of the sexual revolution. Even if we stay single all our lives, at least we've got our memories . . .'

The sexual revolution encouraged our generation to take Germaine Greer's admonition to act irresponsibly, even promiscuously, and to try it out in our own lives. Where had it taken us? Having paid out so much permissive rope in our own relationships with men, we of all people were best qualified to question the wisdom of what we had done. If the pill had allowed some young women to sow wild oats in the way that young men did, was that what they really wanted, and what had they gained or lost by it? As Oscar Wilde pointed out, most people simply collect experiences, but those of us who fell in with the sexual revolution had to learn by them. Whether the light was on or off, we had been groping in the dark.

We had been naive enough to believe Richard Neville when he recommended in *Playpower* (1970) that we should let ourselves go and told us how easy and uncomplicated this would be:

No more tedious 'will she or won't she by Saturday?' but a total tactile information exchange, and an unambiguous foundation upon which to build a temporary or permanent relationship. The pot of gold at the end of the rainbow comes first; later one decides whether the rainbow is worth having for its own sake. If the attraction is only biological, nothing is lost except a few million spermatozoa, and both parties continue their separate ways. If there is a deeper involvement, the relationship becomes richer, and so does the sexual experience.

If some of us responded to the pleasure principle when relieved of the pressure of anxiety about pregnancy, we did so in part because we recognized the hypocrisy in the old values, where the girl treated her body as a lure to bribe the man into a committed relationship, whether he had grown to truly care for her or not. We were idealistically in search of purity and honesty within relationships which we equated with freedom and openness, as glowingly extolled by Richard Neville. Experience taught us otherwise, perhaps because the new consciousness merely covered up older, deeper social conditioning on both sides, or because real intimacy, on whatever level, is not so effortlessly and spontaneously achieved.

In *The Illusory Freedom* (1978) Graham Heath, while examining the intellectual and social consequences of the sexual revolution, and deploring them, quotes from Dr Rollo May (*Love and Will*, Fontana, 1972):

> What we did not see in our shortsighted liberalism in sex was that throwing the individual into an unbounded and empty sea of free choice does not of itself give freedom but is more apt to increase inner conflict. . . .

an inner conflict complicated by the overlap of two different approaches to morality, where theoretically one had replaced the other.

In the kind of frank, soulbaring conversation women indulge in, one friend of mine had the guts to admit the superficial, unsatisfactory sexual relationships she had with men, which stood in the way of any real expression of her sexuality and actively precluded the development of any real relationship, reinforcing with every rejection her loneliness and need for affection, trapping her inside her inhibitions and defences, while she pretended to be so liberated on the outside: 'I lost my virginity when I was 18, but until my umpteenth boyfriend, at the age of 25, I'd never actually seen a man's prick. I hadn't dare look! Sleep with them all, yes, but never actually look at it. Sadly, it was easier to say "yes" than "no", so I plunged straight in before I could allow any real intimacy, any trust, to develop. No wonder I didn't dare look at them. I slept around at university because it was the only act that made me feel not so lonely, gave me more personal contact. As regards physical pleasure, I got next to nothing out of it. I know that sounds like a cliché, but it's true all the same. I didn't know any better. Once you've opened the door to your own sexuality, you can't bolt it up again and pretend it's not there, but you don't know how to handle your own urges at that age. Those embarrassing unhip conversations because you'd already left it too late to object. In the old days, at least there were rules to the game that allowed you to develop some sort of relationship before sex took over. I literally burnt all those relationships up until I met the man I'm with now who bothered to try to get to know me. I'd never met anyone like that before.'

Even when that punitive, prejudicial element was missing, the enforced intimacy between strangers often blocked deeper involvement, rather than paving the way towards it. The coins in the pot of gold were counterfeit – the rainbow's colours painted on to please: 'It's so important how you're introduced to sex. Mock bravado led you into appearing more liberated than you were. A friend of mine was amazed when I said I had problems about sex; she said, but you were always so liberated, going and picking up the guys and I said it was all a defence, a front; all I thought about was appearing sophisticated and pleasing them. You put on a performance, did your "number" on them. They could have been anyone and so could you.'

The total tactile information exchange became a faked-up show with masks behind which both parties did not readily reveal themselves and so drifted their separate ways, having acted more stereotypically than they realized – the woman yearning to be coquettish, sexy and the man playing the seducer obliged to lunge lest he be thought slow, the woman responding for the same reason and thinking only to please the man, never of her own pleasure: 'We thought we could hold on to the man, impress him by pleasing him. A friend of mine said that she thought for years that she'd had a good sex life because she'd learnt what you do to please men in bed so that they had a really good time and all of a sudden the light dawned that *she* got no physical pleasure at all, apart from seeing them looking as if they'd been enjoying it! She'd been doing the old self-effacing trick without even realizing it because she was getting used to encounters with men where you didn't get anything back. You gave and gave thinking you would, but you didn't, so in the end you stopped expecting anything.'

They took it all and moved on because the essence of what was exchanged lacked the tension of true-life encounter, the tentative feeling towards attunement of two separate beings – the careful, gradual taming of the Fox in Saint-Exupéry's story, the dance of distanced mutual attraction, the game of fitting jigsaw pieces into place and building up a picture instead of brutally, damagingly, forcing together bits that didn't go. And all because the freedom of expression of the sexual revolution was initially so one-sided – the man dragging the woman along at his pace. Those who allowed themselves to go along with it can criticize it now: 'Sex became a sort of masturbation. That's what the pill did, I think. It didn't liberate women; it made them into sex objects more than ever. Sex became like sucking sweets or something, no meaning. You're a sort of sterile object on the pill. OK, I can't say I didn't enjoy the thrill of discovering a new body but it didn't last; it got in the way of what I really wanted – a relationship – but it wasn't fashionable to admit that. We were never in relationships long enough to mature emotionally, develop with the kind of intimate trust that never comes if you go from one short burst to another. I think that's against a woman's nature, because sex happens really deep inside you. In the act of opening yourself up you are giving all, whereas what is the man doing? Just getting rid of something. And you used to think that by giving all, it must have an effect on them, but what happened? They just walked out and wouldn't speak to you again. Let's face it, at least the whole issue of women's sexuality has been forced out into the open over the last ten years – the right to have your own pleasure. I'm convinced though that sexual pleasure is not something that just happens, like the media led us to believe. It depends for enjoyment on both sides, on a woman taking longer for arousal, otherwise what's to stop it being all over in five minutes? And for a woman to get satisfaction depends on a man who's willing to take the trouble – and how do you find the words to talk about it with someone you hardly know?'

Like the woman who never tells the man he's too hasty, doesn't satisfy her, some of us never made our own demands known in those early days, on any level. We learnt, defensively, not to ask for more than the man was prepared to give. And the overintensity of a precipitated physical intimacy threw a strain on a tenuous relationship that essentially immature adults could not handle. Both sides tended to revert, unwittingly, to another old stereotype – that of the clinging, insecure female seeking the reassurance of affection and the frightened male, running a mile. It led some of us to ponder whether there wasn't perhaps a subtle difference between male and female sexuality after all, a difference which created tension as a vital ingredient for the interaction that forms the relationship.

Graham Heath quotes Konrad Lorenz as saying that diminished sensitivity to pleasure, caused by its overavailability, leads to a demand for instant gratification which militates against imagination and creative tensions in a relationship. Love, as Rollo May says, comes to seem 'tremendously elusive, if not an outright illusion'. Sex, in the mature person, is integrated in the underlying, more powerful need for 'relationship, intimacy, acceptance and affirmation'.

We were so brainwashed by the desire not to appear repressed and old-fashioned. Yet as the sexual revolution ground on, whether through put-on bravado or real sexual self-assertion, women began to throw off the passive body stocking – whereupon the coins in the pot flipped over and showed their other side: 'Sex as a deliberate performance to satisfy the woman de-automizes the sexual reflexes and can disturb the involuntary process of orgasm', wrote George Frankl, neatly summing up the principle of sexual repression under which *women* lay supine for so long. Men were now exposed to the pressure of trying to please a discriminating partner, and the consequent inhibition of their sexual response was more tangibly measurable.

In *The Failure of the Sexual Revolution* (1974) George Frankl, a psychotherapist, claimed that more and more men were suffering from impotence – his major premise being that the new self-assertive liberated female intimidated the man. It was not simply that this sexually demanding *Cosmopolitan* reader was insatiable but that the new liberated lady who was emerging in the mid-seventies (the confident young woman in her mid-twenties who supported herself, paid for herself and whose solidarity was towards her sisters rather than the passing lover) clashed with the traditional need of the man to dominate, creating a 'crisis of masculinity' in which men inhibited their anger, and therefore their sex drive, and, to make matters worse, the whole issue was aggravated by her persistent desire for a sexually aggressive male.

Intellectually we demanded to be equals; deep down, emotionally and sexually, we were still looking for the awe-inspiring Mr Right – a man you could put on a pedestal which was where you eagerly elevated every new lover. But when the romantic aura dissolved, his irritating habits pockmarked him as less than divine to your increasingly discerning tastes. We fell for the fantasy of Mr Wonderful at the same time as intellectually rejecting the notion because we were the first generation fully exposed to the media hype of television heroes who were larger than life: 'We grew up in an age when romantic love was very important – endless teenage magazines and then the whole idea cashed in on by the media, of sudden dramatic fatal attraction – he's wonderful, the only one for me. And if he thinks you're perfect, then your own doubts about yourself are dispelled, but the two people are not real, they're projections of each other. I messed up relationships because I couldn't see the man as a separate being because anything that's separate is out of your control and I was frightened of that.'

Superficial, narcissistic love, wanting total fusion with the love object, projecting one's own ideal image on the other person is essentially immature and insecure. The added insecurity of opting for personal freedom and brutal honesty in relationships, reinforcing every failure, encouraged us to paper over our real needs with the pursuit of false images, rejecting the fallible human being underneath.

There's a Feiffer cartoon where a man at a party is chatting up a girl, telling her how wonderful she is, and instead of the glowing, credulous response, the balloon above her head betrays what poor taste she thinks he has. A more equal balance of power, unfortunately, lent us the capacity to feed our self-criticism by feeling contempt. Unused to power, we did not know how to handle it. True to the counter culture ideal, we even pretended a power struggle in a relationship could not exist. You simply bemoaned your fate, that you always attracted men you didn't fancy, always fell for the ones who were out of reach. We frittered away the chances of making a real relationship because we tended to trample the first tenuous links underfoot. It was too easy to take it or leave it within co-operative living arrangements, because we didn't need it.

The counter culture has yet more crimes to answer for. Frankl pointed out that the counter culture's blurring of sex roles and the understating of sex differences promoted by the ethos of women's liberation dissipated the magnetic tension of mutual attraction of opposites. The over-familiarity of sharing lives and clothes encouraged platonic relationships. Unisex, which rendered our parents' sons and daughters indistinguishable beneath long hair, embroidered velvet jackets, T-shirts and jeans, was a symptom of the safe, desexed and defused level at which relationships tended to settle. There was something repressive about living platonically with men, denying dangerous sexual tension under the guise of personal freedom. I began to sense this, mainly in the dereliction of the shared spaces of our flat, the uncaring under the easygoing façade. Having polished up different facets of myself, I felt my identity splintering – no one really knew me with the depth of daily contact.

Within the flat, you could so easily avoid your own emotional growth by turning to another person when you didn't get on with someone. We also coasted through relationships with the opposite sex, muffling our need in the conviviality of the house which was never empty. The counter-culture philosophy discouraged full relationships because it discounted commitment, the vital catalyst fusing the otherwise unstable elements of attraction and affection. We shunted into an emotional siding because it was all about 'getting on' rather than opening up to change yet we were still explorers, long after others had settled down. One mother worried, voicing the fears of the others: 'I've given my daughters the freedom I didn't have, but sometimes I wonder if I gave them too much. Once they leave home, that's the end of your influence with them. Did we go wrong, letting them go like that? Because neither of them are very secure, and I do worry about that.'

We had begun worrying too. Jane: 'The advantages of being single are wearing thin . . . I did gain a fair sense of who I am and found out what I wanted to do and did it, but since I got to 30 I've had to admit my feelings, because time is running out. You could always align yourself with radical feminist views before, and say it's fine to be a woman on your own. But I now know very few people who are still single. That selfish sixties thing failed because it tried to ignore people's need for security in relationships. A lot of good things came out of the alternative society but a lot of people used it as an excuse for not growing up . . .'

We may have felt the panic at 30, but we didn't all rush into marriage with the nearest man. Having faced the vulnerable feminine in ourselves, we also began to enjoy the very real achievements we had made, in the way that Joan Armatrading exulted in being by herself in the album, 'Me, Myself, I', released in 1980. My friend, who'd written proposing marriage to her boyfriend, rethought that sudden urge in the light of all her freedoms – 'It wouldn't really make any difference to us; did I really say that?'

The sudden surfacing of submerged doubts enabled us to recognize the independent spirit we have all built up, in defiance of the social conditioning of our upbringing. When my parents moved, I rushed straight out and opened a building society account. Shortly after that, I met an older man, who could have offered me all the material security I needed, but the price was too high for me to pay. I imagined myself seduced into accepting his lifestyle and my own easy existence within it, as an ornament, and then saw the relationship breaking down, and facing not merely emotional bankruptcy but the knowledge that I could never support myself in the manner to which I would have become accustomed.

I wanted something much more equal where I could retain my capacity to fend for myself. I have friends who have much more to offer materially than I have, because they embraced the masculine ethos of carving out a career, and acquired mortgages, rather than my feminine lateral exploration in pursuit of variety. Perhaps we don't need a relationship with a man as much as we think we do. Looking at the wreckage of some marriages, perhaps it's better to survive on your own than be trapped in something unsatisfactory because you're frightened of standing on your own feet. There's a kind of complacency in getting on with your own life. As one woman says, she feels torn between getting on with writing her novel or going out on Saturday night to the party she won't enjoy, in the hope of meeting the husband who won't be there . . .

Where are all the single men of our generation who actually outnumber us, apparently, by two to one? According to the Office of Population Censuses and Surveys, most of them are in the armed forces. However, there is also a large pool of single men in their late twenties and early thirties who live on their own. I've met some of them. They seem to have given up on women, retreated into traditional male preserves, drinking beer, listening to rock music, watching football and, yet, ironically, there is something emasculated about them, and in a way it's our fault. We never asked them to shoulder any responsibilities, and they never had to struggle for independent status, like we have. Yet there are some men around who are as motivated for it to work out as we are, but, as one sighed over his cup of coffee, 'We're all such complex people now.' And we are attempting to peg out ground with no plan to follow.

It's only when I try to accommodate another person in my life that I begin to realize the true extent of my independence, my liberation, that perhaps, like Joan Armatrading, I don't want a man that close any more. Potentially, we're capable of making the most liberated relationships, but when we try to combine forces, share our lives, there's a tendency for a lot of territorial toe-treading.

For me, domestic equality becomes a life-or-death issue. I

enjoy housework at home as a relaxation, but I'm scared stiff if I lift one finger too many times in his kitchen, or sew on a button and he'll expect me to do it all the time, even though I'm much better at it than he is. It's as if the struggle for women's rights has reached First World War level, bloody hand-to-hand fighting over a muddy strip of no-man's land that other women wouldn't think twice about relinquishing. It's hard to act out total interchangeable equality, and I think I'm about to give up. Competitive hostility looms up because we don't have separate testing grounds for our egos, like my mother and father did. And I have to admit that not only is he better at putting up shelves than I am, but I quite frankly would prefer to leave him to it, while I do the sewing. Does that make me a traitor to the cause? There is something very sterile about being all-round self-sufficient.

Just as there is something very fixed in my insistence that I can produce a meal single-handed while he's reading the Sunday papers, but when it's his turn, I have to act the willing assistant, drop what I'm doing to trot back and forth, laying the table, making the gravy. OK, he says, producing thick but astonishingly unlumpy gravy, dashing backwards and forwards from the kitchen while I sit uncomfortably unable to concentrate on what I'm reading, haunted by the ghost of the girl who wanted someone to cook Sunday dinner for. Or am I simply acting like my mother, wanting kitchen omnipotence so I can do it all my way? Perhaps I should see chores as a shared thing, like he does, instead of wanting to claim all the credit myself.

I met a man recently who accused women of being unable to negotiate, citing the example of his wife, who talks herself, and him, into a corner, from which neither can emerge gracefully. I opened my mouth to protest, and then closed it again, wondering whether he had a point. If women haven't learnt the art of negotiation, it is because they've not had much experience of having negotiating power. Women are accustomed to having to act the injured party rather than the put-out partner, prepared to give way a little.

And yet I'm not the only one wanting total control. He gets upset that I've not put his kettle back where he keeps it, the teatowels aren't draped over the eye-level grill, and – worst crime of all – I left the milk bottle out of the fridge. I smile and say (to myself at the same time), 'You say you want to have children, but how on earth would you put up with them? They won't put your milk bottle back in the fridge . . .'

This is why we're trying so hard, why my friend goes to the party instead of writing her novel, why we gave up on the alternative lifestyle before many of our male counterparts, and reject them as immature – because we can't see them as fathers for our children, and that's what we're looking for now. This is why we felt the panic at 30, because the spool of our relationship to our bodies suddenly stuck and started winding back the other way. A man can carry on fantasizing having children by a younger woman, but for a woman 30 is a fact of life where you wake up and realize the thing that you always took for granted (and dodged) won't be there for the asking much longer.

Part of the sudden panic we feel is that it caught us unawares. All our freedom and independence had been based on the fact that we didn't have to consider pregnancy, babies, the ultimate adult responsibility which polarizes the masculine and the feminine, casts a woman in the vulnerable role, falling under the man's protection, his domination, trapped in the domestic prison created by his consumer society.

The key to all that freedom we had in our twenties, to walk in the world of men, was the pill. We could coast on a series of casual relationships, go out exploring our potential because we didn't need to build a nest. The choice was ours, and we turned our backs on motherhood because it represented everything that trapped a woman. The most emotive issue of the women's rights movement of the seventies was not equal pay. The cause that got women out on to the streets showing their solidarity was the threat to the Abortion Act, that safety net under our irresponsibility. Although the slogan was 'a woman's right to choose', there was little doubt which way many of the women present would have chosen. Just as the women's movement was concerned with entering the world of men, it encouraged us to play Peter to ourselves as lifegivers, creators, nurturers – mothers.

For that is what we did to our biological function of creating life; we held that side of our nature in suspension. It was frozen, forbidden, a monster looming over the horizon instead of the happy event, because it represented everything we couldn't face about being a woman. Each one of us suffered that nagging anxiety when a period was late, the fear that you couldn't share with him because the relationship wasn't on that level, so you were frightened of scaring him off, until the sighing relief at the show of blood, or the claustrophobic panic of invasion when your worst fears were justified. Some women never told the man, paid for the abortion themselves, almost as if it was some terrible crime they had committed, which was nothing to do with him. Only when we woke up to the fact that the choice might shortly be taken out of our hands did that side of our natures unfreeze like a spring flood.

Anna Coote wrote in the *New Statesman* (26.9.80):

I have been blessed throughout my grown-up life with a large and strong network of women friends . . . A fair amount of marrying and divorcing and cohabiting and separating has gone on (over the years) but – mercifully – very little in the way of reproduction. Until now.

I visit Mary . . . and with me comes Angela . . . As my two friends exchange notes about labour pains and feeding times, locked in a wonderful conspiracy of expertise, I look on with rising panic. There are suddenly *an awful lot* [her italics] of babies about. I've subscribed for some time to the Domino Theory of maternity and now my fears are being confirmed.

It hasn't been easy for any of us to take the plunge. Well-educated and middle class, we are not the sort of women for whom babies can just 'happen along'. So we have played with the idea endlessly – longing and dithering like children at the edge of a chilly sea. But of course the goddam tide is coming in. And soon there'll be no beach to dither on. Thirty-two . . . thirty-three . . . thirty-four, in they go, one after another, waving and beckoning to the next. One more pregnancy and I'll order the bombing of Mothercare. Or the rest of us will not sleep soundly in our beds.

Some did leap in deliberately, because desire overtook them so compellingly in a situation in which it was practical to indulge for the first time that luxury of feeling great, my period is late, perhaps I'm pregnant. Some of us, though, have lives too complicated to contemplate complicating them further: 'Look at me at 30. I'd intended to have six children, and I haven't got any. I live with a divorcee, who's got a wife and children to support. They have the house and we live in a bed-sitter and I sometimes look at his wife and think which of us has got the better bargain. I don't know.

'So many women find fulfilment through children, which perhaps they can't get through a man. I think children must complete a woman – that's what we're all here for. It's stupid to have the whole of your body geared up to it and not do it . . . and it's not just a female thing. More and more blokes seem to want children, only they don't have the time limit. That's what being 30 meant to me. Help! What if I never have children? I think the hangup for women of getting old is, unfortunately, tied up with the idea of childbearing. I don't know what men feel about having sex with a woman who can't conceive.

'We were all too bloody intellectual about everything. It makes me sick when I see some pathetic women dragging round a load of kids and I think look at us, physically and intellectually all right, what a loss to the world if we haven't managed to reproduce. The trouble was, I was just too clever to do it and now my situation is just too complicated to go ahead. Being too intellectual, we were so far from the reality of our own needs, because our problems simply became something we talked about and analysed, instead of feeling and getting on with solving them.'

It is hard to follow your body where it leads you, instead of clinging to the controlling force of your intellect. Is the tendency to cuddle the man of the moment the only broodiness we can allow ourselves? Will the real physical experience measure up to the fascination of fantasizing about the mystery of bearing a child who will become a person with whom to rediscover one's own childhood, all those buried memories? Is one simply being narcissistic, longing for a sliver of oneself animated in another being, fused into a likeness with one's lover? Is it simply nostalgia, wanting to repossess the family teatable familiarity lost when we grew up?

For those of us still waiting for the right situation, it is a difficult time. Our settling instinct may have surfaced too late, so we have to remind ourselves that although children vivify your life, they steal some of your own luminosity to do it. Beneath the frilly knickers is the dirty nappy; behind the angel smile the demon crying that won't stop to let you sleep. That sweet-faced toddler is the one about to poke fingers in the electric socket, pull down the saucepan from the stove and snatch your pen when you try to write. They'll whine and disobey, argue and dictate, then leave without a word of thanks and finally dump you in an old people's home.

Yet still we want to find all these things out at first hand, and share the experience with a man who matters. We believe children need fathers, active ones with whom to recreate the stocky drama of family life, not those gangling, out-on-a-limb puppet-show-with-no-strings relationships. Single parenthood seems so much of a constraint, such a betrayal of the opposite sex, denying the romantic essence of procreation, the embodiment of an act of love.

Part of the old terror of pregnancy was the fear of invasion by someone you didn't truly love. For those of us who are far away still from the blood and guts of life, who have our lives under such control, who are still holding back for that reason: we have a little time left. Perhaps when we reach 39 (the age my mother had me) we'll have faced the dilemma and resolved it, but then if we're still single we really will have to make up our minds. Do I want to do this so much, that I'm prepared to do it in the fiercely independent, somewhat stoical and self-defensive way of a woman alone?

9 Who'd be a Mother?

expectant teenagers – not all home birds – wastage of women teachers – putting it off, with the pill – choosing motherhood – teething troubles and turning points – where are we now?

> *So it is that for the begetting and bearing of three or four children, a matter of a few minutes in the life of a man and of a few months in the life of a woman, the sexual shape is imposed upon almost all their activities . . . For that much practical outcome our whole lives are obsessed. And if it were not for that obsession, for its hopes and excitements and collateral developments, I do not know where the great majority of lives would find the driving force to continue.*
> (H. G. Wells, *The World of William Clissold, 1933*)

Sheila: 'I'm a housewife, I don't go out to work, I've got plenty to do at home. I've got three children, all boys, and they're quite time-consuming, one 9, one 7 and the baby's 2. We haven't really got any hobbies, we don't seem to have the time, do we? Life revolves around the children, and I do all the housework. Greg's not at home a lot, he works long hours, so it does tend to fall on me most of the time.

'All I ever wanted was to get married and have babies. I really longed to have a child. It's when you've got them you sometimes think twice! I don't think women's lib had come out then, had it? It was the natural thing that everyone expected to do. I suppose I have missed out on other things I could have done, but you don't realize, at that age, the responsibility it's going to be, having to put your children first. Having them young, we've had no time on our own, or been able to go out spontaneously on our own. But then I think not having children must make you very selfish.

'They're lovely when they're small – oh dear, kiss it better! – like this one. But then it becomes a battle of wits. I prefer them when they're babies, up to about twelve months. It does tend to spoil them, growing up. They're not yours any longer, they've got minds of their own and they learn such a lot that you don't teach them. But I've enjoyed looking after them, seeing them grow up, taking an interest in all they do. It's your whole life nearly, isn't it? I've not thought what I'll do when they're older, it seems too far ahead. I should have to do something that fitted in, part-time, but it would have to be something that means something to me, not just something that pays. I'd quite fancy nursing . . .'

I hadn't seen Sheila since she left school, when we were 16. Fourteen years later, we were 30-year-old women facing one another on the three-piece suite they've had since they were first married: me perched on the edge of my chair, she next to Greg, sinking into the soft cushions of the settee, secure in the cosy clutter of her own home, surrounded by her children, everything she had ever wanted. Her fantasy future had been real for so long its edges were rubbed and worn, while mine was still pristine and polythene-wrapped inside my head.

I had just started out researching this book, meeting women I hadn't seen for over ten years, and it was surprising how little they had changed. Figures were perhaps filled out a little, faces delicately etched with a tracery of tiny lines, but the girl I remembered vividly re-animated before my eyes. And yet there was one dramatic difference. Most of the women I was beginning to re-encounter now that we were all 30 were mothers. The startling difference was the small shy face claiming a hold on their skirts, or the self-absorbed adolescent, running in with something to say, ignoring me, although I could not ignore them.

My unresolved feelings about motherhood were rising to the surface, not simply because I had reached the age at which I could no longer push them away, but because I was faced with so many mothers introducing me to so many small strangers. My friends who have children tend to drift out of my social circle. The most daunting aspect of interviewing my schoolfriends was not wresting their attention from these arrogant little Napoleons, whose insistent hecklings punctuate my tape recordings, at times totally obliterating a fascinating and thought-provoking response, nor the way in which these tiny terrorizers of attention could triumphantly shatter a stream of thought with some deliberate distractive strategy. It was confronting my own utter ineptitude and inadequacy, faced with something I knew nothing about.

I was in my mid-teens when my sister and sister-in-law produced. Babies embarrassed and bored me. I resented the assumption that I should coo over them and want to hold them. Motherhood spelled an ugly, bloated body, then a messy, fractious millstone. It was easy to reject babies because you expected they would come along anyway. In pre-pill days pregnancy was the expected outcome of sexual relations. Families were hopefully planned, but babies also happened along. The very word 'expecting' seemed to be used more often than it is now.

When Sheila met her future husband, at 15, most girls expected motherhood as a matter of course. You carried on working after you married, but only until you started your family. The young wife who discovered she really was expecting, eagerly gave in her notice and looked forward to the happy event. The teenager, torn between going away and training to be a teacher or staying at home and marrying her boyfriend, chose marriage because, like Christine, she always imagined her future 'settled and content with a family. I gave up the idea of being a teacher because I knew what meant most to me'. Christine worked as a teaching assistant for a year before marrying. 'It didn't seem worth looking for another job because I knew I would be starting a family. It just seemed the natural thing to do.'

Lured by the attractive aspects of motherhood, young wives forfeited their freedom without a second thought, and the real life responsibilities of dirty nappies and sleepless nights cemented them, more than anything else, into the traditional female role, because being a wife and a mother was the natural, expected thing to do, and these young women had hardly done anything else. However, in most cases the name etched on one's ruler did not turn out to be that of Mr Right and in his absence many women who had gone out to work at 16 did not marry until their mid-twenties. They still expected to start a family, but that expectation was more psychological than biological now that most married women were taking the pill. It was natural for thoughts to turn to children when you had finished feathering your nest. Julie had been a bank clerk for seven years when she and her husband arrived home from a holiday abroad, looked around and decided that all they now lacked was a family. Julie had no idea what it would be like, but it was something she had always wanted and it disposed of the burden of running a home as well as having a full-time job. Julie: 'Just after I left work, I was stopped on my way to the ante-natal clinic, for a social survey. They asked me what I did and I hesitated and was about to say bank clerk, but then I said housewife. I thought no, that's what I am now.

'The responsibility of the baby frightened me at first, because there's never a time when anyone's so dependent on you. But I'd found my vocation. Steve said "You're really enjoying this, aren't you? You've found something you're good at." I'm not the perfect mother, I shout and bellow and they get me down, but I just enjoy bringing them up, especially babies, because you're the whole world to them when they look up at you. You just give them a cuddle and all their troubles go away.'

Losing the status of being at work didn't worry Julie; she had found something that meant so much more. Andrea also married in her mid-twenties and had a family. I remember Andrea as a talented comic at school, mimicking the teachers or the voices of the Goons. Her ambition had been to become a doctor, but the narrowness of the 'A' level science syllabus stifled her, and she left in the sixth form, for a job as a lab technician. She loved the practicality of her work, but preferred freedom to the prospect of promotion: 'The firm would have paid for me to go on, but I didn't want to. When you go out to work you discover there are men, don't you? I was more interested in my social life than trying to be ambitious.'

Mr Right turned up when Andrea had tired of skating over the surface of life and felt ready to stop and dig her heels in. She gave up her job without any regrets and confided to a friend, when her second child was born, that she thought she'd found her destiny. Kath and Glenda had both trained as teachers and been working for several years when they turned to motherhood, equally naturally and easily, but not because they were leaving a career to which they could return, as part of Betty Friedan's three-phase life-plan. For them motherhood was an easy way out of an uncomfortable work situation from which marriage alone had not rescued them. Glenda had always wanted to be a teacher, but found classroom discipline difficult to enforce and her husband's resentment of her higher earnings hard to handle. Both problems melted away when she became a mother. Brenda, too, found class discipline a bit of a strain.

Unlike Glenda, Brenda had gone in for teaching because 'the only alternatives were university, teaching, nursing and secretarial work, in that order. I've often thought since that working with computers would have suited me better. I was going to try and get out of teaching but I got married and for the first time in my life, when I had the baby, I felt right, whereas I never felt right in teaching. I like feeling needed, the only person who can do this particular job, be mum to my children.'

Some women who became mothers didn't automatically become contented, homecentred housewives. There were the girls who, in pre-pill days, discovered they were expecting when they hadn't particularly longed for a child nor seen motherhood as the natural next step. Not that they didn't discover maternal feelings when the baby did arrive – Margaret, whose son was born when she was 19, had always seen babies as something that made a lot of mess, 'but the unique feeling when they put him in my arms really did surprise me, the feeling of joy that went right through my body when I held him and he was mine. Having maternal feeling aroused for my own child, I could feel it for others, when I never had before' – nor that they didn't see motherhood as their primary responsibility.

When Viv discovered she was pregnant, the bitter realization of being among the unlucky ones who had been caught out was shortlived, because this compelling and irrevocable commitment neatly disposed of another gnawing dilemma. Having failed to get the 'A' level necessary for the career she had set her heart on, Viv had turned to teacher training, very much as second best. She had already decided to withdraw from the course when she found she would have to, because she had also discovered, with the first teaching practice, that she wasn't cut out to be a teacher: 'So really, all I was feeling was what else could I fail at? Getting pregnant was the making of me, because it gave me a real goal in life.'

Viv had always been one for going out, looking for excitement, but she realized, with a family centre of her own, that she had been simply after an image, out of insecurity: 'I didn't miss going out in the evenings, but maybe that was because I was coming in tired from work and having a baby to cope with. My life was suddenly full of responsibilities, working, running a home, looking after a baby.' Viv went back to work when her baby was only three months old.

In the mid-sixties, whether conception happened shortly before or after marriage mattered much more than it does today. Because of the social stigma of illegitimacy young couples would hastily marry and so, either way, the unplanned arrival of a child followed too closely upon marriage for the couple to act out their respective roles of breadwinner and homemaker. Viv put her baby in a private nursery and went back to work because her husband's earnings could not support the family: 'My boss was most disapproving, I was an evil woman leaving my child. And the nurse who took me to the medical was really caustic, too, but it was either that or the family splitting up. I was doing my best for Mark.'

Clouded career aspirations had evaporated before the challenge of making a go of family life. People mistrusted mothers with young babies and when Viv finally did get a job where she was promoted and sent on a course, 'I couldn't reduce my hours when Mark started school. I had terrible trouble finding anything part-time. It just became a battle for survival; all that motivated me was earning the money. OK if I actually enjoyed the job, but that was a bonus.'

Viv claims she would have stayed at home, had she had the choice, content to be a wife and mother. But being a housewife and mother wasn't enough for Margaret, when she moved to a neighbourhood where she didn't know anyone. She'd always seen work simply as a means of survival but suddenly the prospect offered social contact and stimulation. She found a nursery when the baby was 2 and went out to work, not because they needed the money but because she felt cut off and bored at home all day. Housework was easy; being with the baby wasn't enough.

Teenage girls were rushing into marriage and motherhood in the late fifties and early sixties, but the percentage of working mothers of pre-school age children was also increasing, from 6 per cent in the 1950s to 45 per cent in the mid-sixties. Society still frowned upon the working mother, but financial necessity, the decline of homecrafts and neighbourliness with household gadgets, instant foods, supermarkets and increased mobility and higher standards of living all conspired to attract the young mother away from the cloying demands of her child.

Mother had needs of her own, and home was no longer a place which could provide them. Education had enabled some young wives to find jobs that were important to them. Being pregnant took Sylvia by surprise, 'because I got pregnant in spite of taking precautions. I wasn't ready to give up my job and stay at home.' Long before the maternity leave provisions of the Employment Protection Act, Sylvia arranged for her job to be kept open for her and went back to work three months after the baby was born. Her sister minded it with her own, and then when she was 2, Sylvia's daughter went to the same nursery as Viv's son. Sylvia doesn't remember much criticism at the time, but then she says she was used to going against the tide, so she probably didn't notice other people's attitudes. She was simply aware of her own needs dictating the quality, rather than the quantity, of care she could give to her child. Sylvia: 'I didn't feel my daughter was deprived, because I would have been the wrong person to stay at home all day. I needed to be at work and with adults. You sparkle a bit more, then, you have more to offer in the time you do spend together. Nursery children got the reputation of being deprived because some mothers did just dump them there. I think it's a personal thing, for each mother to determine which arrangement is best for her and her child. I would have been quite happy not having children, there were so many more important things at that stage. But the responsibility of having a child that young does make you mature earlier, it made my growing up happen in a different way.'

Motherhood met Sylvia head-on, but it did not deflect her
from her own path in life because she had already gripped a
firm enough hold to carry on, without feeling she was neglecting what society saw as her primary responsibility. Kath, whose
career plans had anticipated motherhood, nevertheless also
faced the prospect before she was entirely ready. She had
married straight from college (in preference to taking a BEd –
studying was never her strong point) and fell pregnant while
she was still doing her probationary first year in teaching:
'We'd planned that I should work for a few years first. That
first year was quite a strain, suffering someone supervising my
classes when I wasn't very confident, as well as having a home
to run and my mother-in-law to look after, which was possibly
why I was a bit careless! And in a way, I was glad to get away
from the pressure at work. But I was only off work for eighteen
months altogether.'

Kath had been released from the pressure of having to prove
herself in her first job, but, like Margaret, she didn't find that
home life or motherhood absorbed or satisfied her: 'I went back
to work when my second child was three months. I'd intended
to wait until they were both at school, but I got bored, just
sitting around reading all day, and very withdrawn, without
realizing it. It got so I couldn't conduct a conversation.' Unlike Viv and Margaret, Kath found it relatively easy to get
part-time work, but soon changed to full-time 'because you
feel out of it as a part-timer'. Oddly, her elder child reacted
more strongly to the separation. It was only later, when she
saw more of him, that she began to feel guilty that his problems might have been her fault: 'Maybe it was the strain at
work while I was pregnant, rather than going back to work –
you never know, do you? You just live with the guilt and hope
they turn out all right.'

It was relatively easy for Kath to return to work, when she
discovered she wasn't happy being a full-time housewife and
mother, because she was a teacher. Margaret had found it
quite difficult to get clerical work – employers were so wary of
mothers with young children needing to take time off. And
Viv's good job had to be given up because school hours didn't
fit in with the normal working day. Teaching was the ideal

occupation for a working mother (if she didn't mind working with children as well as coming home to them). The hours synchronized with the times her children needed her at home. She could apply the skills of dealing with children she had developed while away.

In the late sixties, however, opposition to married women teachers still existed within the profession itself, from some members of the National Association of Schoolmasters (which had lost the battle against equal pay for female teachers). They claimed that the intermittent career pattern of married women detracted from the status of the profession itself. The woman teacher could not win. Either she was whooping it up on the Costa Brava as a single woman, or betraying her commitment to her work by marrying and having a family while her male counterpart was struggling to support a wife and family on an equal but low status salary.

Brenda and Glenda were both culprits in the status-lowering syndrome in teaching known as 'wastage', whereby recruits left within a short time of qualifying. In part this problem reflected the halfhearted way in which arts graduates, male and female alike, drifted along the academic conveyor belt to be wafted into teaching when no other option presented itself. But Brenda and Glenda's ostensible reason for leaving teaching accounted for the greater proportion of wastage in the profession, hence the NAS attack, brushing aside the fact that they were thereby providing the essential raw materials for the profession, and that many mothers would return when they had seen their own children off to school.

Whatever the justification, wastage did cause concern. Reports on the 'Demand and Supply of Teachers' attempted to forecast future recruitment needs by assessing potential wastage rates, the age and rate at which women would leave teaching to start a family. The forecasts for our generation (published in 1965, just as the potential teachers among us were about to embark on their training) allowed for our statistically assessed difficulty in finding husbands, but not for our facility for our work, as the next ten years were to show.

In 1965 the wastage rate for our generation of women teachers by the time they reached 25 was estimated at 20 per cent; actual wastage only touched 16 per cent. We were 27 when wastage did reach 20 per cent, by which time it should, by the 1965 forecasts, have reached 27 per cent.

What the forecasters could not have anticipated was that some women's lives were careering away from their mothers', boosted not only by a better education and job prospects but better control over their bodies, in the shape of the coil and the pill. Ours was the first generation of women to turn to the pill as a natural form of contraception in our twenties, the years when a woman is most likely to conceive. That made us the guinea-pig generation for hormone contraception, but it also made motherhood a much more conscious choice. Julie, the proud mother, was equally proud that all her pregnancies were planned, and that women shouldn't have children if they didn't really want them – which would have been a rather impractical suggestion in pre-pill days when part of your mind adjusted to the mother persona every time your period was late, in the way that women adjust to many things.

With the pill you could confidently put off parenthood, despite all the social pressures around you. Would-be grand-parents, their ears to the ground, waiting for the patter of tiny feet, were likely to be a long time in that position. Liz, who got married at 21, planned to teach for four years before start-ing a family, and remembers the general comment being 'I'll give you about two'. But, having been apart so much while she was at college, Liz and her husband wanted time to do things together; and even though time went on, it never seemed the right time. Parental expectations prompted them to think about it, but 'we realized we were thinking we ought to, rather than we wanted to, and that didn't seem the right reason to have a baby'.

All through the 1970s women were getting married later, and then putting off having their first child. One observer noted in 1974 that births had been falling by about one thousand every week and predicted that this trend would effect actual population decline by the end of 1975, the reverse of the Registrar General's predictions over the last decade.

As the general upswing of births during the late fifties and early sixties had gathered momentum, population forecasters must have thrown up their hands in Malthusian mock horror as to the outcome when the postwar 'bulge' generation reached marriageable age. But the anticipated 'second bulge' didn't happen. The tidal wave of bulge 'bulge' babies subsided somewhere out at sea, leaving forecasters splashing about for a solution, while concern mounted as it had done during the thirties.

> There has been a strong downward trend ever since the end of 1964 – apart from a period from summer 1970 to autumn 1971, which presumably reflected the scare over high oestrogen contraceptive pills, the fall has tended to become more rapid. During most of the past decade the numbers of females aged 20–29 (who account for two thirds of all births) has been rising. In 1973 it was about 17% above the 1964 level.
> (*Recent Trends in Births and Deaths and National Population Predictions*, Eric J. Thompson, 1974)

Abortion and the pill had mopped up what had previously been the spilt milk of accidental motherhood. Women who could choose were choosing independence, and enjoying it. Successful teachers like Pauline, who'd survived a period of disillusion with the profession (during which she might, had she been married, have succumbed to having a child), actively shrank from the prospect of babies. Women like Angela, living in London surrounded by friends with busy social lives, never thought about babies. These were the years when mothers least understood their daughters, and we them. Against our alien (to them) worldly expertise, their homespun (to us) wisdom appeared so naive and limited, their blunted home-centred tastes so cosily suffocating. You rejected motherhood like you rejected mothers and everything associated with domestic life. And besides, how could you consciously take such a step, now that you were mature enough to realize its enormity?

The first two years of marriage showed the greatest fall in fertility. Wives were now no longer naturally turning to motherhood as soon as they were settled. During the years when our bodies were most finely tuned to fulfil their biological function, many of us turned our backs on it. These were also the years when the women's movement most vociferously denounced the trap of staying at home to look after children in its haste to disentangle women from the washingline stranglehold of nappy-goo and baby-gossip. Having been educated to benefit a future family, it seemed that our education had simply produced individuals who had no intention of encumbering themselves with children when they had a job, money and the freedom to do what they liked. A 1972 forecast predicted that the reduced fertility rate was simply a deferment of births, concluding smugly (or was it anxiously?) that 'continued childlessness' was still 'largely involuntary' – that it would only be a matter of time before we fell.

And it was. While questions concerning the declining population were being asked in the House of Commons, and also at the Strasbourg Council of Europe in October 1977, women had started quietly to capitulate, yet again foiling the statisticians who couldn't read their minds.

> Britain's beleaguered toy manufacturers, teachers worried about redundancy and the entire babywear industry can afford to be cautiously optimistic . . . 1980 looks like being a boom year for babies . . . the birth rate could reach fifteen per thousand head of population this year . . . a considerable number of women now expecting first babies are in their late twenties or early thirties, products of the career-orientated and homebuying 1970s.
>
> This has led some demographers to feel that the babyslump – a one third drop in births from 1966 to 1976 – was in fact misleading. Many women, they now believe, were merely delaying families.
>
> (*Guardian*, 26.2.1980)

The tide had begun to turn in 1976 and the actual upward trend started to show at the beginning of 1977, the year that we were 30.

Catherine's first child arrived three days after her thirtieth birthday, in January 1977. Catherine had married in 1974 and carried on in her demanding and absorbing job, now a twelve-mile bus journey away. Simon shared all the domestic tasks, but there seemed little time to relax together, after travelling, marking, cleaning, shopping, cooking. Catherine developed a mysterious virus, which left her tired and depressed. While this was being investigated, she visited her doctor about a slight side-effect of the pill: 'When he heard I had no children, he said "At your age?" and pushed me out into the waiting room, saying "Go on, go on, get on with it tonight!" He was right of course.' Catherine resigned from work and got pregnant straight away. She enjoyed home life, 'after spending so long in less congenial surroundings', housekeeping on a tight budget and all the things she had never had time for before – cooking, baking cakes, sewing. The mysterious virus vanished. It had taken her body to tell her what to do.

Similarly Hilary was advised, for health reasons, to come off the pill for a year. As a teenager she'd sworn she would never have children, but was conscious when she married that her husband appealed to her because he was very good with children. Still, the decision always seemed such a terrible ir-reversible responsibility until: 'I thought I'll have to go for promotion pretty soon if I'm going to make anything of my career, yet I'm almost 30, am I going to have a family or not? I thought I would give myself the year the doctor suggested, and apply for higher posts if nothing had happened. I did it like tossing a coin and I didn't know which side I wanted the coin to come down. I didn't think work was everything, al-though I was happy there. I just needed something to make up my mind.' Hilary got pregnant straight away and gave up worrying about the terrible responsibility and losing her in-dependence. She swam with the tide, looked forward to the change, 'a new life, if you like'. Both women had needed a change in their lives, but both had also needed to trip over the impending milestone of 30, with its label of elderly primi-gravida for the childless woman, to deter them from carrying on in the same smooth progression, locked into the security of sameness, whereas those who'd turned to motherhood before them had found the way ahead too rough and unmarked, or simply prairie dull and monotonous.

Procrastination, the powerful momentum of carrying on the way things were, even pushed Susan, who'd yearned to be saved, to sail on past 30 before playing her trump card, by accident: 'I'd always imagined myself with children, even had names for them. It just seemed the natural thing to do after you married, but when I did marry, I wasn't really bothered,

I was happy to carry on at work. I only started to think about it when I was 30, that I did want to have children, but even then I'd push it into the future, because I knew Kevin wasn't keen. Every year I'd think next year, perhaps, until I was advised to come off the pill for a while. I didn't even realize I was pregnant until I started feeling sick at work!' Like marriage, motherhood was not at all the roseate fantasy of her imaginings. The dependent state she'd once longed for now became an enjoyable homebased hiatus before resuming work and independence when her child reached school age.

These women all settled down to bringing up their children knowing they would be able to resume the careers they had interrupted, as teachers, when they were ready. Was it this knowledge that enabled them to make the gear change so smoothly? Motherhood could be a worthwhile sabbatical, a chance to recreate home life out of what had been a dormitory shell of snatched meals, flicked dusters, bulging laundry baskets, a mountain hut halfway up the slope of two self-orientated lives. A women could happily lose sight of her work status and independence while she saw a light at the end of the tunnel: Betty Friedan's three-phase lifeplan, the perfect solution to the female dilemma.

Motherhood didn't come so easily to Monica, who had gone to catering college at 16 and worked her way up to become cook/supervisor for school meals. She'd been married for nine years, enjoying sharing an active social life with her husband and the stimulation of her work. Then, when she was nearing 30, they realized that if they did want a family, it was now or never. But leaving work wasn't what Monica found difficult; it was relaxing into her new role: 'I was terrified when I came home with Sara. And I was so used to having things the way I wanted; it was awful confronting buckets of dirty nappies and baby clothes. I think I actually spoilt it. I'd got so used to being busy at work, but you've got to devote time to being with a baby and playing. My life had been under such control before.'

Work had coiled her into a tight spring of tension and it was hard to let go, allow the baby to disrupt her carefully ordered life. Monica blamed her feelings on the fact that she'd gone into motherhood without feeling broody or maternal, simply to start a family before it was too late. Valerie had made a similar choice, to have a baby before it was too late, rather than wanting to be a mother. Even when she married, she'd never envisaged having children, because she saw the bank as her career: 'People expect you to have children. If you don't, they think it's because you can't. I suppose the pressure got quite great so that we were forced to think about it. I was approaching 30 and I began to think about it from the opposite point of view, and all my friends had children, which decided me. If it hadn't happened, though, I wouldn't have been bothered.' Valerie had felt the need for some sort of change, however. 'We'd both been having a whale of a time, earning good money, doing what we liked, but you do reach a sort of plateau, and you probably slow down a bit and conform more . . .'

Valerie's personal plateau didn't protect her from the precipice that opened up before her. She had thought it was all going to be roses, and still feels bitter that nobody, not even her friends, warned her about the problems; that after the antenatal attention she was left to her maternal instincts – and felt guilty because she hadn't got any: 'There seemed nobody I could turn to for help. The health visitor made me feel like a bumbling buffoon and my mother couldn't understand that although I had a loving husband and a beautiful child, I felt as if I was walking along a cliff with a sheer drop on each side.'

It was a vicious circle. The more inadequate Valerie felt, the more she withdrew from other mothers who seemed to be coping, and the more she resented her loss of freedom, everything that work had given her. Then after a few months it cleared. 'It was post-natal depression, but I'm sure it was worse because I'd had a career for twelve years and gone into having a child halfheartedly, and Alan was such an awful baby. I just felt stuck in a boring role as a wife and mother. I still miss work, I'd go back tomorrow. Some women are just chiselled out for motherhood, but for the first three months, Dave was more of a mother to Alan than I was.'

The thought of being a mother had appalled Pauline in her twenties because of the way it seemed to narrow your life. She was nearing 30 when she began to want to have a child, but fending it off into the future was quite easy, while she was still enjoying stretching herself in her teaching career. Then, when

204 *Now We Are Thirty*

she got to be head of department and things were running smoothly, Pauline realized she didn't want to go on and be an administrator. At 30, what did she want? 'I felt terrible when I was 30, because one or two friends had left work to start families. I felt if I didn't get on with it, I'd never have any and I really wanted a child. But I got terribly fed up after Frances was born.'

Pauline really resented the loss of her status, her independence, faced with the overwhelming demands of a tiny baby. 'It was a very selfish thing, but up to then I had been able to be very selfish in my life.' Threatened and inadequate in her new role, she was forever rushing to consult her mother, looking in baby books, unable to trust her own judgement. 'I even clutched at the possibility of going back to work far too soon, because there I'd got expertise. From being on top of everything in my life, suddenly I was at the mercy of a tiny baby I didn't know how to cope with because I'd had no contact with babies. I didn't even have the compensation of looking well.'

This was not like starting a new job, where momentum from the old one, the success of having been selected, carried you forward on a false crest of confidence until you had mastered the new situation enough to feel at ease, having fuddled along and faked a lot of it, with home to retreat to at night. Here, knocking around in a dressing-gown, feeling like nothing on earth, was a life and death responsibility you couldn't escape home from, because it had taken over your home in the same way it had snatched the props of salary and status away from you. Rationalizing that it wouldn't go on forever didn't do any good. You'd chosen this thing you were failing at.

I could sympathize with Pauline's predicament only by extending the gloved hand of the clinical enquirer, dabbing at her details with the swab of my imagination, but I did discover a strange parallel with my own experiences in that of another mother. Shirley and I had taken separate paths after school, she to a different northern university and then to qualify as a teacher. She became a successful head of department at a distinguished progressive school in London, and although I also moved to London, our paths never accidentally crossed. Why should they?

When I took the first step towards writing this book, some time after conceiving the idea, I advertised in the local newspaper to make contact with those of my year at school who had stayed in the town where we all grew up. The ad produced two letters, one of which came from Shirley. She'd long since moved to London and had no intention of returning to her home town and even less interest in the goings-on there. She had bought this issue of the local paper because the announcement of the birth of her first child was in it and, out of mild curiosity and amusement, had scanned the small ads. It seemed a strange coincidence, particularly since so few women who regularly saw the local paper responded to the advertisement. But perhaps it wasn't so strange, since we were both announcing the birth of our first creation, except that mine was my brainchild, not the child of my body.

And the difference between a baby and a book is that you can always smother the latter if it becomes too difficult to handle, escape the frightening commitment that both represent, because they confront you head-on with your failings, you can't fake anything. All your mistakes show, and you have to come to terms with the fact that each has a life of its own, you cannot control it, make it fit into what you thought it would be. This loss of control, coupled with loss of status, seems to be central to the problems of mothers who found it hard to adjust to the birth of their child. The powerful demands of the child are only matched by the powerlessness of the mother, deprived of everything that signified her identity: social status, financial autonomy, freedom of movement, stimulation, all the controls that independence grants. Ambition, born of energies focused in a concentrated direction, sharpens abilities to succeed and, once acquired, is as selfish a force as a newborn baby.

Women whose own life chances didn't give them so much power in their own lives warmed to the parasitical dependence of their babies rather than resenting the way it encroached upon them, because the power and importance it conferred was something the outside world had never offered them. Julie could freely disown social status, because she had never really tasted it. Work had given her stimulation and variety, but had never involved her as deeply as motherhood. Her

clients at the bank could never have gazed across the counter
into her eyes with the contentment with which her baby gazed
adoringly at her when she satisfied his hunger, soothed his
hurt.

When Julie was 30, she faced her younger child's growing
independence of her, her own loss of control over his life. 'There
was a spate of babies in the village, and I thought it's now or
never, I just got very broody.' She couldn't resist having another
baby, in spite of the economic climate. Julie freely admits that
her children have been the main satisfaction of her life. 'It's
given me confidence, having a family centre of my own, and
it widens your outlook on people, understanding what makes
them tick, seeing how they grow and develop and how they're
cheeky back as they get older. I don't feel I've missed out on
anything.'

I remember a dream, at a stage in my life when I was beginning to develop ambition rather than simply passing from
one thing that 'meant' something to another, growing in
myself through variety. I began to want to risk becoming
something through what I did, confirming myself in outward
expression rather than inner significance. I dreamt of a house,
the house of my husband/Regency terrace fantasies, but it was
standing alone, its elegance marred by the jagged innards of
the ones which had been demolished on either side of it. Three
people emerged from this house: a small child, a plump,
motherly figure and a slim girl dressed in party clothes. The
mother and child instantly clung together, though which was
the magnet and which the iron filings it was hard to tell. Each
became the focus for the other, secure in their self-contain-
ment, unself-conscious because they had each other. The girl,
meanwhile, could only pace up and down, uncomfortable in
her conspicuousness. She had drawn attention to herself but was
now paralysed by the fear of it, of now having to perform to
strangers.

No doubt this dream was a repeat, seven years on, of the
diary entry when I was 21. It does seem to be relevant to
starting out in life, the impulse to merge into safety pitted
against risking the dangers of self-discovery through the outside world. Perhaps Julie is right, that when she faces the
time her children no longer need her, her education and her

valuable experiences will have given her the resources to fill the gap in her home-centred life. Perhaps, like Sandra's mother, she will develop some natural extension of her present outside activities, helping to organize the local playgroup. She has put off that phase, and so has Sheila, who has had her fourth child since the interview which began this chapter, born when the third had just reached school age. But as Julie says, 'You can't keep on having them.'

Mothers like Viv and Karen, who had to go out to work when their children were young, now feel, however much they might have liked to have had more than one, that they're too far-away from the constraints of bringing up young children ever to have any more: 'It's much too late to start all over again with nappies.' Yet Sylvia, the one who chose to rush back to work, says she would stay at home this time, if she chose to have another, because her needs are different now. And Gillian, who was a stay-at-home wife and mother for twelve years says, 'Very selfishly, I don't want the reality of a family and babies any more. I want to travel, enjoy doing my job and getting out, that's what I want now.'

Since I began researching this book, when we were all 30, most of the women who figure in it have been undergoing a seachange in their lives, centred around their childbearing capacities and themselves, as individuals or mothers. And the way in which they have been weathering their dilemma does reflect upon the space society allows for women to act out their dual roles.

Valerie began to enjoy her baby when he ceased to be a sponge, soaking up all her energies and giving nothing back, but she has never adjusted to the fact that motherhood forced the housewife role upon her. 'The satisfaction that I get from Alan is in some ways more than I got at work, when he does something on his own, or comes up and throws his arms around you, it's more tangible. I don't mind being financially dependent on my husband, but I do feel in a rut, I've never enjoyed housework. I feel it's my life I've had to sacrifice, more than Dave has. Not in a nasty way. People go on about women's lib, but when it boils down to it, it's still the woman who bears the children and has the full brunt of bringing them up.'

Valerie has found that a part-time job at the bank where she used to work, helping with the night-safe work on Monday mornings, forces her out of herself, to take trouble with what to wear, go out and mix with people. But the job itself is at a much lower level than when she left. And because she plans to have another child – 'I don't crave another baby, but having committed myself to a family, I want at least two, for the child's sake' – she'll have to wait until they are both at school before she can get a proper job. 'I thought of social work, but I can't really see anything that I'm going to be able to commit myself to as a career. You can't say, either, what opportunities are going to be like in five years time.'

Monica has also adjusted to the freelance freedom of the housewife, and enjoying family life now that her children are much more responsive, but although she feels she has plenty of time to think about what she will do next, part of her dreads it, because opportunities are so limited. She's thought of doing voluntary work, or something at home, although she doesn't know how lonely she'll feel once the children start school. Her old job as cook/supervisor would be too much responsibility. 'We thought about running a guest house, but it would be too difficult to start financially.'

Pauline has also been toying with the idea of going into business with her husband. Becoming a mother, once she had adjusted to the new way of life which it forced upon her, has effected a change in her attitude, and direction, a new growth in herself. 'When I was in my twenties, I would have looked down on someone who could ONLY describe her life as staying at home all day and bringing up a child, seeing friends. But although it can seem stultifying at times, there has been an important growth for me. I have learnt to absorb the moment, live in the present more and enjoy it. I've had time to reflect and sort out my priorities, as well as enjoying doing childish things with my daughter, watching her respond and develop, getting to know my friends better, because I can spend more time with them. I feel as though I've sidestepped for a time, just to think out what I want to do. I'd reached a point where I was going along a clear line and didn't want to go any further.

'When I was pregnant with Frances, it all seemed so simple that I would probably go back into teaching, part-time, after two or three years of being at home with her. Now, although that's the only career that fits in with children, I'd like to do something different. I envisage having two children and going back to work when they're at school. I know I'll be nearly 40 then, but when I've got there I'll think about doing some sort of retraining, possibly doing secretarial skills as a means of branching into something else, but it's so difficult to look ahead because everything may have changed with all the new technology. We've talked about doing a small mail order business together, but in a way I'd rather bring something fresh into my life.

'I've got over feeling the loss of status now, although I haven't yet had to put Housewife on any forms. It's difficult to say whether I may lose my confidence, but I think as you get older, you do get a stronger sense of your own identity. All I'm doing at the moment, which sounds a bit simplistic and dull, and it isn't, is bringing Frances up and just living from day to day. I'm more patient, more flexible now, more domesticated in one sense, but not as an end in itself, I don't want to be home-orientated all the time.'

Having a child has enriched Pauline's life in more ways than simply seeing her child develop. It has given her an opportunity to stray from the tramlines of her career, discover a different side of life and search for a new direction. Shirley, who had problems similar to Pauline's in adjusting to the sudden loss of status, expertise and independence when she had her first child, also found time to reflect that she had gone into teaching without really exploring other possibilities, but it's difficult, practically speaking, to branch out. Teaching is the one career which does fit in with having children, especially if granny is getting too old to cope, or is too far away and babysitting contacts are difficult to build up. It's also difficult to start again after 30. 'I get worried when I look at job advertisements in the paper and realize all the things I'm too old for now I'm over 30,' Susan says. 'It wasn't until a couple of years ago that I realized that whatever I was doing would have to be regulated by the fact that if I was ever going to have kids, I would have to have them fairly soon. It's difficult for women to be, I won't say equal, but the same as men, because whatever provision the law makes, having a baby takes a big chunk out of your life. You don't go into hospital and come out as if nothing had happened.'

Most couples who've had children late automatically made the choice who would be the one to give up their career to look after the child at home; it was implicit, not only in their conditioning but in the career structures which dictate that the man has the greater promotion potential, that the most practical thing is for him to continue as the breadwinner. Shirley and John did discuss the possibility of his giving up work because they were both enjoying successful careers when they decided to start a family, and had always made joint decisions and had shared ambitions. But there were practical aspects of mothering that John couldn't do, which would disrupt Shirley's career several times if they had more than one child, and, the deciding factor, John's earning potential was greater.

Society is geared in this way to encourage the separate breadwinner/homemaker roles, because most job structures, in the present economic climate, treat pregnancy as a temporary disability and do not allow for sabbaticals, however much, in theory, the provisions of the Employment Protection Act allow for women to return to work after having a child. This strategy would only work if a woman who shares her child with an active father has an equal or greater earning capacity, thus enabling the father to take a greater share of childminding, because most parents prefer to enjoy bringing up their children themselves rather than farming them out to strangers.

Present choices propel women with talent and initiative into becoming more and more dependent upon a husband who spends longer and longer hours at work, coming home exhausted because his responsibilities shove him further and further into his role. It's not that men don't feel the urge to step off the career ladder, along with the ulcers, receding hairlines and business lunch bellies and heart attacks they accumulate on the way. The midlife crisis, the what's-it-all-for? reaction to a bland routine when you suddenly find that work, in taking over your whole life, has edged out its meaning, is a familiar landmark in a man's life. But he tends, given the present relationship between work and family life, to resolve this dilemma by bending the circle into a spiral, climbing to a higher niche, a more demanding, better paid job. While his wife, with the ever-present option to turn to her traditional childbearing role, ambles down an overgrown siding to explore a neglected aspect of herself. If the couple are both facing similar plateaux in their lives it becomes a natural, neat collusion, solving both problems – except that each has to compromise with the degree of change that is introduced into their lives, the woman too much for her own good perhaps, the man too little. He cannot afford to stop and explore himself, take stock, change direction, expand. She is given so much space to do so that she is likely to flounder, and as yet there aren't many lifelines to be flung in to help her back into the swim.

I visited Shirley on one occasion, where they now live on the outskirts of London, a house with more room for the children, of which there will be, by the time this book is published, three. The waving rose bushes, the potting shed, the vegetable patch, the sturdy rambling Victorianness of the house with its moulded ceilings and large, airy rooms, panelled doors with intricate beading, rounded knobs and doorplates, the carved wooden bannisters and boundless space, carried me back to my own childhood. For Shirley, this house means everything she did not grow up with, everything she and John have jointly attained.

Shirley was now feeling too emotionally dependent upon John, waving him off at the door in her dressing-gown, egging him on to fight for that promotion, yet wishing he had more time at home and she had a little less. The trouble with this polarization of men's and women's roles is that it does trap us in separate worlds, the separate worlds that men and women have inhabited for a long time now, so long that their valuations of those worlds are equally separated and divorced from one another; the woman's world, because love and trust are not currency in the marketplace, the one that has tended to be belittled and devalued.

Julie: 'Having children really makes you think about the mystery of life. I used to watch them playing in the garden and I couldn't take it in somehow, that we'd created them and there they were. There's nothing more rewarding than the first year because you see so much, they come from a little thing to a being. I'm not particularly bothered about going back to work. I think it's a lot to do with personality, whether you need to go out and mix with people, need status. It doesn't bother me at all, describing myself as a housewife.'

Julie knows the value of her own world, and yet she still measured it against society's values, protesting that she was only a housewife, her life was very ordinary and boring, at the beginning of our interview. Likewise, women who have left careers to turn to motherhood experience the loss of status as an internalized, personal problem, but a growing number recognize it as something imposed by society's belittling of the female role. Susan: 'I opened my mouth to say teacher, and he looked at Julian and said "housewife" and I had to nod, but I felt really resentful. I'm working just as hard as anyone else.'

Shirley: 'I feel a lot more confident now about me and my children, but I still feel a sense of inferiority in that society doesn't regard me as a very important person. They think it's an easy option, an anybody-can-do-it kind of job, something that doesn't take much time, effort or imagination and thought, whereas most mothers know that it does. I get frustrated and depressed when people don't know what I am capable of. They pin this label of housewife on you and a whole set of assumptions goes into operation, that determines how they treat you.'

Like Pauline, Shirley found it difficult to adjust to the birth of her first child, floundering in feelings of inadequacy while at the same time suffering the loss of those things which had previously supported her self-esteem: status and financial independence, the stimulation of the demands of her job. Although Shirley adjusted to the new way of life, like Valerie, she continued to feel, in spite of valuing the experience of being a mother as much as she valued being a teacher, her loss of status. It was probably because she was able to translate these separate valuations that she came to see how demeaning it was, first at the ante-natal clinic to be herded together and kept waiting for hours as if her time did not matter, and then to feel the way in which society paid lipservice to the demands of her new responsibilities as a mother and the talent and expertise it requires, while at the same time dismissing it as a soft option, something anyone can do.

Shirley felt most strongly about the fact that, in choosing to leave her job to bring up her child herself, she was forfeiting a sum of money which, under the maternity leave provisions of the Employment Protection Act, would have been paid to her had she decided to return to work within twenty-nine weeks and entrust the major part of the care and up-bringing of her child to others. The provisions of the Act are there to ensure that the woman who wishes to continue in her job when she has a baby can do so, physically, without suffering the loss of her job or her earnings during the time in which she is physically incapacitated by becoming a mother. Shirley's argument, that in choosing to leave her job she is automatically losing her entitlement to the salary she would receive had she chosen to return to work after having the baby, is not quite so illogical as it appears. In rewarding the mother who chooses not to undertake the care of her own child while it is most dependent, society is by inference penalizing the mother who chooses to devote herself for a few years to her responsibilities as a mother. None of the women who have had children since the Employment Protection Act became law has chosen to utilize its provisions, partly because, unlike Sylvia, they did not feel the pull of work at a formative stage in their lives. Sylvia herself says she would stay at home now if she had a child, because her own priorities have shifted.

Presumably most people prefer to take the major part of the responsibility for the care of their children themselves; otherwise why have children? As long as women remain in careers and jobs which have less earning potential than men's, it is still the woman who, in Valerie's words, sacrifices most, by giving up the continuity of her working life and then finding it difficult to rejoin the swim.

Some of the women I have interviewed found that 30 marked the point at which they reached the third phase of their lives, when the large part of their mothering role was accomplished and they could turn to themselves, in Janet's words, 'the next few years are for me'. And yet Janet has deemed herself lucky to land a part-time librarian assistant's job; Eileen, with a degree in computer science, can only find part-time work selling cosmetics; and Rosemary writes gloomily: 'I know now that my biggest mistake was not to realize that I'd want to go back to work after bringing up the family I always expected to have. Being a mother is very important to me, but the most important thing in my life now is to regain some of the personal freedom and independence I feel I lost through having children. I am sure this will strengthen rather than weaken my marriage. I have more outside interests than my mother who always lived through her husband and children and I hope my life will continue to differ from hers, with more independence. I'm taking a secretarial course, but the chances of a good job for a woman with children are very small. I've accepted that I'll have to take what's offered, probably at a very low rate of pay.'

The women's movement is only just coming to grips with these problems, the problems that ordinary women face, para-doxically, through a new softened stance which extols the virtues of the domestic life and the mothering role. Betty Friedan claims that this is because the movement has now reached a 'second stage', that women have now proved themselves sufficiently in the world of men for working life and family life to be weighed equally, that women now feel certain enough of their advances to be able to retreat a little without losing ground. But I would argue that articulate voices in the movement have been experiencing for the first time and at first hand that which Pauline and Shirley have been experiencing, the positive benefits of the feminine world, and speaking out on a subject they once belittled.

A recently published feminist work, *Women's Work, Men's Work* (Virginia Novarra, 1980), sticks to the old feminist line that:

> while men are acquiring valuable experience, women are dulling their minds by . . . almost ceaseless exposure to the demands and the concentration-destroying cries or chatter of babies and toddlers. At worst, years of this can result in a woman's needing a refresher course in being a mentally active human being . . . I hope I shall not be accused of being a child hater if I describe children as the final fetter.

Somehow I cannot believe Ms Novarra has any children of her own, whereas Mary Kenny (*Woman X Two*, 1978) freely admitted the root cause of her conversion to the 'second stage': 'Until I was 29, I was a doctrinaire women's liberationist . . .' It was then that she was caught on the tide of those not wanting to miss out on motherhood. She planned to return to work after having the baby, but didn't, because 'the whole focus of politics and sociology changed for me . . . I suddenly saw the point of the family', which led to her writing a book about women's two roles, rather different from the first, in which she declared:

> the next phase of women's liberation is not to have to prove how tough and unassailable you are, but to be unafraid of showing your needs and your vulnerability not because this is slavishly 'feminine' in the helpless sense, but because it's what makes us all human.

Millions of women, she says, feel that their families come first, but 'men aren't allowed to feel like that . . . if they were they'd be dropping out all over the place wouldn't they and that wouldn't do, would it?'

The women's movement has struck a new note that harmonizes much more with the voices of ordinary women, urging men to acknowledge the positive value of what women do, and share in it. Anna Coote and Ann Oakley see this as the solution to struggling to play supermum, that it should free more women to devote time to fighting for their rights, attending union meetings while their husbands bath the baby. Anna Coote (*New Statesman*, August, 1979) points out that men buy off their responsibility as fathers, in spite of the fact that nearly fifty per cent of married women go out to work:

> If men saw themselves as full-time parents (as women do, even when they go out to work) with a commitment to their families in terms of time and energy rather than primarily in terms of cash, they might view their interests from a new perspective. Is it inconceivable, for example, that a man should *want* to spend more time with his kids if he could work a twenty-five or thirty hour week and rely on a second, equal wage to support the family?

Men continue empire-building because they have hitherto been locked out of the feminine world by their own experiences as well as their own prejudices. At a recent Women's Action Day in London, a woman doctor (who received the longest ovation) not only stressed the need for upgrading the status of childcare, but declaimed that it was high time that the woman doctor who took time out to have a child was recognized as making a positive contribution to her professional empathy and expertize, rather than detracting from it, and that a good many men would perform their jobs more effectively if they had the same experience.

Erstwhile confident careerists, like Shirley and Catherine, are echoing this sentiment. Catherine: 'I was happy being a working woman, and I know if the need arises, I can go back. But I still deem the most important role a woman has is to bring up her children, which is almost a full-time job, and I don't intend to resume work until I'm satisfied that I've done all I can to set my children on the path to independence. I do not intend to sit and vegetate at home.' This is intellectual, articulate woman speaking out at last, not the dried-up old spinster or the harebrained housewife but whole people whose values, tarnished by the desire to earn money and be recognized in the outside world, have yet not been dulled to the values and virtues that grow through the interchange of real relationships, rather than fake treaties based on exchanging money, guns, ammunition. It is up to us. We cannot expect the chances our mothers had in the last world war in the next one.

And yet perhaps we have lived through a war, the confrontation between the sexes in the early 1970s when, armed with education and the pill, married women suddenly flooded the job market and put off having children, tomboys climbing the tree of career aspirations our mothers had planted for us. Suddenly it seemed up to society to make us a more attractive offer before we would turn to our mothering role. The falling birth rate must have influenced the passing of the maternity leave provisions in the Employment Protection Act. This was a first step towards making motherhood more attractive to working women, but, ironically, like the recommendations of the Royal Commission on Population in 1946, coincided with our voluntary turning to motherhood, thereby losing our foothold in the working world and our bargaining position, like our mothers did.

But this apparent capitulation need not necessarily mean we must defer our hopes to our daughters, like they did. Our mothers' generation made the gains that it did, the ones we benefited from, in the absence of the men. Men have rushed to keep women out of their world because they saw women's desire to wander over the boundaries as a threat to their jobs, their status as breadwinners. If men were encouraged to value home life more, the positive advantages of the female world which they miss, as fathers, husbands, brothers, family members, might induce them to shed some of the burden of being lifelong breadwinner. As things stand, money and status seem more important. The basic working week has been steadily falling, but the average working week is still forty-six hours, despite the fact of ever-increasing unemployment.

We live in a society that seems to demand all or nothing of its workers, in which countless men and women feel the strains of work while three million others have no work at all. We live in a society in which home for some is a centrally-heated, insulated shell on an anonymous estate, where the only welcoming glow at night is the on-switch of the slowcooker, and for others a comfortable trap or a demeaning cage.

One professional woman, whose husband was made redundant, carried on doing most of the domestic work, in spite of the fact that he was at home most of the day, because she didn't want to add to his problems by demeaning him with women's work. Do we have to adhere to these mutually exclusive demarcation lines determined by our self-images as men or women? The reality of the present situation is that 50 per cent of married women go out to work, only two-fifths of all households comprise breadwinner father, housewife mother and children, and traditional men's jobs are declining faster than women's, even though women tend to be the ones made redundant before men. With opportunities dwindling all round, jobsharing and part-time work seem the fairest solutions. Even one hour knocked off a working day would help marriage partners to share the responsibilities of work and home, solve latchkey-child problems, spread the load, so that if one loses work, the family need not automatically go to the wall. Where is the leisured society in Britain that we have been hearing about so much, for which men, in their alienated state, are so ill-prepared?

The technological revolution which is contributing to the recession in employment hit the home first. Specifically, it hit our mothers, in the late fifties. Some of them responded by going out and getting jobs, like Sandra's mother, making up, in a small way, for the disappointment of their own ambitions. Many of them responded to the erosion of skills and community networks, which once gave women's work its intrinsic satisfaction and purpose, by focusing on the family, becoming unhealthily overdependently childcentred, to the exclusion of their husbands, emphasizing and underscoring the separation of women's and men's worlds in their own fear of the shrinking one they inhabited.

Their daughters recognize this trap. Janet: 'My mother-in-law was like that, and she's lost now. It's a lesson to us all. When they get to be teenagers, you've got to stop and think, what exactly is my role, am I here just to look after them? I shan't like to have them strolling in saying where's my tea, mum? It must be so easy not to question it, and continue to role-play at home, but I feel strongly that the next years are for me.'

Our education has given us the resources to throw off the housewife stereotype and handle the open-ended freedoms of home life. Andrea: 'I think if you do your job properly, it's like being a teacher. And it is a job, isn't it, having children? We read and draw and paint. I do tend to be on my own a lot, but I like the variety, planning different things each day. Women themselves have devalued the idea of bringing up children. I'm not bored, probably because of the resources my education gave me. I can think of nothing more boring than standing chatting over the fence for two hours, just as if you get caught up in a career you get narrowminded, a company person, whereas I can voice my opinions freely. I don't feel I've missed out, because I chose to do what I've done. I think you can tell an educated person, they're interested in the outside world. When I was in hospital having Martin, someone gave me a pile of Barbara Cartlands to read. That was when I discovered I was an intellectual! I suppose I would like to go to college, just for the interest, to keep me sharp, because you do go stale when you leave work.'

Some of the women I have interviewed are still very family-focused, but others, reaching 30, are now exploiting their leisure time, the spare-time nature of household responsibilities, to extend themselves. Margaret recognizes that she does not need to go out to work and realistically predicts that she would not get a worthwhile job if she did, so she is taking a degree course, purely and simply for her own interest and enjoyment. Pauline and Shirley have had time to reflect on a change of direction. Catherine has been extending her organizing skills and the local family involvements she had as a teacher, into valuable community work, vital and necessary to the quality of people's lives, as well as being enjoyable and in spite of (or perhaps because of) being unpaid. In this respect, men are the losers.

Thirty is a watershed for most people. The boat of their chosen direction begins to rock with the shifting ballast of neglected dreams and changing attitudes, and women face a possible change of course not open to men. A woman, in becoming a mother, effects a change in direction for which, however ill-prepared she is, she needs no formal qualifications, apart from fulfilling the upper-age-limit requirements, and rationalizes the loss of remuneration because she is choosing something positive. The man who tries to step sideways faces a void of recrimination – the humiliation of retraining even if he can afford a drop in salary. Only the drop-out can negotiate such a path. For the family man, it is of course impossible.

Pat swopped jobs various times – including trying teaching – before finding a career that satisfied her, working in town and country planning. She felt the panic, too, at 30, wanting to start a family right away before it was too late, but put it off (encouraged by meeting women who were having babies 'almost in middle age, so I don't think it's now or never, I rather hope there's another six years at least') so that her husband could engineer the switch to *his* preferred career, while she acts as the major breadwinner.

And just as women are excluded, by their involvement in bringing up children, from participating in careers, it seems tragic that many men function as fathers solely in a materialistic sense. Husbands are becoming more active fathers, many women assure me. Glenda: 'Mick gets on the floor and has a rough-and-tumble with Paul, whereas my father never spent much time with us.' Jackie: 'Ken was used to children. He would do the middle feed when he didn't have to go to work the next day and dirty nappies as well, although he wasn't so keen on that! If he's had a hard day at work, the best thing for him is Harriet looking out of the back door with a big smile – that can relax him more than anything.'

But paternal involvement is still kept to the twilight zones of bedtime and bathtime and Sunday afternoon outings, rather than knowing their childen at the intimate level their wives do. Valerie: 'However good your husband is with the children when he comes home at night, so you can relinquish the responsibility for an hour, it's still you who knows intimate little details like how much they have to drink, when to give them a drink during the day and things about their toilet they're particular about. Your husband never knows these things, so you're bound to still feel it's your responsibility even if he takes them out. Dave's very good, he pulls his fair share, but I still feel the responsibility.' Some men are recognizing what they may be missing:

> To spend all day in an alienated environment which fed me, defined technical challenges and offered material comforts (phone, restaurant, central heating, secretarial labour on tap) was the easy option. Pauline at home was confronted continually . . . by human demands . . . The great thing about work is that I'm released . . . from the necessity of trying to live like a whole human being . . .
>
> ('Disappearing into The Company', Mike Hales, *Guardian*, 2.12.80)

The edges have begun to overlap, but husbands and wives, when they become parents, still inhabit scparate worlds, the one dominated by the necessity to manipulate, exert power and control by asserting the self, and the other encouraging spontaneity and the generous denial of the self in service to others.

I passed a secondhand furniture shop recently and picked

three hardbacks, twenty pence each, from the rack outside. One of them was the H. G. Wells book from which the quotation at the beginning of this chapter is taken, while the other two were more familiar journeys into nostalgia. *Joan Goes Farming* was a Bodley Head career novel – not to be found in our school library, presumably because farming wasn't a fit career for a high school girl. The third, that I couldn't resist buying, was called *This Feminine World* by a lady called Mrs Robert Henrey, published in 1956, the year that *Women's Two Roles* was also published. It is, as the title suggests, a celebration of the traditional female preserves – fashion and nursing, cameos of different kinds of women whose only common characteristic was that they were women and therefore shared the qualities of sensitivity to the arts and receptivity to the needs of others, the vanity and selflessness which co-exist in the freefloating interplay of emotion and imagination. The book purported to be truth, in the arrogant way of non-fiction, but it posited a kind of science fiction of two parallel worlds, mutually dependent but utterly opposed.

Housewives tend to underplay their world. So many women dismissed themselves with this label, protested that their lives were very boring within the first five minutes of our interview, that they lived from day to day and didn't do very much, and yet the thoughts and feelings winkled out of them show how much satisfaction they derive from their lives and how misleading the title of housewife really is. The trouble is that it is hard to translate into society's terms, and perhaps they do not try because they do not care about status, are unused to playing competitive games. The task of nurturing children, of operating at the hub of the interplay of close human relationships is immediate and ever-renewing itself; it leaves no visible trace.

Women who come to motherhood later in life, pass from one world to the other, would seem the ideal champions to reinstate the status of the stay-at-home mother and wife, but it seems that once you pass through the looking glass, the old values of the men's world cease to matter. Why bother with what other people think of what you do? Status doesn't matter, nor money; it's who you are that counts and whether you feel what you are doing is worthwhile.

Perhaps the main rationale against the three-phase life-plan for women (training and early work experience – motherhood – back to work) is the very contaminating effect of the separate worlds upon those who inhabit them. Not only is it hard, in one's teens, to have an overview of life, but the time spent in the mothering phase is likely to alter one's life goals anyway. Mothering is not simply an opting out of the mainstream, a selfless decision to stand out of the game for a few turns, before returning unscathed and unaffected, to one's former place. The experience of mothering and homemaking changes a woman because it allows her to explore a side of her nature denied to the full-time worker; it encourages her to grow and develop, and affects her view of life, careers and all.

The battle some women of the 'bulge' generation are facing, now that the mothering phase of their lives is coming to an end, is the battle for equal opportunities with men, not to threaten them but to relieve them of some of the burden of their own role. While we were growing up more and more married women were going out to work, contributing to the family income. The most marked increase happened between 1971 and 1976, among wives in the 25 to 34 age group (the age at which our mothers were at home with us), this group actually overtaking all others to represent more than half all working wives in 1974.

In taking the pill, putting off motherhood, my generation took the first step, in the seventies, towards fusing the separate worlds of men and women, by infiltrating the world of men and then rediscovering the feminine world, by choosing the unique experience of having children. It is up to them now to articulate the value of this world, just as it is up to women like Lesley to demand a place in the working world dominated by men.

Change, however, only happens gradually, almost imperceptibly, like physical growth. Perhaps we do not appreciate how far we have come, since we are still our mothers' daughters. Perhaps there is a limit to which we can cease to identify with sex-roles. Perhaps in responding so readily to the choice which recently drew many of us back into the home, and closer to our mothers, we are expressing our greater suitability for nurturing, for the business of sympathetic human caring. After all, physiologically, we are receivers, containers, while men's bodies are tuned to externalizing themselves, making a daub on the world. Perhaps our chemistry of cyclic mental states is more suited to the imaginative, self-starting, freelance activities of the childraiser. There are strong arguments for the importance of the mother-child bond at an early age, but why should human beings who want to bring up their children for a few years suffer subsequent ostracism from society?

Liz and Beryl swam against the current in preferring their working lives to the experience of having children. For Liz, who works with children, it was simply a decision she and her husband put off, until they realized they were putting it off because they didn't want to have a family; they valued their lifestyle and their freedom more. Beryl, now district community health administrator, responsible for forty health centres and clinics, also anticipated that she would have a family, and gave up the idea of going to university for that reason. But then, after a few years of marriage and one or two wistful remarks from her mother, went off the idea: 'I kept putting it off, because I valued my own income and freedom and independence and now I'm really glad, because I really enjoy my job and it's not the sort of job where you can take a break for a few years and come back and pick up the threads. There's too much competition for middle and senior management positions, which is probably why I meet so few other women at my level. But I had no idea I would enjoy having a career and telling other people what to do, because my mother always stayed at home and I took it for granted I would do the same. All that happened was that when it came to making the actual choice to do that, I realized that there was more to life than stopping at home and having babies.'

Sylvia would agree, but from a different point of view: 'I quite enjoyed going out to work, but I'm happiest in the times spent as a family. I've been surprised at the satisfaction I've got from having children, taking them places or the little chats we have, simple things like making things for them and seeing my daughter's face light up when she sees me. I can't see working at a career would satisfy me as much, but you don't know, do you, when you're young? You can't plan these things, you don't know what you're going to get pleasure and satisfaction from.'

Most of my contemporaries have children. As I had guessed when I started the research for this book, I am eccentric in that I am unmarried and childless, as yet. Perpetuating ourselves, having children, is what life is basically all about, it is the rationale of the attraction between the sexes, and as such soaks into our very being. For most people having children is the most real thing they do, as my grandfather put it, the only reality, apart from death. But must that reality dictate so much of our lives that it forces all of us, men and women, into a straitjacket of interdependent, yet strangely separate, worlds?

I once had an idea for a painting I wanted to paint. It was based on the car I saw in front of us, travelling up the motorway. The view through the rear window showed the parents in silhouette, immobilized in the front seats while two children sat in sunlight in the back, playing and jumping about. The father was too intent on the serious business of driving the car to pay much attention to what was going on behind him, while the mother sat passively at his side, dividing her time between amusing, feeding, placating him or the children, and reading the map. There was something in this tableau vivant which made me shudder, because it implied that becoming a parent kills your own capacity to enjoy life. For parents who change places in the driving seat, I am sure this needn't be so. Time alone will tell. Perhaps, when we 'are forty-two', I shan't feel like painting that picture any more.